EMPTY TUBES
AND
BACK SEAT MEMORIES

A LIFE CHANGING EXPERIENCE

Russ Warriner

Outskirts Press, Inc.
Denver, Colorado

Empty Tubes and Back Seat Memories
A Life Changing Experience

Outskirts Press, Inc.
http://www.outskirtspress.com

ISBN: 978-1-4327-5324-5 (paperback)
           978-1-4327-5325-2 (hardback)

Outskirts Press and the "OP" logo are trademarks belonging to Outskirts Press, Inc.

PRINTED IN THE UNITED STATES OF AMERICA

PREFACE

The contents of this book are about the life-changing events that I experienced as a young man eager to serve my country in the Vietnam War. In short, I was one of those soldiers who managed to survive the casualties of war and the lasting influences of the Southeast Asia war games on the rest of my life.

Physical injuries, be they internal or external, caused by a hostile environment and enemy gunfire are visual remnants of war. However, many mental injuries go unnoticed because they are deep inside the minds of our veterans. Because we are all comrades-in-arms, I would like to share with you my life while serving as a crew chief assigned to duty aboard an armed helicopter. The setting is in a land far from family, friends, relatives, the smell of fresh air, of country life, and the small town where I grew up. My innocent, joyful, and serene life was taken away when I landed in the middle of war torn Vietnam.

I wrote this book from memory with the use of photos and research to make the story as authentic as possible. I did not keep a journal while I was in Vietnam. Some of the stories may be out of order or pieces may belong in another chapter. I believe that if two people were in the same spot at the same time, they would remember something differently. My experience in Vietnam occurred more than forty years ago but it still seems like yesterday.

My story covers the period in my life from the day I decided to enlist in the United States Army until just after I returned to the United States from my one and a half year tour in Vietnam. It includes the missions I flew and activities in which I participated. I changed a few names so as not to incriminate anyone due to ignorance or stupidity.

Many things happened that most likely will forever be etched in the memories of those who served during warfare. Family members will never hear about many of the memories and even fewer will be put on paper.

I hope that you enjoy the story of my life as an American Vietnam Veteran, find it enlightening and leaving you with a deep understanding of the lifetime experience of one soldier.

Every time one of us tells any of our stories, we are sure to catch incoming. I am sure this book will be no exception to the rule; therefore, I have my helmet on even though it is full of holes already.

DEDICATION

I dedicate this book to all the men and women of the United States armed forces, for their willingness to serve and protect our great country, especially those veterans who gave their lives to make our country safe for our families.

FOREWORD

In the early 1960's, as the Army developed its Air mobility concept, it was determined that the Airmobile Infantry needed the support of Airborne Artillery. The Army met this need by creating the Aerial Rocket Artillery (ARA) and achieved it by arming the UH-1 "Huey" helicopter with the M3 Rocket System. The system consisted of two rocket pods, one on each side of the aircraft. Each pod consisted of four modules with six rocket tubes each (24 rockets on each side of the aircraft), totaling 48 rocket tubes. As Artillery, they dispatched us on "Fire Missions" with a full load of rockets and most of the time returned with "Empty Tubes". From this comes the first half of the book's title.

The concept of an "airborne artillery" outfit made perfect sense once you saw it in action. Characteristically, "Charlie" (the bad guys), when encountering a good guy force, would turn and run. The good guys would crank up conventional artillery, or "red leg", as it was affectionately known. The artillery could shoot from any number of firebases and simply put, rain on the enemy. So "Charlie" got smart. Learning that running from U.S. forces was a bad idea, they simply changed their tactics and "snugged up" as close as they could to the friendlies. This worked because U.S. artillery had a "range probable error" with most artillery pieces. What this means is that when shooting, say, a 105mm Howitzer, the round might land plus or minus 50 meters from its intended target. Therefore, not a good tool to use, if the enemy is only 10 meters from your location. Hence, the ARA was born. Sincere kudos to the military genius who developed the concept and with it, created the capability to surgically remove the bad guys from the good guys.

Pilots wrote most books that were about helicopters in the Vietnam War and their views were from the "front seat". As an enlisted man, my views were from the "back seat" and these are my recollections of combat actions that I participated in and/or observed while serving as Crew Chief/Door Gunner of a UH-1 (Huey) Gunship. We were 2nd Battalion, 20th Artillery (ARA), 1st Cavalry Division (AM). My assignment was with C Battery of the unit. Until 1968, it was the only unit of its kind in the Army. These are my "Back Seat Memories."

ACKNOWLEDGMENTS

The author is grateful to the following persons for their help: my wife Terri Warriner. Without her by my side, I would not be where I am today. I wish to thank N. G. Brown, for his book, which gave me the encouragement to write this book. I wish to thank all my ARA Alumni friends for their encouragement and help to make this book possible. The 1st Cavalry Division Association for giving me a column in the 1st Cavalry Division newspaper "Saber", in which I could write about Aerial Rocket Artillery history in Vietnam for the past 16 plus years.

A special thanks to the pilots and enlisted men with whom I had served. They gave me their side of some of the stories and permission to use their names. This made the book as close to the facts as possible. Without their input to jog my memory, I am sure this book would never have gone to print.

I wish to thank Art Jetter (an ARA pilot 1970-71) who helped edit this book to make it more interesting reading and Jerry Barloco (one of the pilots with whom I flew 1967-68), who assisted on mission details. Without these two, I am sure that the language utilized would not have been as correct as that used by the pilots.

I would like to thank Barbara Krull, Bonnie Roberge, Richard P. Grenier and Daniel P. Gillotti for their help in editing this book.

I would also like to acknowledge my Junior High English teacher, Mrs. Anna B. Curtis (ABC) who instilled the basic knowledge of literature and writing.

Without her, I know that I would be seriously lacking in the skills to write this book.

TABLE OF CONTENTS

PREFACE
DEDICATION
FORWARD
ACKNOWLEDGMENTS

CHAPTER

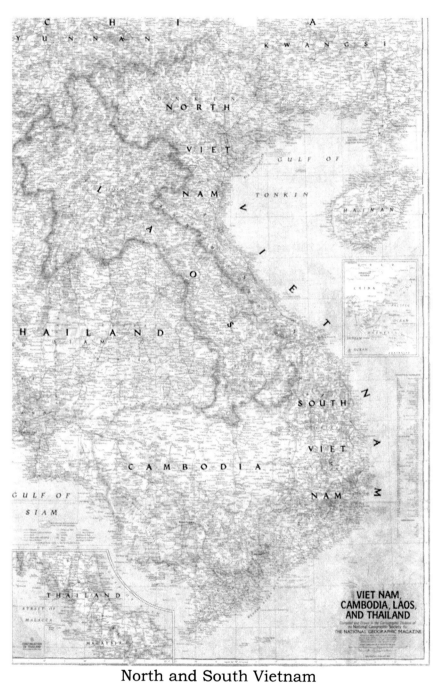

North and South Vietnam

BIG DECISION

Growing up on the outskirts of the small town of Williamsburg, Massachusetts, I attended the two small town schools. I enjoyed the outdoors and spent every waking moment that I could at the nearby farm. I raked hay with the John Deere 50, drove the truck while picking up the hay, and harvesting corn. I helped with milking the cows, and during the snowy months of winter, did the milking while the owners -- father and son -- were out doing their snowplow routes with their tractors. My dad had started working for the VA Hospital in Northampton way before I was born and my mom worked for W. T. Grants Department Store in Northampton from the time it first opened. After I finished junior high school, I elected to go to Smith Vocational Trade School and take up auto body as a trade. I dropped out of trade school because I did not get along with one of the teachers and thought I already knew enough to get along in the world. I found myself a full time job working in a local blacksmith shop and worked at a gun manufacturing plant part time as well as a local gas station. I owned my own car and was proud that I had paid for it with my own hard-earned money.

During the 60's, things were beginning to heat up in Vietnam. The draft was in full swing. I had been in Mrs. Curtis' class when the assassination of President Kennedy happened and already knew I wanted to serve my country at that time. I knew that since I had dropped out of school, as soon as I was old enough, my draft board number would be coming up. Dad had worked on Thanksgiving Day as he did many holidays.

On Saturday, I was having a late Thanksgiving with Mom and Dad. The younger of my two brothers had entered the army and got Germany for a duty station and my oldest brother was married, so I was the only sibling left living at home.

As I sat at the dinner table with my mom and dad for our Thanksgiving meal, I wondered how well what I was about to say would be received. "I am sure I will be drafted soon, so I would like to go to the recruiter's office Monday. Maybe I can get a chance to do something I want to do rather than have someone pick what I will do and end up on the ground dodging bullets. I may even be lucky and not go to Vietnam like many of my friends."

Because my brother was already in the Army stationed in Germany, I guess my mom thought she could change my mind and fired questions at me without giving me a chance to reply. "Have you thought about this? What does Gloria think about this? Are you seeing someone else these days? Are you sure this is what you want to do?"

I answered in a low voice, "I am still dating Gloria, but she is not pleased about the war. She says she will wait for me if I go in the service, even though she does not like it one bit. I have a feeling she will not be here waiting for me when I come home, but I will deal with that issue when the time comes. I know my chances are better if I can pick what I would like to do by enlisting. I have been thinking about this for a while. Now, I am sure this is what I want to do. The draft has already taken some of my friends who are no longer in school and I do not want to go that route. Tonight, I will see Gloria and tell her my plans."

Dad smiled and spoke next, "You know, I have been working at the VA since I was a young lad, watched several who served in other wars trying to deal with what they saw or did. You know that some of those that are in the hospital where I work will never leave there. I respect what you think you want to do even though I know it will not be easy for you as you do not even like to hunt. I did not serve in the service because of my job with the VA. You may be lucky and not serve in Vietnam, but I know you will be okay if you do. If you can get into something which involves mechanics, I know you will do very well."

After supper, I headed for the home where Gloria lived. Thoughts of how she was going to take the news flooded my head. Will it be better to get her away from the house to tell her the news? Gloria came from a large family with several children and she was the oldest of the girls. I had dated Gloria for several months and already knew she did not like the war.

As I got out of my car, I spotted Gloria coming out of the house. "Gloria, let's take a short ride. I want to talk to you about something. It will be easier to talk away from your family, where we will not be interrupted."

From her answer, I was sure Gloria already knew what I was about to say. "Okay, but I'd rather stay here," She said. Before the night had ended, we got into an intense argument that left a bad taste in my mouth. I already knew what I wanted to do and there was no turning my decision around.

As I drove home, thoughts of what had taken place moments before flooded my mind. I wondered if I was doing the right thing. I was sure I was doing the best thing, but would Gloria wait for me while I put in my three years! I told myself that if she did not wait for me, then that was okay as I was sure I could find someone else.

When I got home, it was after 10:00 p.m. and I headed to bed. I had a hard time sleeping as my mind went into overtime thinking about things that had happened that day and about enlisting on Monday morning.

The next day was Sunday. After church, I went to the farm next door to tell them I was going into the Army. I learned a lot working on that farm and I was sure it would come in handy, but I just was not sure when or how.

I had another restless night, but it seemed as though morning came fast. After breakfast, I called the recruiters' office in Northampton, Massachusetts, to make sure someone was there to talk to me. There was, so I got ready to go. Because it was mom's day off from work, she asked to tag along. I told her that it was okay but she needed to know that this was my decision and I would tell the recruiter what I wanted to do. The recruiter for the Army was Master Sergeant Watson who was dressed in his Army dress greens, with his medals and awards proudly displayed.

Sergeant Watson met me at the door. "My name is Sergeant Watson. I understand you wish to join the Army rather than wait for the draft to get you. This is a smart move, if you want to get into something specific. By the way, what job would you like to do? The Army offers many."

I thought this would be easy to figure out what I wanted to do. "Sir, I grew up on a small farm and worked on a nearby farm operating the farm tractors, trucks, and a bulldozer. I worked at a gas station doing small repairs. I think being a mechanic on tanks would be something I would like to do. At least, I wouldn't be in the infantry dodging lead."

Watson stopped me, "First, don't call me sir. I am a Sergeant. You need to know when and who to call Sir. Are you sure that you want to do that? Chances are you will be right beside the infantry repairing tanks. How about being a helicopter mechanic? Chances are you would be at a base camp doing repairs if you end up in Vietnam. You could go to flight school and learn to fly them. Whatever you would like to do, I can help you get into and I can help you by getting you a 120 days deferment. This will give you time so you can take care of whatever you feel you need to do before going to basic. The deferment will also help you for promotions because it will give you time in grade ahead of others that just wait for the draft."

I did not believe that being in helicopters would keep me from dodging bullets, but I thought helicopters were interesting and now I wanted to know more, "What will I have to do to get into a job like that? I don't think I want to be a pilot but it is food for thought."

Watson was ready with an answer, "You will have to go to Springfield and take some tests and a physical. If you pass the physical and your test scores are high enough, you should get what you want. The Army needs more helicopter mechanics right now. We should start the paper work now because the slots for this will fill up fast and then you will have to pick something else. Do you want to think about it or are you ready to start things today?"

I was thinking this sounded good. Besides, what did I have to lose? "Sergeant Watson, please set things up right now if you can."

Sergeant Watson must have figured I was ready to enlist. "Okay, but first, I want you to go over to 1515 Main Street and see the Draft Board and let them know you are joining the Army. When you finish there, I want you to come back and I will see when I can get you started."

The following Monday, I found myself on my way to Springfield, Massachusetts for the physical, testing, and to be sworn into the inactive Reserves. Then a few days later, I would need to contact Sergeant Watson to see how I scored and if I could get into aviation or not.

Two days later, I called, "Sergeant Watson. How did I do? Will I get what I want?"

Sergeant Watson wanted to talk in person, "Come see me Monday and I will answer any questions you have then. Would 11:00 a.m. be okay, or would the afternoon be better? I can't see you before then as I have appointments until then."

I wanted the answers as soon as I could get them, but had plans for Monday morning, so I set up an afternoon appointment. I had to wait all weekend to get answers and this weighed heavily on my mind. I found myself not sleeping very much, with a mind that would not shut down. I was so tired after the weekend was over, that it was not even funny. As I headed to the recruiter's office, my mind was still in high-speed mode, wondering what I was about to hear. I did not understand why he could not give me any answers over the phone.

The answers I got were not exactly what I thought I would hear. My 120 days was only going to be105, which started from the first day I talked to Sergeant Watson. I would be leaving on 13 March 1967, which did not seem like much time to get things done, but I figured I could make it work.

I knew my date to report was going to come far too fast, but I knew there was nothing I could do about it. I got busy trying to do what I felt I needed to do, taking time to go visit my aunts, uncles, and friends to let them know what I was doing.

When March 13 came, dad had to work and Gloria would not take time off from school, so mom drove me to Springfield, Massachusetts. I was not sure what to expect, but figured that I would find out shortly. Soon after arriving, I met Stan Walzack and Ron Therrien, who were standing outside and leaving the same day. We stuck together and talked.

Mom was talking with Ron's mom who had brought him to Springfield. All talking ended abruptly when someone I could not see from where we were standing said, "Say goodbye to your families and move inside."

Saying goodbye to mom, I joined the others going inside, which made me feel like a cow in a herd. I must not have been the only one because I heard someone making a sound like a cow. Upon entering the building, I entered a small room joining a group. Stan and Ron, who were right behind me, were led to a group in another area. The door closed behind me and I found myself in a room packed with men. Moments later, I found myself standing at attention and inducted into the active duty army with the others.

Later, I caught up with Ron and Stan and we made a plan to try to stick together as long as we could. Before long, we were on a flight headed to God knows where. When we landed, we were loaded onto a bus and driven to Fort Jackson, South Carolina. We all thought it would be where we would take basic training, but soon found out we were just there for in processing.

The first day at Fort Jackson was uneventful. The second day, things happened to let us know that we were government property. Everyone needed to get a haircut, but since my hair was short already, I thought I would not have to get one. That sure was the wrong way of thinking, because everyone needed it all cut. As the line for haircuts slowly moved forward, I could see soldiers coming out from the back of the barbershop with no hair.

As I climbed into the barber chair, another barber was asking a soldier with real long hair in the chair next to me, how he wanted his haircut. Now, I thought that was funny as everyone was getting it all cut off, so who was he trying to kid? After cutting all the hair from one side of his head, he stopped and started joking to the other barbers about how he looked. This upset the guy and I was thinking, why torment the guy, just cut it off and get it done and over with.

A few moments later, he looked like the rest of us. As he got out of the barber chair, he was complaining as he headed for the door. As I left the building, I found him outside complaining to some of the others who were still milling around. He was making comments about going in and kicking the crap out of the barber. One of the other soldiers told him, "Forget it guy, you belong to the US Government now and can't do anything about it. You'll just end up in the stockade."

I guess it was a good thing that things simmered down because a Staff Sergeant came into sight. I am sure things could have gotten sticky.

A sergeant told us to go around the corner and get into line for army chow. Entering the hall, we found more sergeants pushing us along. "Get your sorry ass around the corner. Get in the chow line. Eat and get outside after you finish. The army doesn't have all day to wait on your sorry punk asses."

Well, that did it and made Mr. I-don't-want-my-hair-cut start all over again.

One of the sergeants over heard him complaining, "You got a problem soldier? If you do, I will find something to correct it."

I guess he figured he had better simmer down, "No Sergeant."

"Now get your chow or go hungry. Everyone get over to building #1592 for 1300 hours".

I had fifteen minutes after chow to find building #1592, which was a theater. Upon entering, I barely got to my seat before I heard attention called.

A sergeant began with, "At this briefing, you will be told what is expected of you here at Fort Jackson. Afterwards, we will be taking a few of you out for further processing, one at a time."

I was among the second group to start processing and being asked where I was born, where I entered the army, how much schooling I had, and where would I like to be stationed overseas after basic, and giving us a choice of Vietnam or South East Asia. Whom were they kidding? Both places were the same thing!

The next day they started to pull people out of formation to attend basic at Fort Jackson. I began thinking to myself that maybe I would be taking basic right here at Fort Jackson just as we originally thought. When formation ended, those of us who remained had to wait for another formation to see where we would take basic training. After heading back to our barracks, I found myself running a buffer in a mandatory cleaning "GI Party" that was waxing an already waxed floor.

There were two more formations called before I heard my name. I returned to the barracks to get my things and be ready to board a bus headed for basic. Once on the bus, I was happy to see Ron boarding but did not see Stan. We had no idea where Stan was or if he would be going with us. Then, I spotted Stan getting on another bus and let Ron know that I felt he was going with us. Still no one knew where we were going. It was not long before a drill sergeant got on board our bus and informed us that the bus was taking us to Fort Gordon, Georgia.

Arriving at Fort Gordon, Ron and I joined B-1-1 for our basic training. Ron got different drill sergeants than I did and had a different barrack. Later after settling in, I caught up with Ron and we got a chance to talk. Neither of us knew where Stan was and figured we would not see him again.

As I started basic, I was thinking that basic training must be the same for everyone else. They marched us for miles upon miles in tough going areas and made it tough on our bodies by carrying our heavy backpacks.

Anyone who was a little over weight seemed to get pushed harder to help them lose the weight. When they went through the mess hall line, they never seemed to get much on their plate. It appeared to be working because I could see the weight coming off. One of the soldiers from the barracks next to mine had exchanged fatigues two or three times because he had lost so much weight.

Those who I thought were nothing but skin and bones had extra food put on their plate and were expected to eat it. However, they usually tried to give some of their food to anyone who wanted it.

On Friday, March 31, we received word, that if we wanted our pay, we had to go to the mess hall where someone would be giving it to us. We had to be in uniform and have our ID card or there was no pay. I thought "Wow" my first paycheck from Uncle Sam. Now I can at least get a few things I need from the PX, if they will let us go.

Arriving at the mess hall, I was standing in line when word came that we needed to know our service number. If we did not know it, they sent us back outside to learn it before we could receive our pay.

From the first day of basic training, they drilled us repeatedly with questions. It seemed like they wanted us to know everything but were always switching everything around. No one had ever asked me to recite my service number. To me, knowing the answers to questions like who is the General of the Army, President of the United States or rifle serial number did not seem to come easy. However, I felt I knew my service number even though I had not even thought about it for a while. As I got closer to the door to go in and receive my pay, I was getting more nervous by the second. I did not want to get it wrong.

At least when I went into the mess hall, there was a chance they would skip me and not ask me to answer any questions because they wanted to keep the chow line moving. Nevertheless, I knew they would ask for my service number. Learning your service number was like learning your rifle number. If I got it wrong, I had no one to blame but myself.

Word was that most of us would not get much pay, but any money would help because I did not have any left. I still had problems with remembering my rifle serial number, but felt I could not mess up my service number.

As I stepped up to the pay officer, proudly standing at attention, I said, "Sir, Private Warriner RA11960898 reporting for pay sir!"

The Lieutenant snapped back, "What are you here for Private?"

I did not understand. "Sir, my pay, Sir!"

Now the Lieutenant was laughing, "Private, you have no pay. You owe the government. Now take your pay stub, stop wasting my time and get out of here. Come back when we owe you some money."

I was floored! What did he mean I owed the government money? I had an allotment going home but it was only a few bucks a month. When I looked at my pay stub, I found out how little we made in this army. My take home pay would not buy a cup of coffee.

As I left the pay line, I headed for the phone booth to call home. When I got the there, the line had at least 75 soldiers waiting to call home. I wondered if they had the same problem. I thought about leaving the line and trying to find another phone or waiting until later. However, if I did that, I could be in the same situation. I also thought, if I tried that, there was a chance that there would not be any time to do it.

Almost an hour and a half later, the line finally was down to the point that I was going to get the phone soon. I was not sure if I was going to be able to reach anyone at home, but sure was going to try. Dialing the operator was my only chance, as I did not have but thirty cents to my name. Placing one of my thin dimes into the slot, I dialed zero for the operator. After several rings, the operator came on, "Operator, may I help you?"

"Yes, I would like to place a collect call to 413-268-7873."

As I listened, I heard it ring several times. I thought, I guess I am out of luck but then I heard my mom answer the other end, "Hello."

Then the operator asked, "I have a collect call from Georgia. Will you accept the call?"

Then I heard, "Yes I will."

The operator then said, "Go ahead sir. I have your party on the line."

I explained to mom that I needed a few bucks out of my savings account, as my pay was zero for the month. I only wanted enough to get me through the month and was not even sure what I needed, but thought $30 should be enough. I went on to explain that I was going to reduce the allotment that I was sending home, so I would, have a little more money to live on after the next months check.

As April started, we were so busy with training that I did not have time to think about much. It was keep your area, and fatigues clean for inspection and repeatedly polish your boots.

On Saturday, April 15, Ron bolted into my barracks, "Russ, you have to report to the orderly room."

I was puzzled, "What for?"

I could tell he knew something more than he was letting on, "I don't know. I was just told to go get you," he said.

As the two of us entered the orderly room, I spotted Stan Walzack standing there in his helmet liner. This surprised me and I was at a loss for words. I managed to blurt out, "What are you doing here?

Stan Walzack and Ron Therrien

Now they were both smiling as Stan explained, "I am in B-3-1, which is next door. I noticed you and Ron going by on your way to the PX, but my drill sergeant is very strict. He would not let me contact you. My mom has been in touch with Mrs. Therrien and I guess she has stayed in touch with your mom. I have tried to get permission to come see you both and today it finally happened."

Now, I was sure about Ron knowing more than he was letting on, but had wanted to surprise me. After a few moments of talking, Stan said he had to get back to his unit. We made plans to meet at the PX whenever we could get permission to go there. We all figured that our times would not match often.

We went on several of what the drill sergeants called a forced march. There were times when several soldiers would fall behind. A drill sergeant would always be near the end of the group and have someone fall back to help these soldiers catch up. The only piece of equipment we seldom carried was our rifles. However, by week five, we were dragging them along.

One day, on one of these forced marches, everyone felt we were going to the range and, sure enough, it was not long before it came into view. As soon as we arrived, they called us into formation and told us, that today we would qualify with our M-14s. If we did not qualify, we would stay there until we got it right or plan on taking basic training over. I was not sure if this was true but there was no way that I was going to find out. I hated hunting and never fired any type of weapon. I was surprised that I qualified the first time around and felt good that I would not have to repeat basic over this issue.

Before leaving the range, we always had to clean our rifles, which made no sense to me because once back at the barracks, we would clean them again. After I finished cleaning my rifle, I turned it in and filed past the drill sergeant, responding with the usual, "No brass, no ammo, Drill Sergeant!"

I moved over into formation to wait for everyone else to return their M-14 to the arms truck and wondered if it would be a long hike back to the barracks. I knew that sometimes we had to clean the rifle all over again after we returned to the barracks.

The hike back to the barracks was uneventful. I placed my gear in my locker just knowing we would be getting our rifles out of the arms truck, cleaning them again and returning them to the arms room.

Within the hour, I was busy cleaning my rifle. I knew that I would fail the inspection by trying to return it to the arms room too quickly, so I took my time. I watched several soldiers who had turned in their weapon and was about do the same when I heard a gunshot. It had come from between the buildings.

Within seconds, one of the drill sergeants entered the building, "Everyone stays in the barracks until told differently. Squad leaders, post a guard at each entrance."

Fifteen minutes later, we learned that one of the recruits had tried to take his life. Now, we were going to have to go through a shakedown inspection to make sure no one else had any live ammo. This recruit had made comments to some others that he did not want to die in Vietnam. Now he was most likely going to die and if he lived, would probably be nothing more than a vegetable.

The following Monday, when we were going through morning PT (physical training), some of the men were having problems doing pushups. Sergeant Maldonado, who was all of five foot nothing, was giving these men a hard time. He started doing pushups with one hand and one leg. Then he did pushups where he would clap his hands together at the apex of each one. He called anyone who could not do it a wimp and other names I cannot mention.

When afternoon came, I found out that I had guard duty at the post motor pool for the night. At least it made more sense to me than walking guard duty around the barracks area. Guarding the barracks was like watching to see if someone spit their gum on the sidewalk or something. I did not think anyone would try to steal a jeep either, but it still made more sense than walking around the barracks.

Now I was pleased because I was down to one week left of basic training. I was sure I had made it.

We were getting shots for everything. Now it was more shots. As I entered the room where they were giving the shots, I noticed they were using an air gun. They told us not to move while we receive the shot or the air gun could cut us. As I stepped up to receive my shot, the soldier in front of me was stepping away from getting his shot and the blood was running down his arm. This scared the hell out of me and I began to feel queasy and worried about passing out.

Some men passed out at the site of getting a shot even though they could not see a needle. I did not like needles either, but figured that if I did not watch I would be fine. I was sure everyone knew I was scared, but no one said anything and I made it through without passing out.

Back at the barracks, I got my equipment ready for the field trip. Then, because I was not feeling very well, I laid down on my bunk. I thought maybe if I rested just a few moments in time I would be okay. When I awoke I found out I had missed formation and everyone had left for the field. I was sure I was going to be in big trouble, would not finish basic and end up in the recycle group.

I lucked out because when the squad leader found me on my bunk he had me shipped to the hospital where I spent three days. The first two of these, I was not sure where I was or who I was. They released me from the hospital on the last day of the field trip. I was still sure that I would not finish basic with the rest.

Basic Training Year Book Photo

However, on graduation day, I was pleased to find out I had completed basic. True to the words of the recruiter, I received my first promotion, putting a few more pennies in the bank. My orders were for Fort Rucker, Alabama and aviation mechanic school. This made me happy because I did not really want to work on tanks.

Taken after graduation

.2.

MOTHER RUCKER

On arriving at Fort Rucker on Friday, June 2, I found myself in a barracks with a handful of others as I waited for classes to begin. On Saturday and again on Sunday, a few more troops trickled in and everyone wondered when the classes would start. I was sure we would start on Monday and when we did not, I began to wonder why I only got two weeks to get to Fort Rucker.

When I arrived at Ft Rucker, I noticed almost everyone was wearing an orange and black patch on his or her sleeve. The patch had something that looked like a torch with wings on it. This must be the Ft Rucker patch or maybe it was a flight school patch. I was not sure what it really meant, but if I needed one, I would get it as quickly as I could.

There was nothing to do so I spent most of the time checking out the area, but staying close enough to the barracks so I could get back without missing a formation. On the first Tuesday after arriving, Specialist Sixth Class Bridges arrived. I just knew that because of his rank, he was going to take charge of everyone and find something for us to do.

Before the week was finished, several more had arrived and soon the barracks was full. Nobody knew what was going on or when we would start classes.

On the third day after Bridges arrived, he became the barracks NCO because he was the only person above the rank of PVT E2. We all had to report to Bridges every morning and every evening.

Ft Rucker patch

Every evening, several of us, including Bridges would sit in front of the barracks and talk. I figured it was a good way to pass the time away. Because there was nothing new to write home about, I joined the group.

I was sure everyone was heading for the Huey course as I expected to. Bridges was sitting on the steps of the barracks talking with a few of us. The subject switched to what each of us was going to do after the basic course was finished.

My response was, "I thought we all were going to be going to the Huey course." After all, the Huey was everywhere around Rucker.

Bridges seemed surprised, "I was sent here for Mohawk school." Hesitating before he continued, "I thought everyone was sent here for the Mohawk course. Must be that we all are going to a basic course first and then some of you will go on to the Huey course. Maybe I am the only one going to the Mohawk course. I am sure that anyone who does poorly in class will be shipped off to Vietnam."

Smith had not said much until then, "Man, that is BS. How can they send someone who doesn't do well off to Vietnam?"

I did not know if he was kidding, but it sure did make me think about how hard I was going to study. I surely did not want to end up a ground pounder.

Bridges added, "Some of you will be going to the Chinook or Sky Crane courses, so don't count on everyone being a Huey mechanic."

Bridges also told us that everyone stationed at Fort Rucker called the base Mother Rucker. I thought that was kind of funny but different. After all, it was kind of a fitting name for the place as I was sure that everyone had to come to Rucker to get into an aviation course.

Every night after classes were over, we would hang around the barracks. If we wanted to leave the area, we had to get permission from Bridges. Then we had to be back by lights out. For me, the days were dragging on. I wanted to check the area out but I was not going to get into trouble by being away from the area and missing a roll call. On Monday June 12, which was 10 days after I arrived at Fort Rucker, we started the basic aviation course of 67A10. This was good because everyone was getting itchy feet to get away from things. When the classes started, they split us into two groups, but Bridges was still in charge of everyone.

I could not get over how easy the school seemed to be, but maybe it was just me. After all, anything mechanical seemed to come easy to me. My mind would often wander into thoughts like, would the Huey be my next course or some other course? Would my next course be this easy?

Now that classes were underway, our nights were free to do as we wished as long as we stayed in the area and made classes on time. This was okay because I preferred to stick around and study. I did not want to flunk out and end up in the infantry. They continuously led us to believe that they could place us in the infantry. Not that I thought there was anything wrong with being in the infantry. However, if you have a "shot" at an aviation career, you will want to give it your best.

Richard Goulette or someone else and I went off to Post Exchange or somewhere else as often as we could. Checking out the area became something I liked to do, but I made sure I made it back in time for lights out. If the Army was going to be like this, then I could do my three years standing on my head.

Every Monday, Bridges inspected us for a good haircut, to make sure our uniform was clean, and we generally looked presentable.

When Friday afternoon would arrive, I knew we were free until Monday morning, but also knew that we needed to be back if they called an alert. Only a very few men had a car and this made it hard to go very far, anyway.

On Wednesday of the third week, I heard a rumor that Private Jones was planning to take his Chrysler wagon to Panama City, Florida and wanted to get a carload. I was hesitant about going because we were not to leave the base without a pass but reluctantly decided to go along.

Bridges said he would cover for us as best he could. On Friday night at 2100 hours, we all piled into the Chrysler station wagon and headed for the beach at Panama City, Florida. About half way to Panama City, the car started to act funny as if it was about to give up on us. This made me sorry that I decided to go along, and I began to pray, "God help us make this trip without any problems."

I was still praying when we arrived in Panama City. The streets were empty. Pulling into a parking lot, we figured we could take a nap while we waited for morning. Within an hour, there was a knock on the window. We had to move or go to jail and pay a fine.

I tried to take a nap as we drove around the area trying to find another spot. Finally, we ran into a patrol officer that was nice enough to tell us where to park.

As the sun came up, we were off to find some food. Nothing was open and no movement anywhere. Walking around we ran into a patrol officer who told us that nothing would be open until almost noontime and we needed to leave the beach area or they would arrest us for loitering.

I spotted a couple of vending machines and decided to grab a coke and a snickers bar to hold me over.

None of us had planned for this trip ahead very much and most of us did not have a lot of money. I figured I had better conserve my funds in case I was stuck without eating, so I only ate half my candy bar.

Shortly after the sun came up, the hustle and bustle of the beach started. It was almost 11am before we found any real food and almost noon before things were in full swing.

None of us had any idea how brutal the Florida sun could be. When I noticed my skin getting red, I put on long pants and a shirt.

Long before the sun began to drop over the horizon, I was ready to go home and was glad when the rest of the men said they were ready also. I was already starting to feel the effects of the Florida sun and I just knew the others were feeling it also. All of us sure learned a lesson about the Florida sun, as most of us looked like cooked lobsters the next day and suffered the consequences of our actions.

By Monday, my skin was starting to blister and I knew it was going to peel. No one dared report for sick call. If we did, we knew we could get in trouble for defacing government property.

On Friday July 14, I finished the 67A10 course and received word that most of us would be going to the Huey course and receive the MOS of 67N20.

We would start this rotary wing training on the following Monday. Bridges was now sure he was going to the Mohawk fixed wing course.

Each of us received the Mechanics Creed and a certificate showing that we had finished the course.

THE MECHANICS CREED

UPON MY HONOR I SWEAR THAT I SHALL HOLD IN SACRED TRUST THE RIGHTS AND PRIVILEGES CONFERRED UPON ME AS A GRADUATE MECHANIC. KNOWING FULL WELL THAT THE SAFETY AND LIVES OF OTHERS ARE DEPENDENT UPON MY SKILL AND JUDGMENT, I SHALL NEVER KNOWINGLY SUBJECT OTHERS TO RISKS WHICH I WOULD NOT BE WILLING TO ASSUME FOR MYSELF, OR FOR THOSE DEAR TO ME

When Monday arrived and the 67N20 course was about to start, I found myself in the position as class leader because I had time in grade out ranking the others. We had to move to another building where everyone from my class was to occupy the second floor. The other half of the soldiers from our 67A10 class occupied the first floor.

I was thinking the Army was not so bad. I have my own room instead of living in the bay with the rest of the men. I guess it's okay that I have to march the men to and from class because I had a little privacy. I picked Private Richard Goulette to be the assistant class leader because he was clean-cut and I had already made friends with him. Now I thought we sure acted as if we were lifers in this man's Army.

Everyone had nicknamed PVT Goulette "The Kidd" or "Kidd" because of his appearance. Kidd and I were starting to hang out together all the time. We checked out the area whenever we were not in classes. We liked to walk to some of the airfields like Cairns Army

Airfield so we could get near the aircraft. By doing this, we thought that we could get a better feel for what our job would be like.

We could not believe how big the area that they called Fort Rucker was. The roads seemed to go on forever. At Cairns, we could see a Huey coming in for a landing, then it lifted off again, came back around and landed again. The second time it landed, it hovered over to a hanger area and shut down. I wanted to go over and talk to the crew but Kidd thought that we would be in trouble for being on the airfield, so we turned around and started the long walk back. Kidd thought we should try a new way back but it was not long before we were lost.

When we figured out where we were, it was getting late and we needed to hurry or we would not get any chow. By the time we were back in our area, the mess hall had closed. Neither of us had any money, but as luck would have it, I had received a care package from home that very day. We found some cookies in my package and got a can of coke from the vending machine.

The next Saturday, Kidd and I walked to Hanchey Army Heliport. On Sunday, we found Lowe Army Heliport. At Lowe, we ran into an officer that told us we could not stay around that area and had to leave.

At the Fort Rucker Museum, we spent a couple of hours looking at the aircraft on display and took each other's photo.

Sunday, after getting back to my room, I was writing to my mom when there was a knock on the door. When I opened it, Private Jones was standing there. "Can you cut my hair or can I borrow your clippers? I need a haircut and I have no money to get one. I know you don't usually cut hair, but I know you have clippers."

I had picked up a set of hair clippers at the Post Exchange to cut my own hair in order to save a few bucks while going through the aviation courses.

I knew what it was like to be short on funds, "I am not a barber so will not cut your hair, but I guess you can borrow them. But if you break them, you owe me a new set."

When he did not return them right away, I found they were making the rounds. I told them it was okay, but to get them back to me that night.

I was sitting in my room writing a letter to Gloria, when I heard a knock on my door. Private Mike Russell was standing there. He said, "Can you help me fix Smith's haircut? I gave him a haircut, but I sure messed it up."

I did not want any misunderstandings. I said, "Mike, you know I don't like to cut hair for anyone. I'm not a barber but I will try to fix it, as long as you and Smith understand that I make no promises how it will turn out".

Mike said it looked good and the next thing I knew I was giving more haircuts. They must have turned out okay because I ended up giving several haircuts the next weekend.

Several of us had talked about going to flight school. It was an option and we had as good a chance as anyone to become a Warrant Officer.

We were sitting on the steps of the barracks, watching the soldiers across the street and I said, "Hey Kidd, let's see if we can talk to some of those guys across the street in the WOC (Warrant Officer Candidate) class." Being a WOC sure had some good points, like getting to be an E-5 when you started, but having to stay in the service longer was not an option that Kidd or I wanted.

I received word that I was getting a promotion to PFC the day of the graduation, so I got a set of the butterfly wings and started to sew them on my uniform.

On graduation day, I was handed my diploma with the words, United States Army Aviation School followed by capital letters; PVT RUSSELL L. WARRINER OF THE UNITED STATES ARMY HAS SUCCESSFULLY COMPLETED THE PRESCRIBED COURSE OF INSTRUCTION FOR SINGLE ROTOR UTILITY HELICOPTER REPAIR COURSE (67N20).

I did not get orders to my next duty station as everyone else had. I was surprised to find out that they had placed me on a hold over list. Now I would have plenty of time to sew the new rank on my uniform.

I always hated to move from one place to another, so I felt lucky that I did not have to move out of my room and start living in a bay again. Kidd was gone and I was on my own.

United States Army Aviation School

PVT RUSSELL L. WARRINER

OF THE UNITED STATES ARMY

HAS SUCCESSFULLY COMPLETED THE PRESCRIBED COURSE OF INSTRUCTION FOR

SINGLE ROTOR TURBINE UTILITY HELICOPTER REPAIR COURSE 167N20I, CLASS 68-9

ON ___28 AUGUST 1967___ AND IS AWARDED THIS

Diploma

GIVEN AT FORT RUCKER, ALABAMA

LUCIEN C. BENTON
Lieutenant Colonel, Armor
SECRETARY

DELK M. ODEN
Major General, USA
COMMANDANT

While awaiting orders, I needed to check in at the orderly room every day. On the following Tuesday when I checked in, I was told I would be placed on guard duty, not to guard the area but to be watching a "screw up" to make sure he did not try to go AWOL (absent without official leave). If he wanted to leave, how could I stop him? I did not even have a weapon. What was I going to do?

On Thursday, October 5, I got word I needed to pack my bags and would be leaving on Tuesday, October 10, if I could clear post by then. I was ready and said I could clear post before that. I could leave on Tuesday. I would clear post fast but not too fast. They could put me on duty doing something.

PFC Warriner October 5

I did not want KP duty or some other duty. Therefore, I took my time and picked what I needed to clear for each day that I had left.

On the morning of the 10th, I was at the orderly room with my bags in tow and would soon be on my way. As I looked at my orders, I read my next assignment was going to be Vietnam. This was no revelation, but when I saw I was to report to Fort Lewis, Washington and had thirty days to get there, I was surprised. There must be a mistake as the army only gives thirty days a year and I had only been in the army seven months.

I was not feeling good about having to say goodbye to my family and friends but I wanted to make the best of it. I headed for the airport and caught a flight out into Bradley Airport in Connecticut. I planned to surprise everyone but changed my mind after I realized I still needed a ride home from the airport. When I called home, the only person I could reach was my mom. I arranged for her to pick me up at the airport.

When my friends found out I was home and would be going to Vietnam, it seemed like everyone wanted to see me. George Hunter wanted me at his home on Sunday, October 29, as it was the only time George could get free to see me. I was sure something was up when I noticed George's car was on the grass, not in the driveway and yet there was plenty of room.

Dan Black

I was correct. It was a surprise going away party for me put on by Dan Black. Dan knew that if he held the party at his home, I would figure out what he had planned.

On the morning of November 5, mom asked, "What are your plans for tonight? You know Mr. Brenick would like you to go visit him around 6 pm. It is the only day when John Brenick has time to visit and he wants to see you before you leave."

I figured something was up but was not sure what. "Funny. Gloria said she was busy tonight, so I won't see her. I guess I'll call her and make sure she has not changed her mind."

My parents said they had a meeting with some friends about a Christmas dinner they were planning in town and left at 5:30. When it was almost 6 pm, I headed for the Brenick home with a strange feeling in the pit of my stomach.

As I drove into the Brenick driveway, I noticed his car was not in the garage and the door was open. They usually entered the home through the garage, leading you through the cellar. As I headed up the stairs, I heard scampering of feet, and then, it all went quiet. Yes, something was up for sure.

When I knocked on the door, Joyce Brenick greeted me with a big grin on her face. "Hi Russ. Come on in. John has gone to the store, but he should be right back. Go sit down in the living room and I will put on a pot of coffee."

Knowing that there was something up, I said, "Sounds good to me. Where are the kids?"

Trying not to let on, she answered, "They are in the other room playing."

As I rounded the corner into the living room, there was all my family and Gloria with a full-lit Christmas tree. Mr. Brenick had gone out into the pasture and cut down a hemlock tree, which they then decorated it for Christmas. They wanted to give me a Christmas before I left for Vietnam.

My brother Lee was the only family member that was not home for the occasion, the army had sent him to Germany. I would be the only family member going into combat unless my brother signed a waiver to leave Germany and go to Vietnam. I knew that would never happen. That was like asking a pig to fly. If I had a way to avoid going to Vietnam, I would not throw it away. However, I would dodge the issue. I would serve my country with pride to the best of my ability. I was scared about where I was heading, but I was not going to let anyone know it, if I could help it.

I was pleased to have my family and friends care enough to have Christmas before I left, but it gave me a feeling that I just could not explain. I was the one getting ALL the Christmas gifts, and it made me feel like I was not going to come home again or they did not think I would come home. Maybe they were right. Maybe I would not come home. No one could predict the outcome of the Vietnam War; much less predict who would make it home. This was the first time I thought that I hated the holidays.

Author by the November Christmas tree

3

VIETNAM

I thought my leave time was far too short. It ended before I knew it. I said my good-byes to my friends and family. Then my mom, dad and Gloria took me to Bradley International Airport, Connecticut.

My dad was a man of few words. As I was about to board the plane, he said, "I am proud of you son. I am sure you will be okay. It looks like your brother will serve most of his service time in Germany, so it seems like you are the only one in the family going to Vietnam. Do your job, keep on your toes and we will see you after your tour ends."

The first stop on my flight to Seattle, Washington and the Fort Lewis area was going to be O'Hare International in Chicago. I knew that I had a two-hour layover before the next leg of my flight. As I stepped off the plane, my mind was on getting a bite to eat and I asked where I could get some food.

I found a small eatery. As I sat down to eat, I was facing the bar and saw two men in army dress uniforms coming out of the bar. They were a little under the weather. I was not old enough to buy booze legally and had had only a few drinks in my life. The sight of these two did not leave a very good impression of military people in my mind.

An hour and a half later, I got on board the flight to Seattle. I found my seat and settled in for the flight. I was still thinking about those two soldiers as I fell asleep to the hum of the engines. I woke up to the sound of the pilot announcing that we were landing and had no idea how long I had slept.

Stepping off the plane, there were many thoughts going through my head. Where do I go from here? Where is Fort Lewis, Washington? I guess I will need a taxi. Spotting several taxies close by, I flagged one down. "Sir, I am headed to Fort Lewis. Can you take me there?"

The answer I got from the cab driver told me he had made the trip between Fort Lewis and the airport for military guys many times and knew what he was doing. He said, "Yes, I can take you there, but you should wait until morning to check in because it is too late to check in tonight. If you want to get any sleep, I suggest getting a room near Fort Lewis. I will pick you up in the morning and take you the rest of the way."

True to his word, the cab driver was there early the next morning and took me to Fort Lewis.

I was positive that once I had checked in I would soon be on my way to Vietnam. I was surprised to find myself among several others waiting to get travel orders.

As I made formation, I knew I was in for the same old BS, "police" the area (an Army term that meant clean-up the area), being called out for details or heading back to the barracks to sit and wait. Being in the army was always a game of hurry up and hang on we are not ready to do that yet. However, I was getting used to it. I spent most of my time checking the list every hour to make sure my name had not been added or walking around the area to pass the time.

On the second day, it was more of the same, police call and then going back to the barracks to wait. On my third day, they picked me for KP duty at a mess hall that was set up for Vietnam returnees. The sergeant in charge said, "Don't get any ideas. This mess hall is for the Vietnam returnees and none of you look like you just came home."

I was not sure what he meant by those words until I noticed what everyone was eating. They were eating steak! Never had I been in an army mess hall where steak was on the menu. This gave me a bad feeling about where they were sending me. I thought that if I worked the dining area on clean up so that I could get some answers, so I asked for that job.

Each group of Vietnam returnees was small. I got a chance to talk to one of the soldiers, "Why is it that I see so many guys come home and most of them bypass the steak meal?"

The answer did not really surprise me, "Most of us would rather get out of this place and back to our families. I am because I have to wait to leave, so I may as well have one last meal on the army. I have finished my service time and now I have to wait for my discharge orders."

On the morning of the fourth day, I found myself getting on a bus that would take us to the airport where I had to board a Boeing 707. I just knew there was no turning back now.

The flight to South East Asia was long and boring. There was the steady hum of the turbine engines. Every time we hit an air pocket, the aircraft would dip and I could see the wings flex. How anything like this aircraft could fly was nothing but amazing. As I sat in my seat next to the window, my mind went off to thoughts of what Vietnam was really like. Was it as hot as I had heard? Did it rain a lot or was that just another rumor? Would I have to sleep in a tent or were there buildings? Would I make it back alive?

I came back to the real world when the pilot's voice came over the intercom. "We are landing on the island of Guam. If you will look out the windows on the left side of the aircraft that little island is where we are going to land."

Looking out my window, I thought there is no way we are landing on that little airstrip. I knew I was not the only one thinking this because someone aboard made a comment, "What, is this guy nuts? We can't land there!"

I held my breath until the plane was almost to a stop. I commented to the man next to me, "A few more feet and we would have been swimming."

As the plane came to a stop at the terminal, the pilot informed us, "Everyone must deplane while we refuel. There is a snack bar inside but do not leave the terminal. Leave your belongings on board unless there is something you need with you."

Almost an hour later, we were back on board and taking off. Knowing how short the runway was, I sure was glad when the wheels of the 707 finally lifted off the runway. I heard the wheels as they folded up inside the bottom of the aircraft.

I decided to kick back and try to rest. Then I dozed off. My dream world ended abruptly by the voice of the pilot, "Welcome to the Republic of South Vietnam. It is cool today and is 101 degrees in the shade. We will be landing at Cam Rahn Bay. When we land, please exit the plane quickly and follow the instructions of the people on the ground because they were just hit by mortars."

In processing was at Cam Rahn Bay.

As everyone got off the plane, those in charge sent everyone to an area without a bunker. We needed to stay there until further orders came down. I thought to myself, no one seems to be concerned except for those who are telling us where to go. There was no shooting, no explosions, and no one was carrying a weapon, so maybe this was a way to make us alert to what could happen.

After some time had gone by, they told us to form up near what must have been the operation center. We needed to get bedding from supply, go find a bunk for the night and be out in the same area the next morning at 0700 hours (7:00 am).

The next morning, I joined the rest and waited to see where I was going. They did not call my name so it was back to my bunk area to wait for the next call. We had to come out and check three times a day to see if our names were on the roster to leave next, but also to listen in case they called a special formation.

Two days later, I was standing in formation when I heard, "The following people are the lucky guys going to the 1st Cav. Good luck as you are going into a unit that always sees the action. Turn in your bedding, grab your bags and be ready to leave for your units."

As the sergeant called the names, I was thinking, what am I in for now? Please do not call my name this time. My thoughts were soon broken into as I heard, "Private Warriner, 2nd Battalion 20th Artillery." What was this sergeant saying? I am in aviation not artillery. There must be a mistake. As I looked at my orders that they handed me, I noticed that the orders did read 2nd Battalion 20th Artillery. I thought I should ask someone if maybe there was a mistake and decided to ask the sergeant passing out the orders.

I approached Sergeant Brooks, "Sergeant Brooks, there must be a mistake, I have an aviation MOS, not artillery."

Sergeant Brooks spoke abruptly, "Private, that is what your orders say and that is where you are going. Now get your bags, get over there and be ready to go!"

I was still not used to calling sergeants by sergeant so I replied, "Yes, Sir." Then grabbing my bags, I ran to the designated spot, thinking this sure is BS. I hope I can get this fixed because I do not want to be in an artillery unit.

I found myself boarding a C130 headed for God knows where. As the plane landed at An Khe airstrip, I found Specialist Pickwell waiting for me in a jeep. He would take me to the base camp of the 2nd Battalion 20th Artillery.

I thought that since this is a lower ranking person, maybe I could get some answers. "Specialist, what kind of unit is this? I do not have an artillery MOS. I went to school to be a helicopter mechanic."

The Specialist started to laugh, "If your MOS is aviation, don't worry, we are an Aerial Rocket Artillery unit. We have UH-1 B and C model Huey helicopters. Do you know to which Battery you are going to be assigned?"

After his answer, I was feeling better. I responded, "My orders just say 2nd Battalion 20th Artillery".

The Specialist came right back, "If that is the case, Battalion will tell you what battery you will be sent to. Usually, new recruits go with the next mail bird and I am sending a batch out tomorrow or the next day. I am the Battalion mail clerk."

When we got to the base camp area, they sent me to supply to sign for my gear and then find a bunk to sleep on. I thought this is the way of the army, hurry up and wait. The next morning, I had to help Specialist Pickwell inventory some things that belonged to someone who had died doing his job for his country. There were things like his wallet, writing paper, and even letters that must have been from his loved ones. Doing this inventory made me think how his family would feel when they got his things back. I told myself that I would survive this crazy time in my life. I would do whatever it took to stay out of harm's way.

The next day, I found myself on a Caribou headed to another area with no idea of what to expect. Soon we landed on this dirt runway they called LZ Two Bits.

As I got off the plane, the Crew Chief instructed me to go over to the operations bunker, which was on the side of the runway. A sergeant came out of the bunker and asked me, "Where are you headed, Private?"

I now had orders for Charlie Battery, so I said, "Charlie Battery 2nd Battalion 20th Artillery, do you know where they are located?"

The Sergeant was quick to reply, "Oh, you are headed for the ARA! Two of their aircraft are working out of here today. I do not know if Charlie Battery is the one working the area, but I will find out or, if they will take you to the unit. They are flying support for one of the lift units. Put your bags here, and I will contact them on the radio."

I watched as several aircraft came in and then left the LZ. I wondered if any of those were from my unit. Time sure dragged on. Then the sergeant interrupted my thoughts. "Private Warriner, this is Captain Neeb. He is from the ARA. He is going to drop you at Tam Ky." I did not know it at that time but he was from another battery and not Charlie Battery.

Captain Neeb spoke with a voice that told me he commanded respect, "Private, grab your bags and head for that Huey over there. The Crew Chief will tell you where to place your bags."

As the Captain went into the bunker, I picked up my bags and started towards the aircraft. As I got closer to the aircraft, I noticed some red marking on the aircraft. The tips of the skids had red paint and the stinger was red. In addition, there was an area just behind the front door where the cargo door met the fuselage and markings on the cargo. This aircraft looked like it would have a red square or box shape if they closed the cargo door. I thought this must be how our aircraft were marked.

When I reached the Bravo model Huey, the Crew Chief was unhooking the main rotor blade. He already had his flight helmet on and helped me with my bags as he told me where to sit.

As I watched the Crew Chief doing his duties, I thought, he must have been a Crew Chief for a while. He called out, "Clear and untied!"

The right seat pilot was ready and responded, "Coming through!" as he hit the starter. The turbine engine whined as the main rotor slowly started turning. I watched the Crew Chief as he went out back of the aircraft. Later I found out that he went to watch for leaks and in case of fire. As the engine got up to speed, I could see the pilot doing his checks to make sure everything was okay.

The main rotor was reaching full RPM as the Captain was getting into his seat. I was watching the

Crew Chief going about his job of sliding the armor plates forward and closing the doors. He was checking to make sure all was okay around the aircraft so they could lift off.

Once the Crew Chief had taken his seat on the left side, he plugged in his helmet and grabbed his M-60.

We picked up to a hover and soon we were in the air headed for Tam Ky airstrip. I was enjoying my first flight in a Huey and deep in thought. I could enjoy this type of job. Then, the Crew Chief interrupted my thoughts as he leaned toward me so that I could hear him above the whine of the transmission.

The Crew Chief yelled, "Hang on, Private. It looks like you are in for treat. We have some bad guys that have our guys pinned down." I was not sure what the Crew Chief meant but I was about to find out. We circled this area and the Crew Chief yelled, "Hang on, we're rolling hot."

I did not know what he meant about rolling hot but I was about to find out. As the aircraft went into a dive, I felt the seat come out from under me, just as it does on a roller coaster and then there was this roar as a pair of 2.75" folding fin aerial rockets left the tubes. As we pulled out of the dive, the Crew Chief opened up with his M-60 rat-tat-tat. The noise without a helmet on was deafening. My ears hurt because I did not get them covered soon enough.

After we pulled out of the dive, we circled again and went into another dive at which time the pilot punched off several more rockets. This time I was ready and covered my ears to block the noise better, but the roar of the rockets as they left the tubes still hurt my ears. Again, when we pulled out of the dive, the Crew Chief opened up with his M-60 rat-tat-tat. As we circled the area, I could see the pilot talking on the radio and figured he was in contact with the troops on the ground.

We were circling the area and went into another dive, which I was not expecting, making me rise up off my seat. Again, I heard the roar of the rockets followed by the sound of the M-60. I could not see what they were firing at but could see smoke drifting up through the trees from the impact.

After the third rocket run, I was sure they had released us from the mission because we flew out of the area. The Crew Chief seemed to be relaxed as he looked over at me. As we continued our flight towards Tam Ky, I was thinking about how loud the nose was and wondered how it would be with a flight helmet on.

When we landed at Tam Ky, the Crew Chief jumped out and motioned to me that this was my destination.

I noticed we had landed on another dirt strip used as a runway for aircraft, but this time, there were several "B" Bravo and "C" Charlie model Huey helicopters along both sides of the runway. All these aircraft had the red marking, but these had a red circle instead of the square that I had noticed on the aircraft I was riding in. This must be marking for Charlie Battery and this must be my new home. I later found out that each battery had separate markings with a red X for Headquarters Battery, a red triangle for Alpha Battery, a red square for Bravo Battery and Charlie Battery used a red circle.

Sergeant First Class Cole met me as I got off the aircraft and grabbed my bags. "I am Sergeant Cole, welcome to Tam Ky, home of Charlie Battery 2nd Battalion 20th Artillery, and the best damn ARA unit in the 1st Cavalry Division or for that matter in the US Army. Let us see where we can put you up for the night and get you some chow before the mess hall is closed. Tomorrow you will be going into maintenance, so we can see what you learned in school."

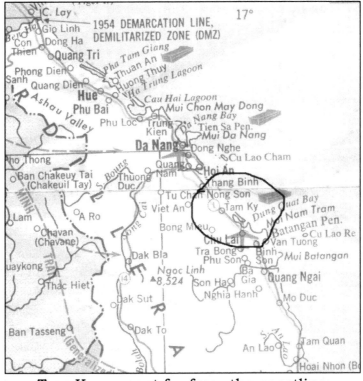

Tam Ky was not far from the coastline

4

CHARM SCHOOL

I had been in Charlie Battery only a few days and had already made friends with two men that I met at Fort Rucker. PVT Jerry Boerm and PVT George Padilla had been in my 67A10 class but were both in a different 67N20 class. George had been the leader of another class at the same time as I was a class leader. It felt good to know somebody from the Fort Rucker classes.

I had been in Charlie Battery less than two weeks and had already pulled guard duty three times. This made me wish I could get a chance to be a Crew Chief and get out of maintenance. They seemed to be the lucky ones and never seemed to pull guard duty. Being a private as well as being the new guy, I expected to get the bad end of the stick. When I pulled guard duty, they expected me to be in the maintenance hangar by 1000 hours (10:00 a.m.) the following day. This was because there was always plenty of work and not enough people to get it done. They expected us to get enough sleep while on guard duty by pulling a shift on and then one off until the night was over. Each person had either bunker duty or flight line guard duty. To top it off, Charlie Battery had no other unit to guard the area around the battery, which meant even flight line needed to be guarded in case the bad guys got through the wire and did damage to the helicopters.

Our enemy, Charlie, would sneak through the wire and place a grenade in the fuel tank of helicopters, with 100 mile an hour tape wrapped around the handle and the pin removed. The fuel would soften the tape, releasing the handle and the aircraft would blow up where ever it was at the time. I never was where it happened and I never wanted to be either. Therefore, if I had guard duty on the flight line, I was extra careful to keep an eye on the fence line.

Right after lunch at 1300 hour (1:00 p.m.), I saw SFC Cole coming towards me. I thought to myself; not again, I just got off duty this morning. "Private Warriner, I have good and bad news for you, depending on how you feel about it. Tomorrow, you and Private Padilla will be heading back to An Khe for Charm School. You should be back here within a week or two."

"We are short Crew Chiefs in the battery. Many have completed their tour and have gone home. Others are getting short and will be rotating home soon. We need new Crew Chiefs. Right now, we need replacements for two of the Bravo models. Are you interested in being a Crew Chief?" Before I could answer, he said, "Even if you are not interested that is what you will be when you return from Charm School."

I did not want to sound too interested, "Sergeant Cole, I wanted to stay in maintenance at least for a while first. I want to learn more. Can't I fly as a gunner a while or something before I get my first crewing job?"

"That's the breaks Warriner. I think you will be crewing 054. It is one of our older B Models but a good aircraft. Padilla, I think 050 will be your aircraft. Both of you be ready to start flying as a Crew Chief when you get back here. Warriner, Kellogg will train you. But, I am not sure who will train you, Padilla."

The next morning with my bags in tow, I waited at the flight line with George for our ride. At 0645 hours, Warrant Officer Comer came onto the flight line, "You guys better go grab some chow if you haven't already. We are not leaving for about another half hour. Put your bags in 054 as that is your ride to An Khe."

PVT Padilla answered, "We already ate sir, so I guess we will just wait."

Mr. Comer smiled, "Still time to grab a cup of that great mud they call coffee. But be back here ready to go in 20 minutes."

I remembered my trip getting to Tam Ky, "George, maybe we can find a little something in case we are late getting to An Khe. You know how things get turned around here."

There were no delays in leaving or along the way to An Khe. Once there, Specialist Pickwell met us and took us by jeep to Charm School to sign in.

We both thought the school was a joke; at least for us fly boys. Learning how to repel from a helicopter seemed ridiculous. When would we ever want to do that! We were going to fly in them, not jump out of them. I thought it was interesting watching two ARA aircraft putting on a demonstration for Charm School. I thought that will be me in a few days. I even wondered if they were Charlie Battery aircraft. Maybe 054 was one of those putting on the show for us.

That evening after chow, I let George know my feeling. "Now we know what it is like to be on the ground and us up above doing our job. I think being a

Crew Chief would be where I prefer to be rather than in maintenance."

George was not so sure. "Not for me. I would rather be in maintenance. I just don't like so much guard duty, but I will do whatever I am told and try to stay out of trouble."

I did not want to pursue the matter anymore so I changed the subject. "Well, tomorrow we should be headed back to Tam Ky. Let's get some rest."

The next morning, George and I were ready to go back to Tam Ky. However, the Army had other plans and sent us across An Khe to the ARA base camp. We were on our own without transportation.

Specialist Pickwell met us as we arrived. "You may as well get some bedding. You will be here a few days. Everyone is busy up north and you will leave on the next mail trip. Tomorrow, you will guard some locals while they clean up around here. After breakfast, meet me at the orderly room at 0730 hours."

That night, George and I decided to look around the old Battalion area and see what was left of the Battalion buildings. The ARA had used An Khe as base camp since it landed in Vietnam back in 1965. Since that time, everyone had moved except for a small hand full of personnel. Most of the buildings were standing idle such as the Officers Club, commanders' quarters and most of all the platoon and enlisted quarters.

The Battalion Commanders quarters still had a sign that read LTC R M TYSON on the door. LTC Robert M. Tyson was the Battalion Commander when I arrived and we expected him to remain as the Battalion Commander until 1968.

When we got to the Officers Club, we looked in the window. We could see our battalion crest hanging on the wall that read in bold lettering DUTY NOT REWARD.

George said, "Isn't that the crest we wear on our dress uniform?'

I had never seen one. I told him that I thought it was but was not sure.

Next, we went out to the north of our old Battalion area where we found the remains of a CH-54, flying crane helicopter, which gave George and me an eerie feeling. We decided that we had had enough of our wandering and would return to our bunks for the night. When we did, we found a Charlie Battery Crew Chief had finished his tour and was going home the next day. Since he was a Crew Chief, I asked him which aircraft he had crewed. I was very surprised when he said it was 054, the same aircraft I was going to start crewing. I was so surprised that I never even asked his name and did not even look to see what his nametag read.

That night, I thought I would write a letter or two to let those on the home front know I was okay. I also wanted to see how Gloria was doing. I had not heard from her since arriving in Vietnam. I was not sure why. Was it due to the mail not catching up to me, her using the wrong address or my mail not getting to her for some reason? I had not been in any action but did not want to alarm anyone either if I had been. I had already written to my mom but I could not concentrate on my letter to Gloria.

George and I were talking when he noticed that our sleeping bags had a zipper that could be zipped from inside as well as the outside. We had turned off the lights and were still talking about things for a while. We finally decided we had better get some sleep.

As I lay there trying to sleep, I was thinking about that stupid zipper and decided to try out how it worked. I slid the zipper up from the inside and had just my head sticking out. I was thinking that this must be nice when you are in a cold area like Alaska but not for Vietnam.

It was hot inside the sleeping bag with it zipped up, so I went to unzip it. I could not easily get my hands up to where the zipper was located. When I finally did manage to get my hands up, I could not find the zipper. Okay, do not panic. It is there. It could not have vanished. There it is. Now unzip it. When I tried to unzip it, I found that I could not because it was stuck.

Now panic was starting to set in. I did not want to feel stupid because I could not get it unzipped, but the fact was that it would not open. Okay calm down. Try it again. Maybe I just was not pulling on it at the right angle and it will unzip this time. No, it was stuck for sure. Now the panic was really starting to set in. What will I do if I cannot make the zipper work? Do not panic. George is across the room. No, I do not want to wake him, but it still would not open. Now I was beginning to sweat, partly from the heat and partly from panic. I was telling myself, okay calm down, you are just panicking over nothing. You cannot make the zipper work because you are in a panic.

All along, I knew in my mind that it was just stuck and I would get it unzipped. Yet my mind was running faster than a racecar on a high-speed track. I could just see the headlines back home. American military area hit by incoming Enemy rockets. US Army soldier dies in sleeping bag due to heart attack caused by sleeping bag zipper. Would they call it combat related or caused by natural causes?

I was about to yell to George, when the zipper broke loose and I was finally free of the sleeping bag.

I sat up in my bunk. My heart was going faster than my mind had been going before I got the bag unzipped.

The night seemed extremely long after the sleeping bag ordeal and I lay listening to the outgoing artillery. They were firing H&I (harassment and interdiction) to keep Charlie on his toes by shooting into suspected enemy areas. At least, the artillery was outgoing.

The next morning, George and I grabbed some chow and waited to pull the guard duty as instructed the night before. I was reluctant to tell George about what had happened to me the night before but finally gave in and told him. We had a good laugh about it but soon it was a forgotten memory.

After breakfast, Specialist Pickwell arrived with three Vietnamese locals. They tasked us to watch them with our M-16 rifles without ammo because they had not issued that to us. My thoughts went off to when I was at Fort Rucker and had to guard someone without any equipment. I was in a combat zone and they had not even issued me any ammo for my weapon. What was wrong with this army! If the locals did anything, I guessed I could point the M-16 at them and shout "bang-bang-bang!"

Author with gas mask, M-16 and no ammo

The next day, it was more of the same. Just before lunch, Specialist Pickwell came to us; "We are sending the locals home. I will be taking you to the airfield this afternoon. Get some lunch. Grab your bags and meet me by the orderly room at 1300 hours."

After lunch, George and I grabbed our bags and waited for our ride. When the jeep came, we put our bags in the jeep and headed for the airfield.

George Padilla

Specialist Pickwell pointed to a Chinook that was just landing. "See the S**t Hook that just landed over there? They are taking a sling load to another unit and that is your ride back to Tam Ky."

As we boarded the aircraft, I was thinking of how it must be to fly in this aircraft. It had hydraulic lines everywhere and was very noisy. We picked up to a hover and I could see one of the crewmembers looking down through the hole where the cargo hook was located. We must have hooked onto the sling load because the crewmember stood up and he took up a spot in a side window.

Once the payload was hooked on, we lifted off from An Khe. Soon I felt the aircraft turning and coming in for a landing. As we came to a hover, a crewmember was watching out the cargo hole again. I figured he must have been talking to the pilots to let them know when to disconnect the sling load and drop it.

We lifted off again. After a short flight, we seemed to be landing again. As the rear gate lowered, I could see the aircraft of my unit so I knew I was back at Charlie Battery. It was a welcomed sight. At least, we could get some good chow again. Charlie Battery had some of the best chow in the battalion and everyone seemed to know it.

George and I put our bags in our sleeping area and headed for the mess tent to see if we were in time to get any chow. We were too late but the cook was still there and he made us a couple sandwiches.

5

LEARNING NOT ALWAYS FUN

The next morning, right after I had some of the army's famous powdered eggs and a cup of coffee, I went back to my tent and Specialist Fifth Class Kellogg met me at the doorway. "Warriner, I am Specialist Kellogg, but call me Jerry. I will be training you. Before we start, let's go see if we can get you a pistol. You will be glad to get rid of that M-16 once you have two M-60 machine guns to worry about."

I had no idea that both M-60s' were my responsibility; "You mean I have to be responsible for both those M-60s' on my aircraft? I thought my gunner had to take care of one of them."

Jerry looked at me and smiled, "You will find out that most of the time, you will not have a gunner. The ARA aircraft are already loaded too heavy with all the rockets and ammo. Now let's go see about a pistol for you."

As we walked, Kellogg spoke. "You need to learn how things work around here. There are three line Batteries: Alpha, Bravo, and our battery is Charlie. They are all set up the same. Headquarters is Battalion. Some call it Headquarters Battery; it is our control point. Each Battery has twelve aircraft and is further broken down into three platoons of four aircraft each. There are two aircraft in a section and one section usually handles most fire missions. If needed, they call in another section to make sure the job is completed. Each aircraft section has a lead aircraft and carries the section leader. This puts one person in control of the mission."

How our aircraft were set up

"Each day, your aircraft will be assigned a status of HOT, BLUE, STAND-BY ONE, STAND-BY TWO or STAND-BY THREE. If we have enough flyable aircraft, there could be a STAND-BY FOUR section. However, this seldom will happen. When a mission comes down, the HOT section goes first. Then the BLUE section moves up to the HOT status and each STAND-BY section moves up the ladder one slot. You could be on STAND-BY one second and the next could be you on a mission. As the sections return, everyone moves back down the ladder, or your aircraft could even replace another because it is down for repairs or maintenance. Remember, you could be in the last STAND-BY slot and then a second later you are in the HOT status. This can happen for any of a number of reasons. You will catch on real fast. Just be ready when it's your turn because we have two minutes to be in the air when the horn goes off."

"If you go to operations, you will see a status board. On the board, the Hot section is marked by a "RED" dot, BLUE is a "BLUE" dot and the STAND-BY sections are marked by a "YELLOW" dot and a number. It is up to you as the Crew Chief to know the status of your aircraft and be ready when your aircraft takes off."

Kellogg went on to explain. "The commanders of the Battalion, Brigade and even the Division can call a fire mission and they will do it just to test us on how fast we get off the ground. If we were not fast enough to make them happy, we would get a bunch of crap and we could bet that they would test us again when we do not expect it.

At the arms room, we found out that the Battery Commander had changed how he wanted weapons handled. He wanted only the officers to have the pistols. This meant there were no more pistols authorized for the enlisted personnel. Kellogg asked the armament officer, "If I turn in my .38, can you issue it to Warriner? It would still be with an enlisted guy and would be almost like I never turned it in."

The armament officer was worried that he could get into trouble but because the pistol was already in the hands of an enlisted soldier, he thought it would be okay. I turned in my M-16, was issued the .38 and Kellogg was issued my M-16.

As we left the arms room, Kellogg spoke, "I only have a short time left in country. I will not be flying once I train you, so I can live with the change. Besides,

I would rather have an M-16 if Charlie gets through the wire."

When we got back to the flight line, Kellogg wanted me to understand my job. "This is your home away from home. You will live here more than in the Crew Chief tent. I have already done the daily inspection but I want you to do it any way to learn. Get the log book and let's do your daily inspection."

I climbed in, found the logbook and we started to do the inspection.

I was just finishing the inspection with Kellogg close behind me when I heard Captain Ott, "Chief, we are on stand-by one, is this thing ready to fly?"

Kellogg spoke up, "Yes sir, but I am training your new Crew Chief and he is doing the daily inspection so he can learn how to do it."

I was thinking; if the HOT section was still on the ground, I had time to learn; "Sir, if you don't mind, I would like to do the preflight with you so I can see some of what to look for and maybe learn more. I am fresh out of the Huey mechanics course."

Captain Ott held his hand out as he spoke, "That sounds okay to me. I am Captain Ott, the second Platoon leader. I heard you were the new Crew Chief for this bird. She is one of our older birds but she is a good aircraft and one I enjoy flying. Let's get started before a mission comes down."

We were finishing the preflight as the horn went off. This moved me to the BLUE section on the status board. Kellogg was on the left side getting things ready. "Warriner, you sit on the right side today and watch what I do. It will be the best way to learn. The can on the floor next to the ammo on your side is an assault-can that I borrowed from another Crew Chief."

After a moment Kellogg added, "You can make a new assault-can from the container the M-60 ammo came in. That will give you 200 rounds of ammo to use at a time. By removing the cover from the container and making a plate for the end, it would hook on the M-60. Most Crew Chiefs prefer to use it because the rounds do not jam as easily as a belt feed out of a box on the floor and it will give you more freedom. I prefer to use a belt feed and you may find you like the belt feed better also, but let's start you off with the assault-can. Later, if you want to try the belt feed, you can do it on your own time. Hook the assault-can on as you are taking off and load your M-60 once you are airborne. Remember, to leave the safety on until you are ready to fire and put it back on before you land. Try hooking the assault can on and load your M-60. Aim it out as if you are getting ready to fire it."

I sat down and hooked the assault can on the M-60, lifted the cover, put the belt of ammo into place and closed the cover.

As I did this, Kellogg continued, "You will have to tip your weapon on its side a little so the spent brass will fall away from the aircraft. If you do not do this, you will have to replace your tail rotor because the brass will hit the tail rotor. This is why we keep the Crew Chief in the left door and another reason we don't carry a door gunner very often."

Just after I closed the cover on my M-60, the fire mission horn went off. Having the horn go off twice in a short time, I knew that there must be something big happening. "That is good. I think you will be all right. Now put it away because I think we will be bounded soon." Before I could finish putting things away the horn went off again, Kellogg yelled to me, "Get the main rotor blade untied so we can crank and get your gear on."

I ran and untied the main rotor and called, "Clear and untied!" I heard, "Coming through." I grabbed my chest protector, put it on and grabbed my helmet as I heard the turbine starting to whine. I moved to the right side to check the engine for leaks. As soon as the engine was up to a point I thought all was okay, I moved forward, slid the armor plate forward for the right side pilot and closed his door.

Kellogg had already finished the left side and was heading to his seat for the mission. I got in my side, put my seat belt on, plugged in my helmet and grabbed my M-60 that was hanging on the bungee cord. As I plugged my helmet in, I heard Kellogg key his mike, "Clear left rear Sir!"

I took the cue, "Clear right rear sir!" I felt proud that I was catching on quick.

Warrant Officer Babcock, a red haired pilot from Michigan was the pilot at the controls. Captain Ott was on the radio getting clearance and the fire mission information. We picked up to a hover and started to back out of the revetment. "Tail coming left"
Kellogg responded, "Tail clear left."

I could hear Captain Ott on the radio with our wing aircraft asking if they had heard the information on the mission. Then he keyed his intercom and briefed us on the mission, "We have some Grunts pinned down. Six Seven is on station with only a few rounds of ammo left for the gunner and has expended all their rockets. They are trying to hold things down until we can get there. This could be a long day."

Soon, we were on station and Captain Ott keyed his intercom again. "Kellogg, we will be making our run from north to south and breaking left. The bad guys are inside their perimeter and we are firing real close to our guys so keep your rounds close to the target area as we do not want any good guys hurt." Then he followed with, "I have the aircraft", which meant that he was taking over the control from Babcock.

Kellogg clicked his mike twice to let Captain Ott know that he understood. Captain Ott took control of the aircraft and soon nosed the aircraft into a rocket run. "Falcon 68, rolling hot." Swoosh-swoosh-swoosh the rockets left the tubes. As we pulled out of the dive, all I could see was sky from my side, but that was okay because I was not sure of myself yet anyway. When I looked over at Kellogg, he was almost standing in the door and leaning over the rocket pods firing his M-60.

We made three passes with our rocket runs. Then Captain Ott told us that the troops felt they had it under control now and we could go home.

Kellogg keyed his intercom on our way back to Tam Ky, "Sir, our new Crew Chief hasn't fired the M-60 yet.

Can we go to a free fire area and let him fire a few rounds?"

Captain Ott radioed in for permission to go to the free fire zone. Moments later, given permission, we changed course towards the free fire area. We were in an area that did not look any different from any other area to me. "Okay door gunner, see if you can hit that tree at the base." I opened up with a short burst from my M-60. I knew I had to lead the target and hit the tree by the time I had fired about 10 or 20 rounds. Boy was I shaking. Did I do okay? I guess I would find out soon enough.

Mister Babcock keyed his intercom, "Not bad for a new guy. Dump a few more rounds on the tree. There are no moving targets to test you on here. But I guess you will get a chance for that soon enough." I fired a few more rounds on another pass and then Captain Ott said we needed to return to base camp. I was pleased that I had a chance to fire the M-60 and even more pleased that I was able to hit the target after only a few rounds.

When we got back to Tam Ky and we were shutting down, I discovered another lesson. I was not John Wayne or any other western star and wearing a .38 on your side was OK for these movie stars or maybe in the old west. However, it sure was not okay when you were flying in the door of a Huey in combat. My pistol was gone and so was the holster, which gave me a sinking feeling deep in the pit of my stomach. The leather had rotted, causing it to break away from my belt. Now there was no sign of there ever being a holster or the 38. I was sure the stuff would hit the fan and my crewing days would be over before they really began. At the very least, I would be paying for that weapon. With the pay that I was getting, I had nothing left as it was, never mind having to pay for an unexpected cost, I would be paying for it a long time. The imaginary sharp pains in the pit of my stomach now were almost unbearable.

I was not sure how I was going to break the news that I had lost my .38. I knew I had to do it now and not later. If I waited any time at all, they surely would not believe me. If I waited and told the platoon sergeant someone stole my pistol, that was not the truth and I would not have been able to live with myself.

I figured I would tell Kellogg first and let him break the news to Captain Ott. Maybe this would soften the blow. The outcome was not looking good no matter how I looked at it. I sure was in hot water and it felt like it was boiling.

When I told Kellogg, he was upset and rightfully so because he had given me his .38 and now it was gone. When he told Captain Ott, the look on the Captain's face told me all I needed to know. My stuff was sure in the wind.

I went to work cleaning out the brass from my aircraft and loading the rockets. I needed to keep busy so my mind would not dwell on what had just happened.

As the fuel truck pulled up next to my aircraft, I had almost finished cleaning the last of the spent brass from the inside of my aircraft. I stopped cleaning and slid the cargo door forward so I could refuel my aircraft. Refueling the aircraft was something I had never done before, but knew that I would have to do it whenever the fuel truck driver could not. This was another learning process. The fuel came out of the nozzle very fast. I knew from my gas station days that if I did not slow it down when it got to the top, I was going to get a bath. Knowing that getting fuel on one's skin sure could lead to adverse effects, I slowed the fuel down when it got close to the top, as I did want not want to take a bath in JP4.

When I finished Kellogg commented, "That was a smart move. Where did you learn how to do that?"

I explained that it was mostly common sense. I had worked at a gas station before entering the army, and if the nozzle did not shut off when the tank was full, you would get a bath. I knew better because there was no automatic shut off on the fuel hose.

As I was finishing up, I was thinking that maybe tomorrow would be a better day. I sure hoped that it would be.

1st Calvary Division Patch

6

FIRST LAAGER MISSION

I was at my aircraft early the next day. I wanted to try to make a good impression. I just knew my stuff was in the wind and maybe by showing a good effort, they would not be so tough on me.

When I had completed the daily aircraft inspection, which included updating the logbook, I decided to keep busy and added some extra ammo. I also hid some M-60 ammo near the aircraft. I figured I could get it if needed. This would save me time unless someone else found it and used it.

Kellogg had not come out to the flight line yet. I thought this was unusual because he usually was in the flight line before I was. I decided to work on building my own assault-can. I wanted to get the loaned one back to where it came from in case they needed it. I was checking to see how much I needed to remove from the area I had been filing. When I looked up, I noticed Sergeant Cole heading towards my aircraft. I thought maybe if I looked busy and did not look at him, he would go by me without stopping. I just knew he was looking for me. He was looking for me! I just knew it. When he was within hearing distance he said, "Private Warriner, we need to talk." I knew I must be in trouble because he never called me by rank on the flight line.

I thought my crewing days were over and I was going to LBJ (Long Binh Jail). I was surprised when I heard, "I spoke to Specialist Kellogg and Captain Ott. We all feel that it was not your fault. Losing the weapon, should be a combat loss. We stuck our necks out and went to the CO on your behalf. It took some talking but there will be no charges pressed. You will have to get a M-16 to replace your .38. There are no more .38's or .45's being issued to enlisted personnel because the pilots are getting them all. You will have to wait to go get another M-16 because you are in the blue section today and will not have time to get one right now."

I knew I was very lucky. I could have received a court martial for loosing that pistol. I felt a big weight lifted off my back, "Thank you, Sergeant Cole."

Sergeant Cole was quick to reply, "You should thank Captain Ott and Specialist Kellogg, as they are the ones that really convinced the Commander not to press charges." With that, Sergeant Cole turned and left the flight line.

Not long after that, Kellogg came onto the flight line. "I just came from Flight Operations and checked to see what our status would be for the day. We are blue today. If there aren't many missions, we can have some time to teach you a few more lessons."

The rest of the day was quiet. Hardly any fire missions came down. That was the way things were in the ARA. One day you did not get a chance to breath and the next you never got off the ground to get some cool air to breathe. Because we were on blue status, I stayed near the aircraft and did some cleaning in a few areas I felt needed a little sprucing up.

The next day, I was moved to STRAND-BY TWO. This gave me a chance to start cleaning my M-60 machine guns. I did get a chance late in the day to go on a mission and fire my M-60 again. It was a great feeling to know that I put everything back together properly and did not have any malfunctions.

The next few days went smooth with only a few missions. I only got off the ground a couple of times. By the time a week or so had gone by, I felt better about things and my thoughts were on when I would move to the left side into the Crew Chief spot.

On December 11, Kellogg came onto the flight line, "You are now officially the Crew Chief of 054, move to the left side of the aircraft and set things up the way you want them. I will stay on a few days to ride as your gunner. You know you are lucky to have had me to train you. I was handed two M-60s, told I was the new Crew Chief and that I was on my own."

As I was setting up how I wanted things so I could reach them, I looked up and saw Warrant Officer Johnson headed in my direction. He had to be on his way to my aircraft because he had passed every other aircraft and mine was the last one on the flight line. I had heard that he was a good pilot so was glad I would be flying with him and not one of the new pilots that were still not sure of themselves. Having one new enlisted man aboard an aircraft was bad enough without also having a new pilot.

"Chief, I will be flying with you today and Mr. Comer will be your AC. Tonight, we will be laagering at Chu Lai. I do not know if you have ever gone on a laager but you will need whatever you want for the night. We have to go make MACV happy. We will be flying most of the night on mortar patrol. You may want your jacket, as it gets a little cool flying at 2500 feet at night. Grab some chow as soon as the mess tent has it ready and whatever you want for the night and be back here at 1645 hours ready to take off."

I had not even thought about it being cooler during night flying but it made sense. At 1545, I ran to get some chow. Then went to the tent and grabbed my fatigue jacket, my letters I wanted to answer and paper so I could write if I had time. I just made it back to my aircraft in time to meet my pilots. Kellogg, who had already untied the main rotor said, "Next time keep your jacket in the aircraft. You may not be so lucky next time and have to leave without it. Besides you could be out somewhere and not return for a few days."

Mr. Johnson was already to crank. Therefore, I let him know we were all set. "Clear and untied."

We pulled pitch and headed for Chu Lai. After landing, I tied down the main rotor and Mr. Comer headed to operations. A short time later he was back, "Our wing aircraft will fly the first shift. They want us to stay where they can find us. Also, we have been invited to the enlisted club for some entertainment."

The door guard met us at the door. "You crazy 1st Cavalry guys are animals, but because our commander says you are here to protect us you can come in. If you get out of control, you are out of here." The bouncer that was at the door was close to six feet tall and looked like a weight lifter. I was sure they would not have much of a problem getting us to leave. Besides, they had told us we would have to check our weapons at the door. Mr. Comer stayed at the aircraft and kept an eye on my M-60s and all the weapons.

Mr. Johnson went to the club with us but was not comfortable being in an enlisted club. We only stayed a short time and did not see all the show. It really was not that great, as far as I was concerned. Back at the aircraft, I began to read a letter from my mom and did not even get a chance to finish it. My mind was not on that letter, but more on the fact that I still had not received any letters from Gloria.

At just before 2100 hours, I heard Mr. Comer, "Chief, grab the blade and let's crank."

My response was quick, "Yes Sir." As soon as the blade was untied, I called out, "Clear and untied."

Mr. Comer called out, "Coming through." Soon I could smell the fuel as the injectors sprayed it into the combustion chamber and could hear the sound of the igniters snapping. Seconds later, the turbine engine sprang to life and the main rotor started to turn.

As soon as the turbine was up and running, I closed the two pilot doors and took up my seat in the left door. As I plugged in my helmet, Mr. Johnson was looking back at me. "Chief, as soon as we lift off, you may as well close the cargo doors." I must have had a strange look on my face, "I guess you have never flown mortar patrol. We usually close the doors because it is cool up there at night and there is no sense in being cold if you don't have to."

I keyed my intercom, "Okay Sir."

Mr. Comer called for clearance and we lifted off. "Griffin Six Eight Papa, this is Six Eight Golf, we are airborne".

The response came back, "Six Eight Papa. Roger. We noticed your lights when you were cranking. We are turning final behind you for landing."

Our radio call sign had changed to Gallant Griffin, but everyone just shortened it to Griffin. Sometimes, I would just hear Six Eight, Six Eight Papa or Six Seven and not hear Griffin or any other preceding call name. This confused me so I thought I would ask later why this was.

Mortar patrol was boring. The pilots switched off so that whoever flew days would not be flying at night, giving them a chance to rest. The Crew Chiefs never were lucky enough to do that. With my cargo door shut, I had nothing to do until we touched down, unless something happened. I laid my head against the back wall, shut my eyes, and hoped that no one would notice.

I went into a semi sleep mode until I heard Mr. Comer on the radio. He was talking to our replacement aircraft. This snapped me back to reality.

After we had landed and shut down, I decided to ask about the call signs. "Jerry, I notice I usually fly with Griffin Six Eight, Six Eight Golf or Six Eight Papa, but I have heard other call signs within the battery. How does this work?"

Jerry answered, "Each Battery has a set of call signs and each section of the Battery has a set.

"Two Six is the battery commander for Alpha Battery and Two Seven, Two Eight and Two Nine for the platoons. Also, the battery uses Alpha, Bravo, Charlie, Delta, Echo and Foxtrot for section leaders and aircraft commanders."

"Bravo Battery uses Four-Six for the battery commander and the platoon leaders are Four-Seven, Four-Eight and Four-Nine with Golf, Hotel, India, Juliet, Kilo and Lima as section leaders and aircraft commanders."

"Our battery uses Six-Six for our commander and Six-Seven, Six-Eight and Six-Nine plus Mike, November, Oscar, Papa, Quebec and Romeo."

"Any time you hear a call sign ending in Six, you need to know that is the commander of the battery. But if you hear Six and nothing follows it, remember that is the Battalion commander."

Now I was confused, "What about Six-Eight Golf? You just said that Golf was a Bravo Battery call letter, but that does not match the rest of the list!"

Kellogg was not sure, "I guess they ran out of letters to use and still wanted to give him his aircraft commander's spot."

We flew two more mortar patrol missions. Then they released us from duty.

As soon as we got back to Tam Ky and tied down, I told Kellogg that I was heading for the latrine. As I went by the piss tubes, the stench of the urine swell almost gagged me. Why we had tubes stuck in the ground with a piece of screening over the end to piss in making the piss go into the ground did not make any sense, but I never questioned why. I guessed it was a way to make all the entire urine saturating the area. Pissing on the screen made the pee splatter and I think many men used the ground around the tubes. The smell in the outhouse was not a lot better. Under the outhouse, they had placed 55-gallon barrels cut in half and added diesel fuel to mix with the human waste. Every day these containers had more fuel added and then burned, which made no sense to me. This was to help kill the germs or smell. This mixture made me gag and gasp for air.

Piss tube

As I sat there doing my business, thoughts went through my head about how most every latrine I had been in since I arrived in Vietnam had no real toilet seats. Yet, Charlie Battery had nice seats and I began to wonder where they came from.

As I came out of the outhouse, I saw a pilot come running out of the officers' outhouse, with his pants down around his knees and screaming that he wanted to kill Magoo. Magoo was a monkey owned by one of the pilots and it was obvious that Magoo had bit the officer from under the outhouse. Magoo was on a dead run to get away from the officer.

Magoo and one of my pilots

Arriving back on the flight line, I found Jerry and asked him, "How did we manage to get real toilet seats when most of the others can't get them?"

He was laughing as he answered, "Captain Gorham and Sergeant Cole managed to get them for us. You know all our ammo comes in wooden boxes. We use these ammo boxes for everything like building the shower and outhouse. It is hard sitting on just a hole cut in the wood, so they wrote a letter. Sergeant Cole had noticed a stamp of Miller Box Company in Tuscaloosa, Alabama on most the ammo boxes. I understand that when they wrote to the Miller Box Company, they asked them if they could do something about toilet seats, because it was hard to make them out of the ammo boxes. A short time later, about eight new toilet seats arrived. Of course, when the Battalion Commander found out we had them, we had to give up some of the seats. It's better than getting splinters in the back side."

Magoo even had his own dog tags

I thought that was interesting. As I wrote home to my mom that night, I told her about how we got our toilet seats. I thought it was better than telling her a war story that would make her worry.

As I was trying to fall asleep that night, I thought of how hard it was sitting on a hole cut out of wood, and how it must have been in the old days when there were no toilet seats.

On December18, I was standing with Sergeant Cole and few others on the north end of our area, not far from the mess tent when we heard a gunshot.

We knew it was not from the area where we tested out weapons, because it had come from the direction of the tent where the maintenance people lived.

My mind went into over drive. Was this another foolish move by someone trying to shoot himself because he did not want to die in the hands of the enemy? Was it someone who had a gripe with someone else? Maybe it was an accident. Whatever it was, I did not want to know the answer.

Sergeant Cole headed for the tent where the shot came from and I headed for the Crew Chief tent. I sat on my bunk and tried to write a letter home to Mom and Dad, but I could not get my mind off what had just happened.

I could not seem to stop my mind from running. Who was involved? Did someone die? Did someone receive a wound by the round? As I sat there trying to compose myself, I heard one of our aircraft cranking up. Only one aircraft cranked. I guessed that it was going to take the wounded soldier out. I prayed that it was not the body of the person. I cringed at the thought that this was friendly fire.

As the sun went down, I thought that I had better get some rest while I could, in case my aircraft went out on a mission.

I had a very restless night. When I got up the next morning there was a buzz in the area about the day before. The rumor was some sergeant that had transferred in from another unit had shot the supply sergeant. I did not hear the names involved. I decided that it was not my business anyway and that it was over. Someone said it was only a shoulder wound and the sergeant would live but most likely, we would never see him again.

The shooting was an accident, but one of the officers was pressing charges. I was sure the sergeant that shot him would be a private before the investigation was over.

My mind went back to when I lost my pistol. Would this sergeant lose a stripe, get fined or worse yet thrown out of the army with a dishonorable discharge?

I made a promise to myself right then and there that I was going to do my time and try to keep my nose clean. I wanted to be the best Crew Chief I could be, work hard to get more rank and go home walking on my own two feet.

7

FLARE MISSION

I had been flying on the left side a few times without Kellogg and he felt I was ready to crew on my own. As usual, I was at my aircraft early getting ready for whatever mission came my way. I wanted to finish my own assault-can (an ammunition container for the M-60 machine gun, modified to allow the Crew Chief and/or door-gunner ready access) that I was constructing. Then, make a second one to use for the gunner's side. The process would have gone a lot faster if I had the proper tools to work with. I also wanted to build a spare in the event I needed it.

It was a slow day. When I finished my first assault-can, I started on the second one for my gunner. To me, this was important in case I ever had a gunner aboard, or if I had to move to the other side of the aircraft on a mission. I wanted to stay close to my aircraft in case there was a need for it. I knew how fast things could change in the ARA.

In the afternoon, I stored some additional ammo in my revetment to save time during re-arming.

It was a time consuming job getting the ammo set up. Each box held two 100 round belts. I would rip the tops off each 100 round box, tape the two boxes together with 100 mile per hour tape, link the two belts together and then lined them up on the floor. The tape made it easier to grab when I needed them, but if I did not tape them together, I could still manage.

On December 24, some Vietnamese locals came into our area and used our aircraft hanger to put on a Christmas show. Our Battery had worked hard building the hanger using whatever we could find for lumber and now it was close to being finished. The locals spoke poor English, but the show was a break from the everyday missions. Everyone who was not busy went to see the show.

On Christmas day in the afternoon, Specialist Kellogg came onto the flight line. "Tonight your aircraft will be used for a flare ship mission and you will be dropping Mark 24 flares. You will have to unload about half your ammo and half of the rockets to make the aircraft lighter. In addition, you will have to top off the fuel to give you maximum airborne time. (It was a normal practice that each aircraft would be half-fueled, with maximum ordinance. This gave it greater lethality but cut in half the "time on station" – not a problem in the typical combat mission.) The problem was that the aircraft could not lift off the ground in the heat of Vietnam with a full load of ammunition and fuel. I know this is a first for you so I want to warn you ahead of time, do not trust these flares. They can go off when you do not want them to. I will show you how to set the timers and show you how to drop them. The ammo truck should be bringing them here soon. We need to start unloading some of the rockets. Also take the M-60 off the right door and lay it on the seat in the middle, because you will be kicking these flares out the right door." He paused then added, "Both Alpha and Bravo Batteries have had these flares go off on them unexpectedly, just in the past two months. I do not like having to deal with them."

We had loaded about half the flares when the pilots arrived at the aircraft to do the preflight. I had never flown with Lieutenant Barloco or Warrant Officer Jim Krull, but then I knew they both had been in Charlie battery much longer than I had. In addition, I had heard they both were good pilots.

As Lieutenant Barloco put his gear in the left seat, he said, "I will be one of your pilots tonight. We will crank at about 23:50 hours, after the first aircraft is almost ready to return for another load. Kellogg, you have done this before. Are you going to be flying with us?"

Kellogg answered in a way that made me feel more confident, "No, Sir. Warriner should be okay to handle the mission. He has learned a lot and is ready to serve on his own."

All aircraft commanders sat in the left seat and were in charge of the aircraft. I already knew he was in charge unless something was different because of the type of mission. Since this was to be a single ship mission, I knew Barloco was in charge of the mission unlike the two aircraft missions, where the lead aircraft was in charge of the mission.

As the pilots did the preflight, we finished stacking the flares in the center of the aircraft, just behind the pilot. This was to make the center of gravity proper with the added weight.

Barloco noticed what we were doing. "Just the way I like to see the flares placed. Be sure to secure them properly so they will not move around on us."

At 23:30, I was at my aircraft when Mr. Krull arrived. Mr. Krull was almost to the aircraft when he said, "Chief, untie the main rotor and we will crank as soon as Barloco gets here. The other aircraft is returning early because they are almost out of flares."

I had just untied the main rotor when I noticed Barloco coming. I put my helmet on and called out, "Clear and untied."

Taking up a spot near the turbine, I watched with my flashlight to make sure there was no fuel or oil leaks, as the turbine engine began to whine and the main rotor started to turn. Once I was sure all was okay, I noticed Lieutenant Barloco was already in his seat. I walked around the aircraft, slid the armor plates forward for the pilots and closed all the doors except for the right cargo door.

Taking up a spot in the right door again gave me a strange feeling because I had not flown on that side in a week. Even though I would have to kick the flares out from this side, I felt okay, but a little nervous. I buckled my seat belt. As I plugged in my helmet, I checked the right rear of the aircraft. All was clear so I keyed my intercom, "Clear to back out, Sir."

Mr. Krull was at the controls and picked the aircraft up to a hover, "Coming back".

Lieutenant Barloco looked back at me and keyed his intercom, "Chief, once we are airborne, I suggest you turn on the red interior light so you can see what you are doing. Keep it as dim as you can. We do not want to become a target for 'Charlie'."

As we cleared the revetment, I was on my intercom again. "Clear to turn, Sir." Mr. Krull turned the tail, faced into the wind, nosed the aircraft over and soon we were airborne.

Lieutenant Barloco was on the radio, "Griffin Six Eight Papa. This is Six Eight Oscar. We are airborne. You can go get some coffee and refuel. Cookie has some munchies in the mess tent."

The answer came back, "Six Eight Oscar. This is Six Eight Papa. That sounds good. See you in a while. We are turning inbound for short final and have you in sight."

Soon, I knew we were on station and were ready to make the first drop because Barloco keyed his intercom, "Chief, get the first flare ready. We are at 2200 ft so set the chute at 5 and 10 for ignition. I will let you know when to kick it out."

Pulling the first flare over, I stood it up between my legs. I could just make out the settings. They were already set at where Barloco wanted them. I hooked the cable of the flare onto a piece of seat belt as Kellogg suggested and got ready to pull the pin. "Ready, Sir."

A few seconds later I heard, "Kick it out now."

As I pull the safety pin with my right hand, I pushed the flare towards the door with my left hand. "KA BOOM!"

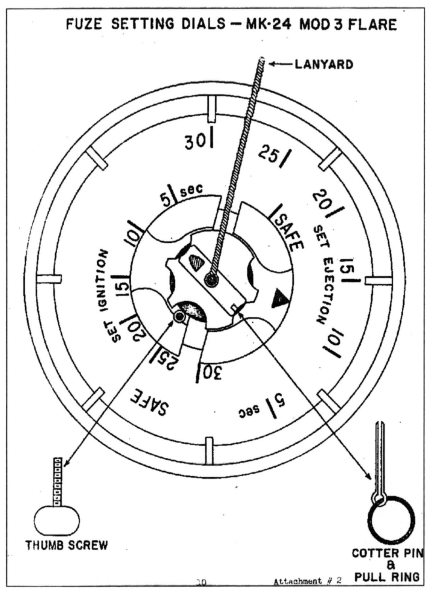

Diagram of top of MK-24 flare

Seconds later, I came to my senses. The first stage of the flare had gone off inside my aircraft, hitting me in the head and knocking my helmet off with the blow.

Now, it was wedged between the floor and ceiling of my aircraft, sending my mind into over drive. I have to get this flare out of here before the second stage goes off or we were all dead.

I began to kick the bottom towards the door. After the second or third kick, it went out the door. Thank God! I had finally managed to get it out of the helicopter. Otherwise, the helicopter would have burst into flames and exploded.

My flight helmet was off and I had no idea where it was. I had no communication with my pilots to let them know what my condition was. A steady stream of blood was running down my face and into my eyes, making it almost impossible to see.

Looking toward my pilots, I could just make out that Lieutenant Barloco was looking back towards me. I was not sure if anyone could hear me but I wanted to try so I yelled, "I'm hurt, take her down." and pointed down with hope that he had heard me or could see my hand signal.

Suddenly, there was a bright light. I knew the flare was hanging from my aircraft. Nevertheless, before I could figure out what was happening, I blacked out.

Going in and out of consciousness, I could sense someone was helping me out of the aircraft. I felt weak in the knees and did not even know they were placing me into another aircraft. I was not even sure where I was or whose aircraft I was in.

Blacking out again, I came out of it as we landed at the Second Surgical Field Hospital at Chu Lai. There, I was placed on a stretcher and taken inside.

Several hours passed before I responded to a nurse who was standing over me. She told me that the doctor would be stitching me up as soon as the x-rays came back. The bleeding had let up and I was going to be okay.

I had no idea how long I had laid there before they stitched me up. I was not even sure how long it was after receiving the stitches that they finally told me that my unit was coming to pick me up.

When they released me, a nurse walked me out and waited while we talked. She informed me that her name was Nancy and that she had been my nurse during the night. She did not think I even knew she had been there, as I was out of it most of the time. She had just got off duty and wanted to wait for my unit to pick me up.

An hour went by before another nurse came out and informed us that my unit would not be picking me up. Instead, a MEDEVAC helicopter was due in to pick me up.

I was not happy about waiting, but at least I was waiting with Nancy, who was a beautiful blond nurse. My wait was cut short as the sound of a Huey soon was heard approaching the helicopter pad.

The flight back was uneventful, until we were nearing Tam Ky. The Crew Chief leaned over and informed me that we were going into an LZ to pick up wounded.

As we landed, my mind went into over drive thinking; I hoped that it was not a hot LZ. I hoped the wounded were not very bad. Badly wounded soldiers could cause us to return to the hospital before they dropped me at Charlie battery. I sure was glad that I was not a MEDEVAC Crew Chief.

Coming to a hover in the small clearing, the Crew Chief helped two wounded soldiers aboard and then we lifted off. Less than five minutes went by before we landed at Charley Battery.

Sergeant Cole met me. "Get chow and some rest. We will put you on light duty for a few days."

Sitting on my bunk, I was writing a letter home to my mom when Jerry Boerm came into the tent. "You're back! They scrambled my aircraft to take you to Second Surge when the flare went off. I bet you did not even know where you were."

"No, you are right. I don't remember much about it and I guess I am lucky to be alive."

Jerry continued, "I guess Major McCloud figured it was faster and easier to fly you to the hospital then to wait for a MEDEVAC. Your pilots flew a sideways 'crab' to keep the intense heat and the flare from the bottom of the aircraft."

I felt very lucky to be alive. I had heard that the Mark 24 flare was magnesium and burned at a million or so candle power. Inside an aircraft that was not only a problem, but also a disaster waiting to happen. Because the flare malfunctioned by going off prematurely, someone needed to eject it from the aircraft immediately. To be able to come to from the blow to my head and kick it out of the aircraft was like God helping me. I owed the pilots a big thank you for knowing they had to fly it in the crab to keep the intense heat from the flare away from the aircraft underbelly or we all would have died.

I figured I would fill Jerry in on what I knew. "I hear we were met by a crew who cut the flare from the skids while they kept it at a hover. Then the pilots set the aircraft down on the ground. It is a miracle! If the parachute ropes wound up caught in the tail rotor, we would have crashed. By the way, who finished the flare mission for me?"

What Jerry said next told it all. "I heard Kellogg was not happy about taking over for you. He took over your aircraft rather than trying to switch aircraft for the flare mission. He also was told to crew your aircraft until you can fly again or someone else takes over."

The fire mission horn went off and Jerry headed for his aircraft. I went back to my letter writing.

Captain Asa Talbot arrived on December 28. Because he was the battalion flight surgeon, he wanted to see how I was doing and to make sure everything with my stitches was okay.

As he read the records and checked over my forehead he commented, "It looks like you have at least thirty or forty stitches. I counted twenty-eight, but I am sure there are more under the top layer. Whoever did the stitches did a good job. I will be back in a week and remove them. I hear the doctor was so busy that one of the nurses signed off for him. The records state that they patched you up at 0230 hours. You received your wounds before midnight. What a Christmas gift that was. I understand, most of Second Surge was off at a Christmas party and they were using people from the hospital next door."

For the next several days, I was on light duty and was not suppose to do anything. I spent my days hanging around the mess tent or my tent and wrote letters.

After a while, I could not stand it anymore and started to help anyone on flight line. Even though they had not released me from light duty, I worked on getting ammo ready.

When Sergeant Cole found me on the flight line, he sent me into the maintenance area to help those that were working on the aircraft in the hanger.

A week later, I saw the Battalion Flight Surgeon again and had my stitches removed. He cautioned me, "You are still on light duty. Be careful not to get the wound dirty."

With all the dust and dirt that the helicopters were stirring up in the area, how was I going to keep it clean! Who was he trying to kid!

Christmas local entertainment

Local entertainment

8

MORE ACTION

There was only one person to receive combat related injuries in Charlie Battery that I knew about and that was Lieutenant Barloco. As the story went, it had been his very first fire-mission after joining Charlie Battery. While on that fire-mission in the Que Son province just west of Tam Ky, the aircraft took a single round through the cockpit just in front of co-pilot Barloco. The projectile's path splintered the cockpit floor, shattered portions of the instrument panel and finally exited through the upper Plexiglas panel of the aircraft. Shrapnel from the flying debris lodged in the forehead of Lt. Barloco. After landing, our medic removed the piece of metal, administered first aid and Barloco returned to his aircraft.

I had heard stories about others receiving wounds in the battalion and knew others received wounds. Some died from wounds, but for the most part, no one ever talked about things like that. From the time I arrived in Charlie Battery on November 17, until the flare had gone off in my aircraft, I had only spent two of the weeks that I had been in Vietnam at the battery. The rest of the time, I had been away at Charm School or traveling.

On December 11, after I had returned to Charlie Battery, it was official; I would be the new Crew Chief on 054. This day was one that I figured I would never forget because it was also my birthday.

Just before the flare incident happened, I had started to crew 054 on my own. Kellogg only went on a few missions with me unless it was something special.

The flare incident would remain etched in my brain forever. Not only because of how it happened but also because it had happened on Christmas night. Even though it was after midnight when they finally stitched me up, my medical records would show December 26. I was sure that we had lifted off before midnight on Christmas night. Even the flight log for the aircraft showed the flight as happening on December 25.

I was sure there would be many things about my tour etched into my brain forever, before my time was over.

Right before Christmas, things had seemed to slow down. Was Charlie trying to fool us into thinking that he had given up in our area? Had he moved to another area or was he trying to make us think he was gone out of the area?

Just before Christmas, we received word that some South Vietnamese people and the province chief would be coming to Charlie Battery to present Charlie Battery with some type of honor for an action that had taken place just before I arrived in Charlie Battery. Rumor central had it that we were getting the Vietnamese Cross of Gallantry.

On December 28, most of the unit was in formation with clean uniforms and boots shined as they waited for our guests to arrive. The day before, everyone had been trying to find polish for their boots with comments made like, "Who were they kidding with shining? Who ever heard of shining boots in Vietnam!" or "A clean uniform is next to impossible. Five minutes after putting on a clean uniform it looks like I have had it on for a month."

We got though the day and only had a few missions. Not only did the unit get an award but some of the officers and enlisted did as well. I felt cheated because I was not in the unit when all this went down. However, on the other side of the coin, I was glad I was not here for the action.

On December 29, I was sitting on my bunk trying to figure out what to write to my girlfriend Gloria. I had heard from her only twice since I had left the states and was not sure why. In my mind were thoughts that I tried to erase. Were her letters to me getting lost? Was she using the correct address? Was she too busy with school and babysitting? Were my letters just not getting to her, so she did not know what to say? Maybe I was addressing my letters wrong when I mailed them to her. No, I am sure that I am addressing her letters correctly. My family was getting letters from me. I was getting letters and care packages in return. I had mail from everyone except Gloria.

Yes, it was very strange that my mom and others had written with answers to my letters. Therefore, I was sure my mail was getting through to everyone. Nevertheless, there were no letters from her.

The sound of the fire mission horn interrupted my thoughts, breaking the silence of the night. I still was not used to the horn and was not sure if it was a fire mission or an alert warning us of incoming or enemy inside our perimeter. None of the Crew Chiefs moved so I figured it must be a fire mission and all those who were hot were already on the flight line near their aircraft. I listened as the sound of feet ran by my tent heading for the flight line. Moments later, there was a whine of the turbine engines cranking but still no one from my tent seemed to be very alarmed. Once the aircraft had lifted off, I went back to my letter writing. I knew that I was not going to be flying for at least a few more days, not until the flight surgeon had given the okay for me to fly again.

Suddenly the tent flap opened as Kellogg stuck his head in the doorway. "One of our aircraft is down. Our section is hot."

Then Kellogg disappeared into the night air.

I knew that Kellogg was letting his wing aircraft know in case the Crew Chief was in the tent. Almost before the flap fully closed, someone left out the back of the tent. I could not tell which Crew Chief it was because of the dim lighting we used in the tent. A few moments later, the horn went off again. This was not a good sign.

This time, I did not move. I could not do anything about it, even if I wanted to. I went back to my letter. I tried hard to concentrate, but my mind only wandered, thinking that Gloria had already started to date someone else. Why had I not seen the signs! No, I have to be wrong. She was probably just busy with her schoolwork. Maybe, she was busy babysitting and the kids were preventing her from writing.

I put the letter to Gloria away and decided to write mom to thank her for the care package I had just received. At least there was a letter in the package so I had a reason to write back.

As I wrote, I read carefully each paragraph because I wanted to be careful not to say anything that would alarm anyone.

Suddenly I realized there was a Maxwell House coffee can in the bottom of the package. A can I had not opened yet. A can that must contain the Congo squares that mom had mentioned in her letter. I had never had Congo squares before but mom had many friends who were sharing recipes. My niece Bonnie made these Congo squares and I was eager to get a taste of some homemade cookies.

Opening the Maxwell House coffee can, I found some very hard and dried up bread but under that were the Congo squares. I was expecting the squares to be as hard as the bread but I found them to be soft and moist. These sure were good. Bonnie had out done herself making these great Congo squares and no one could dispute that. I offered some to Ben who was on his bunk across from me and soon others were asking if they could have one. Everyone liked them and they were soon all gone. I did not even have them one day! I learned that if you wanted to have more than a bite of some goodies you got from home, you had better keep them to yourself.

As I went back to writing, my mind told me that I should tell her how good they were. I could not tell her that I only had two from that batch. Maybe, if I told her how good they were and that the chow wasn't very good here that maybe she would ship some right out to me. Then, I had a second thought, because that would be telling a lie. Charlie Battery usually had some of the best chow in the battalion. Everyone in Charlie Battery said that no one else in Vietnam had better chow then our Battery and it sure did seem that way to me. Maybe I had better leave out the lie about the bad chow. Sure, that would work.

A short time later, word spread through the tent that PFC Lopez was down in his B model Huey. No one knew the outcome. Before long, word spread through the battery that all four aboard most likely had died. They could not get close enough to find out for sure, but it was believed that the Aircraft Commander Captain Larry R. Doyle, Pilot Warrant Officer Ronald Beals, Crew Chief Lupe Lopez and our Battery Cook Corporal Clifton Henson who was serving as door gunner, had all been killed.

Note: ALL above KIA data extracted from the 2002 "Coffelt and Argabright Vietnam KIA Database".

Lopez had been aboard the aircraft because he was returning from An Khe where he had gone to see the dentist. He was sitting in the gunner seat. He had come to our unit as our Charlie Battery cook and now we were without a cook. Our Battery commander was upset when he found out that Lopez had flown as a gunner several times before. Where were we going to get a replacement cook?

We needed a cook and fast. SP4 Johnnie Drew, who had come to us as a generator service man, asked for the position. No one knew Johnnie had worked as a cook. He did not have the MOS to be a cook. Because we needed someone immediately, Drew got a chance.

I did not know either pilot very well. I had not flown with Doyle or Beals. They had just come back from R&R, right after my flare incident. I knew Lopez because he was in my platoon and was on the mortar patrol mission at Chu Lai with me. Lopez was a great guy to be around. He had helped me understand some of my paperwork. I learned about being a Crew Chief from him.

He also had crewed on my wing aircraft on several missions. I just knew I was going to have a hard time trying to put Lopez out of my mind.

I had also known Lopez. I had gotten to know him because I had stayed around the mess tent when I had nothing else to do. Lopez enjoyed giving tidbits to the local kids who were always near the fence that was near our mess tent. When he gave them something, I would hear, "You number one GI". However, if he told them to go away, I would hear, "You number ten" or "You number %*#%*# ten GI". Lopez would answer back with "zin loi", which in Vietnamese means "sorry about that".

A story spread through the Crew Chief tent that Lopez had been standing on his aircraft skid with his M-60 blazing at the time his aircraft crashed. The aircraft went down in the river and no one could get near it because of the heavy enemy infantry in the vicinity.

At first light the next morning, Captain Rivers, who was our maintenance officer and Sergeant First Class Cole took my aircraft with Specialist Kellogg and went out to recover the bodies. They had no luck getting near the downed aircraft. Then the following day, they made several more trips to the crash site but the enemy soldiers were still in the area.

Several days later, they recovered the bodies from the downed aircraft. Specialist Kellogg and Sergeant First Class Cole had to identify the bodies because they knew every person aboard the aircraft. The bodies had been in the water a long time and I know this had to be a tough job for anyone to do. This must have been pure hell and I was sure this would weigh heavy on all their minds forever.

When New Years Eve came, I heard the rat-tat-tat of several M-60s firing at once. I was just sure the enemy was overrunning our perimeter. I had heard that the enemy had tried to get to our aircraft when I was at Charm School, but soldiers had caught them in our perimeter wire before they had gotten to their objective. Therefore, I grabbed my M-16 and was ready. Some of the Crew Chiefs started to laugh, "You new guys can settle down. The bunker is having a Mad Minute."

I was thinking, a Mad Minute, what is a Mad Minute? Whatever this was, I was not going to look foolish so I said nothing. It was my first dose of hearing a Mad Minute but I was sure it would not be my last.

As January 1968 rolled in, I was still walking around with my head all wrapped in bandages, yet was doing what I could to help.

On January 4, I was on the flight line early in the morning when, I noticed a man approaching. I had seen him talking to John O'Brien a few times. I knew he was a navy CB, but I knew nothing more about him. All I knew about him was that John knew who he was, and if John knew him, that was good enough for me. When he went straight to the aircraft that John was Crew Chief, I decided to make sure John knew he was there.

John explained to me that the Navy CB was getting ready to retire and wanted to fly in a helicopter before he retired. He had come to Vietnam to keep his son from having to serve in Vietnam. He had gotten permission to fly as a gunner with John O'Brien for the day. It was not long before he had his chance because the horn went off.

John untied the main rotor as his pilots came running. "Clear and untied", John called as his pilots jumped into their seats.

As I watched, there was the usual puff of smoke that came from the turbine engine as it sprang to life. Soon, they pulled pitch and were gone.

They were gone about an hour or so when I heard some aircraft returning. I headed for the flight line to see if I could help with the rearm. I noticed John O'Brien at his aircraft and headed towards it.

As I got close enough, I could see him busy cleaning the brass out from the mission. He was saying something. As I got within hearing distance, I could hear John talking, but I could not make out what he was saying. I had no idea to whom he was talking but I could tell he was upset. Had his gunner for the day done something wrong or had something else gone wrong? I was just not sure.

As I got to his aircraft, I was about to ask where his gunner was when John spoke. "Russ, I lost my gunner. He did not have a chance. He took an armor piercing .51 round through the chest. It came up through the floor, went through his flak vest, chicken plate (chest protector), and ended right there", as he pointed to the rear wall of his aircraft.

I could tell John wanted to be alone, "I wanted to clean my aircraft by myself. I need some time alone. Talk to you later."

I wanted to give him time. "Okay. Just remember, I am here if you want some help." Neither of us said another word. No words would help and helping him now would only fuel the rage he was feeling. Walking away was best, so I headed for the other aircraft but noticed they had plenty of help. Realizing this, I headed back to the Crew Chief tent.

A few days later, word came down that the 1st Cavalry was packing up and moving to another area of operation. All the equipment needed to be packed. We needed to be ready to move in a matter of days. We were going to have to leave behind the maintenance hangar that all of us had a hand in building. We had to keep enough supplies and equipment to continue to do our job of supporting the troops.

As we were packing, Sergeant First Class Cole came to me, "Warriner, try this helmet on. If you can wear it, you will be flying right side with Kellogg on your aircraft. We are sending you as part of the advance party. You are still on light duty but the flight surgeon has given the okay for you to fly."

When I tried it on, it was big but Sergeant First Class Cole thought it would work. "Get enough gear to keep going for a few days and put it on 054. Take anything of importance with you because you may not see it for days or even weeks, at least until the Battery convoy arrives. Things have a way of getting lost on these moves and you may never see these things again. We are sending your aircraft and one other as the advance party. Since you are still on light duty, you may as well go with them."

Warrant Officer Comer @ Tam Ky

I headed to the Crew Chief tent, grabbed my things and returned to my aircraft to wait for further instructions. The pilots had already finished the preflight before they left to get their gear. As soon as they put their things into the aircraft, we were ready to go. Lieutenant Barloco was the pilot in command and was in the left seat of my aircraft. Warrant Officer Comer was in the right seat. Warrant Officer Bushie was in command of the other aircraft with Warrant Officer Hollister as his right seat pilot and Specialist Roy Gollash as their Crew Chief.

We waited for the other aircraft crew to get ready. Soon we pulled pitch and headed towards the ocean with only the Aircraft Commanders knowing where we were going.

As we arrived at the ocean edge, the Flight Commander radioed us saying we were to turn north. Now, an idea of our destination popped into my mind. I had hopes that we were not going too far north, but it sure was obvious that our direction of travel was toward the DMZ.

.9.

MOVING NORTH

As our flight of two helicopters hit the coast and turned north, Lieutenant Barloco was joking around, "I hope you guys can swim. We will be flying up the coast and staying over the ocean at low level most of the way."

I thought I would give my input. "Nice knowing you Sir. If we do go down, remember I cannot swim." I did not want anyone to know I was having very scary thoughts of drowning if we went down.

Mr. Comer was laughing as he pressed his intercom. "If we have to ditch the aircraft over water, I don't think any of us will be able to swim with all our gear."

Both my pilots decided to slide their armor plate back so they could get out of the aircraft in case we ditched the aircraft in the ocean. Then Lieutenant Barloco changed his mind. "My side is facing land. They could get me with a well placed round. Besides, there is more of a chance of getting hit by an enemy bullet then there is of us ditching the aircraft."

With that, he slid his plate back forward but did not latch it, just in case something did happen. I thought to myself; if anyone in a boat should try to shoot at us at the speed that we were flying and at low level, the enemy would have a hard time hitting us anyway.

We had been in the air for over an hour. When we were part way to our destination, Barloco radioed the other aircraft and told them that we were going to find a spot to land for a short break for fuel, rest, and refuel our stomachs. Barloco picked a helicopter pad near the water that he said was Da Nang and we landed on the PSP.

After shutting down, we broke out some C Rations. This was my first time having a C ration meal and did not like the sounds of some of the choices. I was not sure what was best to eat. I grabbed beans and wieners before anyone else did. I liked beans and hot dogs, so I figured it was a good choice. I sat in the door of the helicopter ready to eat my meal. Suddenly, I realized that I did not know how I was going to get the can opened. Kellogg must have noticed, "You will need one of these. Keep it as I have one already". Then he tossed me a P-38.

P-38

After I figured out how to operate the P-38 and opened the can, Kellogg noticed I was about to eat them cold. "Hey, those are much better heated. If you want to warm those cold things up, you can use some of this C4 I am using."

I was surprised and I think my response showed it. "C4? That is an explosive! How do you cook with that without blowing yourself up!"

Kellogg was smiling as he answered, "Oh, it won't blow as long as you don't try to contain it. Do not ever try to put it out with your foot unless you want to go home early without a foot. Bring your can over and I will show you how to use this stuff. Later I will show you another way to warm those C's, if you don't have any C4."

As we were eating, Comer noticed the dates the C Rations were packaged. They packaged them during the 1950's. The US military started putting up C Rations in July 1945. Mr. Comer made a comment, "The military is probably trying to use up the left over rations".

Warrant Officer Comer

Here are the three basic C Rations as copied from World Wide Web:

B-1 Units
Meat Choices (in small cans):
Beef Steak
Ham and Eggs, Chopped
Ham Slices
Turkey Loaf
Fruit:
Applesauce
Fruit Cocktail
Peaches
Pears
Crackers (7)
Peanut Butter
Candy Disc, Chocolate
Solid Chocolate
Cream

Coconut
Accessory Pack*

B-2 Units
Meat Choices (in larger cans):
Beans and Wieners
Spaghetti and Meatballs
Beefsteak, Potatoes and Gravy
Ham and Lima Beans
Meatballs and Beans
Crackers (4)
Cheese Spread, Processed
Caraway
Pimento
Fruit Cake
Pecan Roll
Pound Cake
Accessory Pack*

B-3 Units
Meat Choices (in small cans):
Boned Chicken
Chicken and Noodles
Meat Loaf
Spiced Beef
Bread, White
Cookies (4)
Cocoa Beverage Powder
Jam
Apple
Berry
Grape
Mixed Fruit
Strawberry
Accessory Pack*

*Accessory Pack
Spoon, Plastic
Salt
Pepper
Coffee, Instant
Sugar
Creamer, Non-dairy
Gum, 2 Chiclets
Cigarettes, 4 smokes/pack
Winston
Marlboro
Salem
Pall Mall
Camel
Chesterfield
Kent
Lucky Strike
Kool
Matches, Moisture Resistant
Toilet paper

I was trying to heat up my meal of beans & wieners when the fuel truck showed up. Kellogg had already finished his meal so he refueled my aircraft.

I was trying hard to get my meal down when Lt Barloco yelled, "Chief, we need to crank. Finish eating and let's pull pitch".

As I tried to get the last of the beans from the can, I responded, "Yes Sir", and headed for my aircraft. Everyone was already putting on their gear so I grabbed my gear and untied the main rotor, "Clear and untied".

Soon, I could hear the sounds of the igniters snapping and the whines of the turbine. Then, the turbine sprang to life and the blades were threatening to beat the air into submission. When we were back in the air heading north, Barloco let us know that our destination was to an area south of the DMZ. The 1st Cavalry Division would be working the I Corp area north of Da Nang. Whatever that meant, I was not sure. I figured I would soon find out.

Arriving in the north in late January, we laagered (temporary lodging) at the 101st base camp called Camp Eagle. We worked from there until the engineers had almost completed Camp Evans.

After receiving permission, we landed, setting the aircraft down and kicking up the usual dust storm that all helicopters made as they land or when taking off in dusty areas. Barloco got out of the aircraft before the main rotor blade had stopped, "You guys stay here while I see what we can line up for some chow and a place to stay. We are the first of the Cavalry to get here. I am sure they will enjoy hearing that the Cavalry has landed." With that, he headed off with the rest of the pilots.

As I waited near the aircraft, I wondered where we were going to spend the night. Minutes later, the answer came. We would be eating chow with the 101st. Barloco was trying to set up a temporary base camp at Evans that Charlie Battery could use after the rest of the battery arrived.

Somehow, I did not think it would be that easy and I was right. Headquarter Battery took control and said this would be their base camp and we would have to move to the other side of Eagle and find a new area.

Talking with the 101st, we learned that the enemy had not hit the area in months. The 101st was not wearing any protective gear, did not keep weapons close by and did not even have bunkers or sandbagged tents. The regulars made comments like, "We must have been sent to the area because there was no enemy action." and "They had the area under control".

After getting a meal, we thanked them and then moved our aircraft to another area that Barloco had chosen, because it was clear enough to set our two aircraft down. Barloco picked an area he thought all twelve aircraft could park. I did not think we could situate half our aircraft, never mind all twelve of them.

Within a couple of hours, a second pair of Charlie Battery aircraft landed. Because we were outside the perimeter of the LZ, we would have to guard our aircraft and the area by ourselves. This was nothing new to Charlie Battery. I was ready to do my job along with the other Charlie Battery personnel. We needed to set up a new perimeter. We would need to string up the barbed wire. It was going to be just like when we were at Tam Ky and were on our own with our defense lines.

Night came fast and it became another sleepless night. As I tried to rest, I found myself very alert to the slightest little sound.

Now that we had relocated to the south-central portion of Camp Evans, I was sure this would be our new base for Charlie Battery. We began the work of laying out the Battery area, flight line, operations area, billets (tents) for the flight crews by platoon, etc. By morning, a group of infantry moved into the area to help secure the area. I was very surprised when a Navy CB team arrived and took over the job of getting a place ready for the tents. Using a road grader and other equipment, they worked on an area for a runway and tents.

At first, I thought the runway was for us. Soon the 1st Squadron 9th Calvary arrived with their grunts, equipment and helicopters. Where were we going to set up our aircraft and tents with them taking over the area? I was surprised when I found out we were going to have our aircraft in the area where we had landed. Our tents would be at the end of the runway and on the other side of the rice paddy.

When the horn would go off, we would need to be in the air in two minutes. I could not figure out how this was possible when our tents were so far away from the aircraft and we would need to cross over or around the rice paddy.

The infantry from 1st Squadron, 9th Cavalry started to string the wire around the outside perimeter of the LZ. This made me feel much better about things as I hated the thought of having to help with that job.

Because we had such a long run to get to our aircraft at the end of the runway to get to where were sitting, we made a bridge across the little rice paddy to our aircraft with ammo boxes. This would sure be faster than going all the way around on the roadway. You just had to be careful not to slip or you would land in the water.

A week had passed since we had first set foot in this area and Headquarters Battery had only been there a few days. I was not even sure how long it had been since they got there. We were still waiting for our other aircraft and equipment. All I knew was that some equipment was coming up part way by boat and then by convoy.

Rumor was that Alpha and Bravo Battery had not even started to move. I had no idea where they would be set up. I wondered if we were close to the DMZ. I had an uneasy feeling in my gut about everything.

Not long after we were in place, the rest of the Charlie Battery aircraft started to arrive. Soon the convoy of Charlie Battery trucks would be arriving. This was good news because we had already been flying missions in support of the troops and needed supplies.

On January 28, the convoy of trucks had arrived from Charlie Battery. Our much-needed supplies had started to arrive and we were in full swing supporting the troops. We still did not have a large supply of fuel for the aircraft.

Everyone went to work putting up their tents and building bunkers. Each platoon had put up their own tent and had to build their own bunker. This was very hard for the Crew Chiefs to do because we were flying so much in support of the troops. Because of this, the maintenance crew helped to erect the Crew Chief tent. However if we wanted a bunker, then we were on our own. For the most part, we were always flying or working on the aircraft. We tried to build a bunker at the end of the tent against the officer bunker. This bunker was not much more than a foxhole and it seemed like we would never finish it. Because there was no roof to cover it, it would fill up with water every time it rained.

The first tent on the right as you started up the hill was for the Crew Chiefs and this put us closest to the flight line. As always, this would serve as home for all twelve Charlie Battery Crew Chiefs. This made the most sense to me. Each of the three platoons of pilots had their own tent with seven pilots in each tent. Each platoon of pilots had built their own bunker using whatever they could find and did it their own way.

The second tent on the right was for the first Flight Platoon pilots. Operations area tent was next. Then the CO had a tent and lastly the mess tent was at the top of the hill.

The left side had a tent for second Flight Platoon pilots. There was one for the third Flight Platoon pilots as well as a tent for maintenance personnel, ammo personnel and motor pool personnel.

Aircraft Maintenance had a tent and a supply connex that was set right across the runway from the Crew Chief tent. We had a volleyball net strung up across the runway which everyone could use when they had time. I suspected that this would not be very often.

Within a week of arriving at Evans, I was back on my own aircraft full time again, and I found that I seldom saw the mess tent. If I did get to the mess tent, I never seemed to finish my meal before the fire mission horn would go off and I would be off on the run. I knew if I did not learn to eat fast, I would be hungry. I managed to put my hands on a few cases of C Rations and picked up a few cans of spaghetti from the PX. I would keep some in my aircraft and hide some under my bunk, in case I needed them. If I came back from a mission and it was between meals, the cook would try to find something for the flight crews.

When they erected the Crew Chief tent, I was off on a fire mission and everyone claimed his own area. I had no choice in placement of my bunk so I wound up at the end of the tent closest to the flight line on the uphill side. This was okay by me because I felt if it was my time to go then Charlie would get me no matter where I was. Besides, getting to the flight line fast was top on my list.

Jerry Boerm and some of the others wanted to be near the bunker entrance so they could get into it fast. Funny, we did not have much of a bunker. Unless someone put some effort forward and worked on it, there was little to no protection from incoming enemy rounds. Word got out that the pilot's tent layout had the fastest person closest to the bunker and the slowest furthest away. This would help to get everyone into the bunker without running over another person. In theory, this made sense. However, would it work? I was sure that when "Charlie" (the enemy) decided to drop a few rounds on the Battery area that they would find out the answer.

Frames for our tents built by the Navy CB's

Our living area after the CB's built frames

Our tents were in place only a few weeks when the word came that we needed to take our tents down. This was because the Navy CB's were there to build us frames for the tents. When the frame was finished, it was the closest thing to a building I had lived in since I arrived in Vietnam.

Now Charlie Battery was at the same LZ with Headquarters Battery but was on the other side of Evans. Wherever Headquarters Battery had their LZ (main base), another line battery had to be also. Alpha Battery had the job in the south and now Charlie Battery had it. Someone had to be saddled with it but why Charlie Battery?

When Alpha Battery moved north, they became the most northern battery at a place called LZ Sharon. Bravo Battery was north of Evans also. Bravo Battery was at a place called LZ Jane which was south of LZ Sharon. Charlie Battery had been the lead Battery with Alpha and Bravo to arrive after we settled into the area.

Knowing that Alpha and Bravo Batteries were north of us gave me a good feeling. At least we were not as close to the DMZ as they were. I felt that we were in a much safer area.

My intuition told me that Charlie Battery was always the leader of the pack for everything the Battalion did. I was sure this was true because my understanding was that Charlie Battery was one of the first to land in Vietnam. Now it was the first battery to move north.

Since my arrival in Charlie Battery, I had learned several things. I learned that Alpha Battery was assigned under 1st Brigade for support, Bravo was assigned to 2nd Brigade and Charlie Battery was assigned to 3rd Brigade.

All this really meant was that when an element of 3rd Brigade was in need of air support, Charlie Battery was called on to do the mission. However, if push came to shove, all three batteries worked together to make sure our troops were supported in the best way possible.

10

TET

As TET 1968 rolled in, so did the weather and the enemy.

On February 4, the second platoon was assigned to be the hot section, which meant they had to be cranked and in the air in two minutes or less. Each 100-hours of flight time, our aircraft had to have a PE (Periodic Examination) performed. My aircraft just reached that mark and the crew just started on the inspection. My pilots moved to Aircraft 561, which was one of our Charlie models. Specialist Reeves was the Crew Chief for this aircraft.

I had just finished removing all the inspection panels, when the horn went off. I was placing sand bags on the panels to keep them from blowing around and I stopped to watch the crew running to the aircraft.

Soon, the two aircraft were up to full RPM and pulled pitch. I knew that as the aircraft went by and lifted off, we were about to get dust and dirt blown in our direction. I decided to hold things down and turned my back to protect my face from the dust.

As they lifted off, I was thinking about the low ceiling that was putting them at a bad flight altitude of about 500 feet or maybe 600 feet. The section was under the command of one of the best section leaders that I had ever flown with, Captain David Whitling (Blue Max Six Eight) and had Lt Jerry Barloco as his pilot. The second aircraft in the section was 516, with

Warrant Officer Ronald Fields (Blue Max Six Eight Papa) as the Aircraft Commander. Fields was a good pilot, but I had only flown with him a few times. His pilot was Warrant Officer Michael O'Connor, affectionately referred to as "OC" because of his age (19), and his youthful appearance.

A short time later, the horn went off again and more aircraft lifted off. This time the Battery Commander was in one of the aircraft. This was not a good sign.

When Captain Whitling returned, his wing aircraft was not with him. This was another sign that was not good. When I asked what happened, they told me that when the two aircraft arrived on station, they came under intense enemy fire. There was a C&C (Command and Control) aircraft on station and the ceiling was only 300 feet at the most. Consequently, they had conducted the entire engagement at low-level. There was naval gunfire coming from the coast, artillery from LZ Bastogne (south and west of the mission area) and F4 Phantom Jets on station.

The flight of two held an orbit one mile away from the action, as instructed to do. As they were orbiting and waiting for clearance to fire, they were receiving enemy fire. Section leader Captain Whitling became increasingly anxious. ARA had a close-in direct-fire weapons capability primarily used in lieu of conventional artillery – as condition on the ground dictated. Here was an ARA section under enemy fire without employment discretion.

After talking to Captain Whitling, I figure the mission went something like this, "Concrete Eight Two.

This is Blue Max Six Eight. Be advised, either use us or release us!"

The Artillery Liaison Officer on the ground stopped all the other artillery. Then he instructed, "Blue Max Six Eight. This is Concrete Eight Two. Place your rounds on the tree line and you are released".

Captain Whitling ordered Lt Barloco to set the aircraft 'intervalometer' to maximum – all 48 rockets that fired in a very short sequence with one trigger squeeze. During the rocket run, the lead aircraft received a fusillade of return fire from heavy automatic weapons. Without hesitation, Captain Whitling called to his wing aircraft to avoid over-flight of the target area. "Blue Max Six Eight Papa, Blue Max Six Eight, expend everything you have in one pass and get out of the area."

With that, Blue Max Six Eight went in hot, expending their entire ordinance into the tree line.

That is when the tree line lit up and Blue Max Six Eight took several hits. Blue Max Six Eight radioed his wing aircraft, "Blue Max Six Eight Papa, break off your run and get the %*## out. We are taking heavy fire."

Blue Max Six Eight expended his ordinance and broke away. As he did, his aircraft received at least one known hit on its' undercarriage. As Blue Max Six Eight completed his run, he pulled the aircraft up hard with a 180° in course reversal and climbed into the clouds.

Even though they were in the clouds, they continued to draw fire for a short while. Captain

Whitling said, "They must have been firing at where the aircraft sound was coming from".

As Blue Max Six Eight flew IFR towards the coast, he tried numerous times to contact Blue Max Six Eight Papa with no response.

Once Captain Whitling was clear of the area and still could not reach Blue Max Six Eight Papa, he radioed operations. "Blue Max Six Three India., This is Blue Max Six Eight over."

The reply came back, "Blue Max Six Eight. This is Six Three India."

Captain Whitling replied, "Blue Max Six Three India, we lost contact with Blue Max Six Eight Papa. Be advised, the area is hot! I repeat, the area is hot and we've taken a hit."

The response from operations was immediate, "Blue Max Six Eight. I am bouncing another section."

More aircraft scrambled and even the Battery Commander, Major McCloud flew back into the area to look for the downed aircraft. Captain Whitling had continued an easterly flight path until he considered it was safe to begin a descent. Once Captain Whitling was clear of the area and could get below the overcast condition, he made his approach to a clear area on the beach. Captain Whitling, his pilot and the Crew Chief exited the aircraft to inspect the damage to the airframe and components. Clearly visible was one entry point of a large caliber round. However, upon further inspection, the crew deemed the aircraft flight worthy. The crew saddled up and took off returning to base camp.

The commanders declared the area of the engagement off-limits due to the continuing intensity of the on-going battle. Charlie Battery wanted desperately to search for the downed crew, but a higher authority instructed everyone to avoid all flights into the area, unless a request for fire mission support came from the ground forces. Days went by without any word of the missing crew and aircraft. The infantry was conducting a sweep through the area and eventually found the aircraft wreckage. Word arrived back to our unit and we bounced a section into the area with Captain Whitling aboard one of the aircraft. Captain Whitling was determined to find his missing crew.

Many of us were lead to believe that both pilots had become POWs and the enlisted that were aboard had been killed. The truth of the matter was that when the aircraft was finally located, a completely different result became evident. The aircraft lay on its right side with its roofline tilted slightly towards the ground. With the exception of Warrant Officer O'Connor, they were able to account for all the crew. In more than one way, this was tragic for the unit. Not only did we lose some great men and an aircraft, but we had also lost Warrant Officer O'Connor, who despite his young age, held the record for the most successful combat launches of the SS-11 guided missile system.

They found the aircraft commander, Warrant Officer Ronald Fields at the scene. Sergeant First Class Henry Adler, who was the door gunner and the Crew Chief, Specialist Reeves, were by the aircraft. Both enlisted people most likely thrown were from the aircraft when it crashed.

Note: <u>ALL</u> above KIA data extracted from the 2002 "Coffelt and Argabright Vietnam KIA Database". Also, Reeves was posthumously promoted to Sergeant E-5.

The right seat pilot, Warrant Officer O'Connor was missing. The infantry said there were tracks showing that someone, most likely O'Connor, had survived the crash and had crawled away. It was not until sometime later that we learned that he had become the first known POW of the 2nd Battalion 20th Artillery (Aerial Rocket Artillery), 1st Cavalry Division.

Note: (When the release of the POWs took place in 1973, Warrant Officer O'Connor was among the group POWs. Where he is today would not be beneficial to this story, but I will say that I have spoken to him on the phone. He exited the army after being a POW for five years. He also gave me his side of the story of that day and that he had plans to be an airline pilot after his service time was over.)

When I learned of this information about the aircraft crew, I made up my mind that I was going to get an extension and stay in Vietnam if I could. To have lost comrades in arms this way was upsetting to me and I could not shake the feelings I got from it. If my aircraft had not ended up having a PE inspection, I might have been the one that went down. My mind went into overdrive thinking about O'Connor and the soldiers we lost that day. I figured it would be better to be dead than be in the hands of the enemy.

They had assigned me to a third platoon aircraft. For some reason, I flew with the six eight section pilots almost as much as I did the six nine section pilots. Flying with any of the six eight section's pilots made me very proud. After all, the second platoon had some of the best pilots in Charlie Battery, as far as I was concerned. Maybe this was because I had flown with some from other platoons and I did not feel as comfortable with or maybe for some other reason. However, for whatever the reason, I just felt second platoon had the best pilots. They did not fly nosebleed high and were not afraid to show their flying skills.

On February 6, Charlie Battery received a replacement aircraft. It was a UH-1B with the tail # 63-12928 from 610th Transportation Company. This replacement aircraft had replaced the one we lost two days earlier. This aircraft had some rebuild work done on it and looked like a new aircraft.

Specialist Roy Gollash, who had been crewing before I had arrived in the battery, was the Crew Chief assigned this aircraft. Before this helicopter arrived, Gollash had been the Crew Chief of 62-01881. This aircraft needed repairs from a higher level of maintenance. The armament section removed the rocket pods from 881 so they could ship the aircraft out for repairs. Next, the crew installed the equipment on 928. Gollash was proud to have a nice clean aircraft with new seats, interior and one without patches all over it. Gollash spent the day setting things up the way he wanted it. The Battery Armorer worked on setting up the rocket pods, making sure that they aligned properly and assured that electrically they worked correctly. Though the aircraft was not new, it was in great shape and to look at it you would think it was new.

In the evening of the day that aircraft 928 arrived, it was flying mortar patrol and assigned to Warrant Officer Comer and Lieutenant Hawkins. Comer was the AC for the mission.

The division G4 had gone on R&R. We had been at Evans a few days and had flown many hours. There was little or no JP4 left for our aircraft because our supplies had not arrived. The Navy had a refueling point set up out on the coast. We had to fly there and refuel.

Captain Whitling had been flying all day on missions. The operations officer instructed him to fly out to the coast and get fueled. They instructed Warrant Officer Kelly to follow him and refuel another aircraft. Captain Whitling did not want to make the trip because he was exhausted, darkness was closing in and the low ceilings made it even harder to navigate. After some pleading, Captain Whitling agreed to make the trip, and asked if he could get some fuel from the 1st Squadron, 9th Cavalry Cav next door. When the answer came back that he could, he hovered over to 1st Squadron, 9th Cavalry fuel blivet and added 400 lbs of fuel. This gave him 600 lbs of fuel to get to the coast.

When both aircrafts were ready, the pair started for the coast. Captain Whitling told Warrant Officer Kelly that if they went IFR to pull a 180 and head back. The flight was 15 minutes and they could track outbound on the ADF (Automatic Direction Finder) on a 90-degree radial. The two aircraft had flown about 10 minutes into the trip when Captain Whitling went IFR. Captain Whitling radioed Warrant Officer Kelly to turn back. Because Captain Whitling was only a few minutes from the Navy refuel point, he was going to continue IFR and see if he could see the lights. If he could see the lights, he would let down, try to go VFR, set the aircraft down at the refueling point and get some fuel.

Warrant Officer Kelly started back and lost his ADF. He was talking to operations and they were trying to use FM homing to guide them back. In the meantime, Captain Whitling and his pilot continued towards the coast but were not able to sight the Navy refueling point and continued flying IFR. They were sort of in and out of the clouds at 500 feet.

Then, the twenty-minute fuel warning light came on and Captain Whitling started to have vertigo. In the meantime, the pilot with Captain Whitling was on the radio trying to help Warrant Officer Kelley. Captain Whitling was struggling to keep the aircraft in level flight but found he was descending and turning. Finally, he reached over and turned off the radios. Captain Whitling quickly instructed his pilot to get on the instruments with him as he was losing it. They had only twenty-minutes of fuel and at least a fifteen-minute flight back. The two managed to get control of the aircraft and started to fly back to Evans. They radioed operations and advised them of the situation.

They were very low on fuel and afraid they would have to set the aircraft down or crash. The idea of all the NVA in the area made setting the aircraft down not very appealing. They contacted operations and asked for the artillery to fire some illumination. By doing this, they thought that it might give them a visual of Evans. As they flew over Evans, Captain Whitling could see the lights from Evans flight line through the clouds, bottomed pitch and landed the aircraft on the PSP runway. Shortly after placing the skids on the ground, the aircraft ran out of fuel.

While all this was happening, Warrant Officer Howard Comer had gotten airborne in 928 so he could help Captain Whitling. When Warrant Officer Comer and Lieutenant Hawkins came back in and landed, the weather was very bad. Navigating at tree-top-level in efforts to find the LZ visually and the Battery landing area, the crew inadvertently struck a tree.

Everyone made comments about what had happened. It was a mortar patrol mission and not a tree-trimming mission. We did not know trees grew that tall! So how did they hit a tree? For that matter, how did they hit a tree and not completely wipe out the aircraft. It was a few days before many of us really knew what had happened.

I am not sure who was at the controls when they hit the tree but they managed to wipe out the left side of the aircraft. The left side of the aircraft, where Warrant Officer Comer was sitting, had no windshield, chin bubble or green house window. The pedals on the left side were hanging in the breeze and the cyclic was broken. The main rotor blade was in bad shape. Other than that, there was little or no damage to the aircraft.

Amazingly, Warrant Officer Comer had only received a few little bruises from the tree strike. No one else got hurt. I knew some felt bad about this but at least we did not lose any more men. We were going to lose our new aircraft and it was not officially our aircraft yet.

Either Lieutenant Hawkins had the controls or he had taken over. Whatever the case, he managed to land the aircraft without any further damage to the aircraft. Everyone was shaken up from the ordeal.

The TET Offensive had started during the last days of January 1968, just as the 1st Cavalry Division and Charlie Battery, was arriving from Tam Ky. Its previous base camp was located south between Da Nang and Chu Lai. One day it was a very casual 100 feet and 30 knots and the next it was pandemonium.

During the battle of Hue, the enemy shot down many aircraft belonging to the 1st Cav. Many more received some degree of battle damage with each subsequent mission. It did not seem to be a question of if you would take a hit, only a matter of how many and how serious.

On one particular mission during the TET Offensive, then aircraft commander Lieutenant Barloco and crew flew an aircraft back from a mission with 76 bullet holes in it. The airframe looked like Swiss cheese. The engine exhaust belched a long trail of fire and smoke as the aircraft approached base camp. The only cockpit instrumentation still operational to give any support was the fox mike (FM) radio.

Before hauling the aircraft away, Ben Stevens who was the Crew Chief wove strings from each obvious entry point to his best estimate of its corresponding exit. The inside of the cabin took on the eerie look of a huge spider web. Most remarkable though was the fact that no one, not a single person of the four-member crew had received so much as a scratch. For the most part, we did not even carry a door gunner. However, for this mission there had been. This increased the odds of how many people that could have been injured or killed. Absolutely incredible!

During the succeeding days, the enemy shot down a 1st Squadron, 9th Cavalry aircraft in the city of Hue. With both pilots badly wounded, no one could fly the aircraft out of the area. A plan went into action. Four pilots would fly into the area and land. Then, the two extra pilots would fly the downed aircraft out of the area with the wounded aboard. All would be okay if they could save the aircraft. If the aircraft was not salvageable, they would extract the wounded and destroy the damaged aircraft.

What unit would this aircraft come from? The ARA aircraft seemed to be the best suited because they carried more rockets.

Because the downed aircraft was from 1st Squadron, 9th Cavalry they would furnish at least two of the pilots to fly their aircraft back to their unit. They chose the aircraft for the mission and adjusted the weight issues by unloading half the rockets. The Crew Chief would have to wait for the return of his aircraft.

When they returned from the mission, our aircraft had several holes but everyone had made it out of the area. It was the talk of everyone for a few days. However, soon it was as if it had happened a long time ago and forgotten.

Things happened this way a lot in Vietnam. What happened on one day, we soon forgot and it became just another everyday thing. It was also the way of the First Cavalry Division. If someone needed bailing out of trouble, someone would be there to help pick up the pieces. It did not matter who was in trouble, the Cavalry would come charging in to help them out.

Author at Camp Evans

Author sitting in open door of his Huey

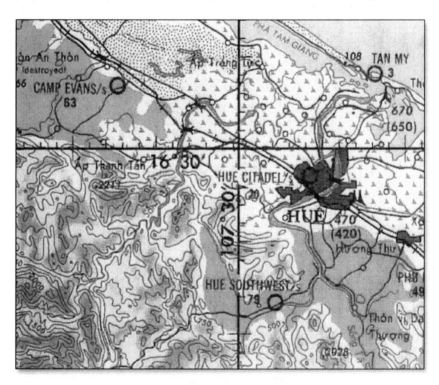

Evans was north west of Hue

11

MONSOON RAINS

Since the onset of the monsoon rains, flying had become tough for everyone. It was extra hard on the Crew Chiefs and gunners because we were the ones sitting in the open doorway, getting wet with the wind and pounding rain making the air even colder on us. The air was much cooler while flying than it was sitting on the ground. My field jacket always felt like it weighed several times more than it really did with the weight of the rainwater added. My jacket and other clothes never got a chance to dry out before I was back out in the rain getting soaked again.

I could never figure out why I was not sick with pneumonia. "Knock on wood", I managed to avoid getting sick. Living conditions were very tough and even staying in the tents was like living in a refrigerator. Some of the pilots manufactured stoves from 55-gallon drums with stovepipes made from artillery shell casings.

We usually did not carry a gunner on the right side. The weight caused by the full load of 48 rockets, a minimal fuel load, 2 pilots, a Crew Chief and ammo for both the M-60 machineguns put our aircraft beyond weight limit stress point. There were days when the weather was so bad that we were not supposed to fly. However, they were still sending us on missions. The pilots did not want to fly any more than the Crew Chiefs did. It was bad enough flying against an enemy virtually every hour we were in the air. Weather was every bit the killer that the enemy was. Frankly, it was scary. Our aircraft flew in conjunction with the navigational aids available to us and did not meet instrument flight rules very safely. Bad weather made flying much more dangerous.

When I first arrived at Charlie Battery, Captain Rivers was our maintenance officer. Now that we had moved north, Major Bloomberg, who was the Battery Executive Officer, was spending many hours working with Captain Rivers. He was performing test flights and helping to make sure that we settled into our new home. Major Bloomberg and Captain Rivers were both getting short and we were expecting a new maintenance officer very soon.

The Monsoon weather was showing me a side of things that I had never seen before in my life. One minute, it was raining and the next, the sun was shining. Out of nowhere, it would start to rain. I mean hard rain and then it would stop. A few minutes later, it would start again.

I was in my bunk area writing a letter home when Major Bloomberg came into the tent. "Men, the aircraft need to be tied down real good. There is a real bad storm headed our way. I want all the exhaust covers installed, the tail rotors tied and both ends of the main rotor tied down. I want everyone on the flight line in five minutes." With that, he turned and left the tent.

Every Crew Chief knew he was serious. There was a mad scramble as everyone headed for the flight line. I dug through my gear trying to find the exhaust cover. I had never used it and did not even remember seeing one for my aircraft.

As I was digging, John came by. "If you are looking for the exhaust cover, you will find it with your aircraft stuff in the connex (a metal storage container for miscellaneous equipment). To cut down on weight, we do not keep these items in the aircraft. You had better get there quickly! If someone is missing anything, they will grab your stuff and you will be without."

I thanked John and headed to the connex. Sure enough there it was. Now I needed to find an extra main rotor tie down which was not going to be easy because we were only issued one per aircraft. It was easier than I expected. Someone had picked up a few extra along the way from who knows where. I found them in the maintenance connex.

The waterfall after the rain had almost stopped.

Once each Crew Chief had secured his own aircraft, he would try to help someone else. No one wanted to be standing in the rain any longer than necessary. Once all the aircraft were secure, everyone headed back to the tent to wait for further instructions and wait out the storm. Moreover, what a storm it was!

It was already raining hard and I had a hard time making my way back to the Crew Chiefs' tent. Back at the tent, I looked out and there was water coming off the hill and over the steps in front of the Crew Chief tent. I thought it looked like a mini Niagara Falls. I could see a large drainpipe at my end of our tent that was so full that the end disappeared from sight. The water was overflowing and running across the runway towards the rice paddy.

Officers' tent flopping in the wind

The wind was blowing so hard, I thought our tent was going to take off at any moment. One of the other Crew Chiefs, James Lashley, thought we had better check and make sure our tent had some sand bags holding it down. As we looked around the corner of our tent, we could see the officers' tent next to ours. The sides started to look like wings as they flopped in the wind. With our tent tied down, all seemed okay. Someone made a comment about the officers needing an enlisted person to guide them on how to do things correctly. Everyone got a big laugh from that comment. After all, they were officers and pilots and could not possibly know how to tie things down very well without help.

As the rain and wind started to let up a little, I opened the flap of the tent and looked toward the flight line. There was so much water in the rice paddy between our tent and our aircraft that I could not see where the edges were. The lower flight line was covered.

Looking toward the flight line and our aircraft

From where I was standing, I could see that several of the aircraft were already partly under water. My aircraft was at the far end of the lower flight line and was in the area where the water was not as deep as where some of the other aircraft parked. I could see it was still deep in the water. I wondered if it was going to damage any of the electrical systems or perhaps something else. I would have to look things over very carefully after the rain was over.

Suddenly, it began to rain even harder than before. I did not think it was possible but it was. I thought that if I held my hand out of the tent flap and tried to see my fingers that I would have a hard time doing it. The Crew Chiefs' tent was starting to leak and everywhere anyone touched the tent it would leak more. Yet, we had no choice but to touch the tent as the wind was starting to catch it. I was sure the tent would take off at any moment.

I had never been in a monsoon rain and had no idea how long they lasted. Would we be sitting like this for only a few hours or would this be a day or two? I did not want to ask for fear of the answer.

At chow time, most of the Crew Chiefs did not want to leave the tent and walk up the hill. It was so much trouble trying to eat with all the rain gear on and water running off it into our food. The mess tent could be leaking as much as our own tent. Most of the Crew Chiefs had stocked up on soda, beer or other goodies. Anyone with a care package from home pulled it out and shared it with the others in the tent. Then it was, hang around doing nothing, writing letters home or play cards and wait for the rain to let up.

Some of the Crew Chiefs started to play cards at the far end of the tent next to the Crew Chiefs bunker that was now full of water. Others were not interested in card games. Someone decided it was a good time to pull out a bottle of Old Grand Dad and have a shot. After all, we sure could not fly in this weather. No one drank while on flight status. When they did have anything, it was usually only one or two beers. Soon, out came a second bottle. It was gone almost as fast as the first one. Of course, there was no alcohol to be found anywhere on the landing zone?

Some of the Crew Chiefs broke open some cases of the beer that were under their bunks. I had so many cases of soda under my bunk that I could not even put the legs of the cot into place. I had my air mattress on top of the cases and my cot folded and tucked into the area next to the cases.

I chose to open a can of soda. Even though it was warm, it still wet the whistle, so to speak. I went back to the letter I was writing to Gloria. Specialist James Lashley was in his area across from me and had pulled out some books to do some studying for a correspondence course he was taking for his A&P (Airframe and Power Plant) license.

Writing a letter to Gloria was not easy. I seldom got a letter from her and was not sure what to write. Frustrated with not hearing from her as often as I would have liked and not knowing what to write, I put the paper and pen away. "Hey Jim, let's join the guys in a drink".

Jim stopped and put his things away. "Sure, why not. I can't think with all this rain hitting the tent and my area is leaking like a sieve".

Then Specialist Roberson opened a bottle of Sunny Brook that he had stashed away and passed it to me. Thinking, I have no idea what this tastes like but it should be okay, I took a big mouth full. I tried not to let on how badly I wished I had not done that, but my face must have told it all.

As someone placed a warm can of RC cola in my hand, I heard, "Here, wash it down with this."

By the time I had a couple shots of Sunny Brook and a can or two of warm beer, I was feeling no pain.

After a while, the fun wore off. Most of the booze was gone and everyone went to bed to let it all wear off.

The next day my head felt like a basketball. It continued to rain hard. However, by mid morning, the weather started to clear up.

Before noon, the word was out that we were to go and take the extra tie downs off part of the aircraft on the hill. The aircraft needed to be ready in case we needed them for a mission. The sun had not shown its face. Before we had the extra tie downs removed, the sun had peaked in on us a few moments here and there. The water level began to get lower in the rice paddy. Every so often, it would start to rain lightly again but it only lasted a few minutes each time.

By noon, the weather had cleared enough. We got the word to get every aircraft ready to fly again.

Some of the Crew Chiefs had already decided to check their aircraft since we were already on the flight line. I looked at all the water around my aircraft and wondered if I should try to get near it or wait for the water to recede a little.

When I looked across the flight line, I noticed Warrant Officer Gary Lackey coming onto the flight line with one other pilot.

I could hear them talking to the other Crew Chiefs. "We are going to move the flight line out of the water and onto dryer land. We will start with those that are on the higher ground. Maybe the water will come down a little before we get to those that are in the deepest water. Warriner, your bird looks to be in less water than the other aircraft. I will move yours first." With that, we headed for my aircraft.

My aircraft had water up to the floorboards. The chin bubble was almost full. I could tell that it had been over the floorboards when the water was at its peak because there were signs of mud showing everywhere.

Mr. Lackey removed his boots and rolled his pants up. I thought this was crazy because his boots were already soaked with water and mud was clinging from them. As he made his way out through the water to my aircraft, I was thinking that I hope he does not step on anything and cut his feet. After all, who knew what was hiding under the water. Once he got to my aircraft, he climbed in and turned on the master switch. He made a comment, "I hope I don't get a shock from the wet wires in this aircraft".

I could see the concern in his actions. He truly believed that he could get a shock from the aircraft.

The expression on his face did not change until he was sure all was OK and the aircraft was at full RPM.

Warrant Officer Gary Lackey

64-14054 BEING MOVED BY WARRANT OFFICER LACKEY

Mr. Lackey moving 054

As he went to pick the aircraft up to a hover, he rocked the aircraft to break the suction that he thought could be holding the aircraft. As it started out of the watery grave, the water began to pour out of the belly of the aircraft. After it was partly out of the water, he hesitated to let some of the excess water drain off before bringing it to a full hover.

Once relocated, the pilot shut the aircraft down. You could now see Mr. Lackey relax. The remainder of the aircraft moves went without a hitch. It was amazing to watch as the excess water continued to run out of the belly of our aircraft for several minutes. The water in the rice paddy was almost back to normal before everyone had left the flight line. Despite all the rain, it only took several minutes for the ground to absorb the deluge. After a few more minutes, dust clouds would be everywhere. Absolutely amazing!

There is a season for all things. It was impossible to accustom myself to the monsoon season in Vietnam. During that season, you learned to expect hard rains – unlike any you had ever experienced.

Unit patch when I arrived in unit

Unit patch in 1968-1969

12

ALPHA BATTERY

I was cleaning my aircraft when I looked up and saw Sergeant First Class Cole headed my way. "Warriner, take whatever you want with you because you are headed to Alpha Battery for a few days. Mr. Comer will be your aircraft commander and you will be leaving in half an hour."

"Okay Sergeant Cole, I will be ready."

I was not sure how long I would be gone so I grabbed a change of clothes, a few things I wanted and headed back to my aircraft. As I arrived at my aircraft, Mr. Comer, or "TC" as he was affectionately referred to by other pilots, was doing a preflight so I knew we were leaving soon. I enjoyed flying with Mr. Comer because he got down close and personal where you could see what you were shooting at. Other pilots liked to fly nosebleed high, as he called it.

As Mr. Hollister was putting his things into the right seat, I got a feeling that this was going to be a good day. I was going to be flying with two people with whom I really enjoyed flying.

Comer noticed me coming toward the aircraft. "Is this thing ready to fly Chief?"

I answered quickly, "Yes, Sir. Who do we have as our wing aircraft"?

Comer smiled, "We are being sent off on this mission alone. We are all here so let's crank."

I put my chest protector on, grabbed my helmet and untied the main rotor, "Clear and untied".

Hollister called, "Coming through".

The sound of the igniters popping, the turbine starting to whine and the blade slowly starting to turn, gave anyone watching a sense that the turbine engine was about to spring to life. Then with a little puff of smoke, she sprang to life.

I slid the armor plating forward, closed both pilot doors and took up my spot in the left cargo door behind Mr. Comer. I listened to Comer talking with Mr. Hollister and waited for the signal that we were about to pick it up to a hover.

Hollister wanted to make sure I was ready. He looked back at me for a moment as he asked over the intercom, "Are we ready Chief?"

I acknowledged, "Yes, Sir."

Mr. Hollister picked the aircraft up to a hover and hovered out of the revetment. As soon as we had cleared the revetment, I called, "Tail clear to turn Sir".

Hollister headed us towards the north, nosed the aircraft over and soon we were in transitional lift.

Comer keyed his intercom. "You ready to settle in for a while? We expect to be at Alpha Battery until some of their aircraft are back flyable and while they have a change of command. They have a Major leaving the Battery and going to Headquarters or something like that."

I wanted to let my pilots know I was ready. "As ready as I can get, Sir."

Moments later Comer was on the radio, "Blue Max Two Three India. This is Blue Max Six Eight Golf, flight of one; zero five from your location, request landing instructions."

The reply came back, "Aircraft calling Two Three India, say again you are coming in broken."

Comer tried again, "Blue Max Two Three India. This is Blue Max Six Eight Golf, flight of one; zero five from your location, requesting landing instructions."

This time we had a more positive answer, "Aircraft calling Two Three India. Understand. Winds calm. Negative traffic. Clear to land at pilots' digression. Two Three India out."

As we touched down at Alpha Battery Comer asked, "Hey Chief, what's up with your FM Radio?"

They had changed my radio twice and I thought they had fixed it. "Sir, I don't know. It seems okay at times and then it quits. Avionics has changed it twice and nothing seems to solve the problem."

Comer was not happy. "Stay by your aircraft chief. I will get their avionics guy out to look at it." With that, he turned and headed for operations.

Moments later, I noticed someone coming towards my aircraft with a head set. "I am Specialist Cauldwell.

I understand you have a radio problem. I wish Frank was here because he is better at this than I am."

With that, he climbed into the front seat, plugged in his headset, hit the battery switch and turned on the radio. "Blue Max Two Three India, this is Alpha Charlie 054, Fox Mike radio check."

Operations responded, "Alpha Charlie 054, Two Three India, I have you Lima-Charlie over."

I knew that Two Three India had heard everything without a problem because Lima-Charlie was radio talk for loud and clear.

Cauldwell shut the radio off and took the head set off. As he climbed out of the aircraft, he was shaking his head. "It is working fine right now. Maybe you have a bad radio. Has it been changed lately?"

I was thinking that if I did not have a problem while on the ground, there must be a bad connection. Maybe it was the wire leading to the antenna.

My response was, "Yes, it has been changed twice. I do not think it is the radio. But I still have a problem every time we are flying."

Cauldwell shook his head. "I don't think it is the radio either. I will put in one of our radios to see if it works."

With the loaner radio installed, Cauldwell tried it again. "Two Three India, this is Alpha Charlie 054, Fox Mike radio check over".

"Roger, Alpha Charlie 054, this is Two Three India. I have you Lima Charlie. Message from Two Six, leave our radio in the aircraft until we send the bird back to Charlie Battery"

Cauldwell shut down everything, unplugged his headset and as he climbed out, he turned to me, "I was told to leave our radio in your bird for now."

I had been listening. "So I heard. Maybe it was a couple bad of radios that gave me the problem."

As I was closing up my aircraft, Cauldwell turned to me. "Let's go to Beer Thirty and get a cold soda."

I had no idea what Beer Thirty was. "I would like to have a cold soda but what is Beer Thirty?"

Cauldwell smiled. "Don't you guys have a Beer Thirty? That is where we keep beer and soda for the troops. I have several jobs in the battery. I am not just one of the avionics personnel. I am also the battery barber and the CO put me in charge of Beer Thirty. I am in charge of giving out the beer and soda when the CO says the guys can have it."

As we walked, we talked about where we were from and how we sure would be glad to be back in the states.

Beer Thirty was nothing but a small tent set up in the middle of the company area with a couple of coolers and a small table. When we arrived, there were some men already there sitting around eating some goodies from home.

It was amazing to me to watch as one of the men used a spoon to take a bite out of a can peaches. Then he passed it along to another. When he was finished, he then passed it to another. I was thinking boy you would never see that back in the world. Mr. Hollister interrupted my thoughts, "Chief, we are on hot status so be ready to go."

Knowing that, I answered, "Yes, Sir. I am ready sir!" Then I turned and headed for my aircraft so I would be there if the horn went off.

There was an aircraft parked in front of my aircraft with the engine cowling removed getting a 100-hour inspection. It looked like the crew had been repainting the engine cowling where it had some damage. There were two maintenance people working on the aircraft so I stopped to talk.

I thought that maybe he was the Crew Chief of the aircraft because he pointed down into the valley. "See where those two gunships were working out. Every aircraft that goes near that area gets the crap shot out of them. If you go out near that spot stay alert because they will punch you full of holes."

Just as he got the words out of his mouth, the horn went off. I ran to my aircraft to grab my chicken-plate and put it on. Then I grabbed my flight helmet, put it on and ran to untie the main rotor. I was untying the main rotor when my pilots came on the run. I helped Mr. Hollister with his gear so he could start to crank. "You're clear and untied Sir."

After the turbine sprang to life, I slide the armor plating forward and closed the pilot doors. I took up my spot in the left cargo door.

A Battery had no revetments. We had an aircraft in front as well as behind us and the battery area was on our right side. We had to take off towards our left in a sideways fashion and turn as we lifted off. This move would put us in an out of ground effect. We would drop before we hit transitional lift causing a feeling that would give me the sensation that we were falling. This was something that I had never experienced before. What was this going to be like?

I plugged in my helmet, grabbed my M-60 and reached up to turn on the switches for the FM Radio and the UHF Radio.

I had learned to monitor all the radios. When I could, I would shut off any radio that I did not need. If we got into a fight, at least I knew better than just waiting for the pilots to tell me.

Hollister was at the controls and picked the aircraft up to a hover. "Coming left".

I was ready for this hairy take off. "Clear left sir".

The take off was one I thought I had prepared for. Wrong! I was trying to load my M-60, was looking at what I was doing and not where the aircraft was going. My first thought was oh crap we were going down. We are going to crash. Then we hit transitional lift. I lost my balance and was sure I was going out the door. Wow, that was close. I sure will pay more attention the next time we take off that way, but I hope it does not happen very often.

Comer was on the radio getting mission information. I caught the end of the radio chatter, "Six Eight Golf, Two Three India, head 270 for 10 minutes, contact Guidon One Seven on 141.5, over."

Comer changed to Guidon One Seven's frequency. He always sounded cool and calm even when the fighting turned ugly. "Guidon One Seven, Blue Max Six Eight Golf, flight of two in route your location. What do you have for us?"

Immediately they responded, "Blue Max Six Eight Golf, Guidon One Seven, receiving heavy weapons fire from our North West."

Then there was a brief pause. "We have wounded".

Comer was still calm. "Roger, One Seven, zero five out your location, request smoke."

I could hear the urgency when One Seven answered, "Roger Six Eight Golf, One Seven, smoke out".

It was important that we identify the position with the color smoke used in case Charlie was listening. If Charlie heard us, he would try to fool us into thinking that he was one of the friendly elements.

Now Comer had shortened the radio chatter. "One Seven, I have purple smoke."

This time, when One Seven answered I could hear the gunfire. "Roger, Max, purple smoke. That is our most northern element. We are receiving heavy weapons fire from our north side from the tree line."

Hollister had the aircraft already in position for the marker rounds. "One Seven, get your heads down. We are rolling in with marker rounds."

Hollister nosed over, punched off a pair of rockets and started to pull out of the dive. Almost as soon as the rounds hit, I heard, "Max, you are right on target. Work that tree line good." I knew it was safe to open up on that area with my M-60 to cover my aircraft.

That is when the tree line lit up. I had no idea how large an element of enemy was in the area but enemy tracer rounds were coming from everywhere. Charlie was trying to shoot us out of the sky!

"One Seven, keep you heads down. My wing is rolling hot."

As I reloaded my M-60, I could see my wing aircraft as he was dumping several rockets into the area.

One Seven was back on the radio. "Max, you have pissed them off now. They are firing back at you. I can see the tracers going up towards the last aircraft."

Now we were in position. "Six Eight Golf, rolling hot."

As we rolled in, I heard a sound that I had heard before. It was real close and I knew instantly what it was. It was the unmistakable sound of an AK-47. I thought I knew were the rounds were coming from so I opened up with some rounds from my M-60 into the area. This must have pissed Charlie off because I could hear the AK-47 as he was firing more rounds in my direction. My thoughts were now racing. Those sure are close! Comer interrupted my thoughts. "Ten o'clock in the tree line Chief. Get that SOB".

The AK made a very distinct sound

Sure enough, Charlie was in the tree line pumping rounds at us. I swung my M-60 around, unloaded the 150 rounds left in my assault can and grabbed another 200 rounds. Now I was wishing that I were using a belt feed instead of the assault can, but I could not switch now.

I thought Comer was going to climb into the back seat and grab the other M-60. Instead, he started firing his pistol out his window. "Get that SOB." Then his voice shifted gears. "You got him chief. You got the SOB."

I turned my attention to another area. Then I heard Comer again. "Must be that SOB doesn't want to die. He just got up and is running across the field." Now Comer was yelling, "Get that SOB"!

Swinging my M-60 back around. I opened up on Charlie again. This time he fell to the ground and the AK seemed to stop. I was checking the area for any more enemy when Comer yelled, "That SOB is shooting at us again. Get that SOB".

Now I was pissed. This SOB was punching my aircraft full of holes and I was not going to let him get away with it if I could help it. I emptied the entire 200 rounds I had just loaded on him.

As my ammo ran out I heard, "Max, your Crew Chief got him that time. He will not be shooting at you anymore."

I had dragged ammo from the right side over to my side. Now I was almost out of ammo and we had expended all our rockets.

Comer let One Seven know our status. "One Seven. This is Six Eight Golf. Be advised we are almost out of fuel and ammo."

The response was more relaxed than I thought it would be. "Max, you did a great job. I think we can handle it now. We have dust off in bound to pick up wounded. Thanks for your assistance. You are free to head home."

Landed at Alpha Battery, Comer was still wound up about what had happened. "Chief, any damage? It sure sounded close. Let's check this aircraft over carefully."

That is when I noticed it. The green house window above Comers head was broken. "Look above your head, Sir!"

When Comer looked up, he said, "No wonder it sounded so close. Check to see where that round went when we shut down. I am sure we took a few more hits also."

After we shut down, I traced the path of the round above Comer's head. It had traveled at an angle towards the transmission ripping the roof of my helicopter open as it went. It had only missed Comer's head by inches.

Both Comer and Hollister helped me look for more damage. Now Comer was smiling. "Do you think any rounds were close to you chief?"

I responded, "They sure sounded close Sir. Why do you ask?"

Pointing to the door track just above my head, Comer said, "Look at the hole in the door track." Then, he hesitated, and pointed to a hole about six inches back from the hole in the cargo door jam and said, "Look how close that one was to your head right there."

I had noticed where the round hit by the doorjamb but had not noticed the one in the door track. I ripped the soundproofing down to expose the damage because I knew these rounds do not vanish, after they hit.

Comer commented, "Good thing that was not an armor piercing. We would have lost our transmission. I will go get a TI, but it looks like we may be out of a job until this is fixed."

Hole just above the door track

The TI from Alpha Battery confirmed that the aircraft was okay to fly to 15th Transportation Corp Battalion (aviation maintenance) for repairs. Comer gave the bad news in operations and soon I was now heading home to Charlie Battery.

I had only been at Alpha Battery a very short time. I had made a few friends that I was sure I would never see again. Then again, who knows? It is a small world.

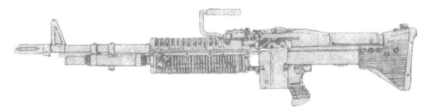

Our M-60 machineguns

Infantry version of the M-60

13

15th Transportation Corp Battalion

(aviation maintenance)

Leaving Alpha Battery, I knew that I was going to miss the new friends I had met in my short visit. My stay at Alpha Battery was not even an overnight, but in the heat of battle, you form quick friendships. On the other hand, going back to Charlie Battery, I was not very excited about being as close to the DMZ as Alpha Battery was. I was also sure that I was not going to get much rest unless you called sleeping while flying mortar patrol "restful".

As we left Alpha Battery for the flight back to Charlie Battery, I was deep in thought. The 15th Transportation Corp Battalion (aviation maintenance) was located at Red Beach Da Nang. The armament crew needed to remove equipment from my aircraft before going for repairs. Maybe I could get some rest while there and see the area. The radio interrupted my thoughts. "Evans Tower. This is Blue Max Six Eight Golf, flight of one for landing at Blue Max pad".

"Roger Blue Max aircraft, Evans Tower, negative traffic your area, winds calm, clear to land at pilots' discretion".

Comer acknowledged Evans Tower by keying his mike twice and changed to the Blue Max push. "Blue Max Six Three India, Blue Max Six Eight Golf on short final".

The response was quick. "Roger, Blue Max Six Eight Golf, Six Three India out".

Almost before we had shut down, the maintenance crew was all over my aircraft like a swarm of bees. I grabbed my two M-60 machine guns and headed for the armament connex to store them while the armament crew was busy removing the rocket pods. All armament items needed to be stored in the armament connex. If for any reason an aircraft went straight from the field to 15th Transportation Corp Battalion (aviation maintenance) for repairs, someone would have to bring the equipment back home. They had no storage space for this equipment.

While the crew was finishing their job, I headed for the Crew Chief tent and my area. Maybe I had some mail waiting and I wanted a few more things to take with me.

Upon entering the tent, Specialist Boerm spotted me. "You have some mail on your bunk."

"That is just what I wanted. Looks like I have several letters. I hope Gloria wrote to me."

The way the letters from Gloria were arriving, I just knew something was wrong. I would get three or four of her letters in one day and then not hear from her for weeks at a time. I was going to study her letters and see if I could read between the lines and figure out what was going on. I knew she was busy but the groups of letters coming in at one time did not make sense. Besides, there were comments and things in the letters that just did not sound like Gloria. I thought the comments sounded more like they were coming

- 161 -

from her sister Brenda but then I told myself I had to be wrong.

I gathered up all the letters without looking to see whom they were from, grabbed a few munchies I had stashed away and headed back to my aircraft.

When I arrived at my aircraft, Mr. Nader was waiting. "Warriner, you ready to go?"

I did not see any other pilot and had never gone anywhere without two pilots. "Yes, Sir. Who else is going with us?"

Reaching for the door handle Nader said, "No one. You will be up front in the right seat. Untie the rotor. I want to be there before dark".

I untied the main rotor. "Clear and untied."

As the turbine engine began to come to life, I noticed Doug Roberson coming towards my aircraft with his helmet on. He was motioning for me to get in, "Get in. I will finish out here". This was something that some of the Crew Chiefs would do for others and I had done it for Doug before.

As I got into the seat, I plugged in my helmet and strapped in. Nader glanced over with a puzzled look but then smiled when he saw Doug.

He went through the final checks and keyed his intercom. "Is that Roberson? Have to thank him when I return. Glad to see you Crew Chiefs work together. Get the pedals and seat adjusted so you are comfortable."

I knew I needed to do that but had never sat in the front seat before. The look on my face must have told him everything, but he said nothing.

Nader called for clearance, signaled to Roberson that we were ready and that we would turn to the right after exiting the revetment.

Roberson signaled all was clear. We picked up to a hover coming forward out of the revetment. Once we were clear of the revetment, Roberson signaled that we were clear to turn. Nader faced eastward. Then he called for clearance, nosed over and soon we were into transitional lift.

As soon as we became airborne, Nader keyed his intercom. "I bet you have not had any stick, have you?"

This comment caught me by surprise. "No, Sir. In fact, this is my first time in the front seat on any flight."

Nader had a smile on his face. "Well, maybe it is time you got a little stick time. Place your feet on the pedals and take hold of the cyclic. It's time for a quick lesson."

I was scared about having the flight controls in my hands. I had watched my pilots and figured it could not be that hard as long as I was not trying to land, hover or take off.

Placing my feet on the pedals was okay. Once I had the cyclic in my right hand, Nader said, "You have the aircraft. I think all you Huey Crew Chiefs should learn to fly. From now on when I do a test flight, the Crew Chief will be in the front seat. It is about time you learn the basics in case you have to help land the aircraft. If the Crew Chief can fly in the front seat and learn what we have to do for a test flight check, they will be better Crew Chiefs. I also think they will take better care of their aircraft. Besides, why should the pilots have all the fun?"

As we continued toward our destination, I thought I was doing okay. Then I could see I was drifting and losing altitude. As I tried to correct the problem, it got worse. This did not seem to bother Mr. Nader.

Calmly he commented, "Loosen up and try thinking of the direction you want to go. You are over correcting. The more it gets off course, the more you are fighting it. Handle her like she is your girlfriend back home, nice and gentle".

I could feel him on the controls with me then. "Now, hold what you have. You'll get the hang of it."

Now I was in better control. The aircraft was not climbing, dipping or drifting sideways as badly.

I was just getting the feel of things when I heard, "I have the aircraft."

I was thinking, am I messing up or is there a problem with the aircraft, when he spoke again. "We are close to Hue and there are a lot of bad guys in the area. We do not want to fly directly over Hue. I will take us around the city. The weather is not good upstairs and at our altitude, we are sitting ducks for

Charlie. We are going to drop down to tree top level. With all the bad guys in this area, we don't want to get shot down with just your M-16 and my .38."

We were flying along at 100 knots almost clipping the treetops. When I looked ahead, I was sure we were going to hit a tree at any moment. Then, I heard a tree brush the bottom of the aircraft. This did not seem to bother Nader. He just pulled up a little as we went over the treetop and then dropped back down. Right away I thought, "I sure hope there are not any more trees in our flight path."

The distinctive pop of an AK-47 interrupted my thoughts as we were flying over this village. I had been looking down and noticed the VC with his weapon pointed up at us. I was not surprised when I heard the pop from the weapon. I was sure Nader heard the shot but was not sure he noticed Charlie. Maybe I should ask him in case he wanted to report it back to operations. "Sir, did you see that SOB shooting at us?"

Still cool as ever, "I heard it but at this speed and with us at tree top level, he did not get a good shot at us and I am sure he missed us completely."

After we had arrived at 15th Transportation Corp Battalion (aviation maintenance) and were shutting down, Nader said, "Warriner, walk around the aircraft and check for additional damage while I go over the books."

I planned to do that anyway. "Yes Sir".

My walk around the aircraft revealed no additional holes. I had never been to 15th Transportation Corp Battalion (aviation maintenance) before. "Well Sir, looks like Charlie missed us back there. Where do we go from here?"

Nader smiled. "Another first for you. Well, as soon as I check radio numbers and a couple other things, we will go turn in the records. They will move the aircraft into their area to start work on it. Someone will show you where you will bunk while your aircraft is being repaired, or they may send you back to the unit with me."

Then Nader discovered the radio serial number did not match the records. "How come the serial number is not correct for your FM radio?"

I explained, "Sir, my FM radio has been intermittent for a while and our avionics guys tried to fix it, but it seemed to still be intermittent. While I was at Alpha Battery, their avionics personnel put one of their radios into my aircraft. Must be we forgot to put my radio back and they never wrote in the log book that it was exchanged."

"Okay, I think I can get that straightened out. It will have to wait until I get back to the unit."

Inside the maintenance office, Nader went to use the phone to contact Alpha Battery. I could not hear all the conversation but I could tell that they were a little upset over the mix-up. Nader was telling them something about not placing all the blame on the Crew Chief as their avionics man was partly to blame. For that matter, he was more to blame then the Crew Chief.

From what I could hear, Nader stood up for me and that sure gave me a good feeling.

Outside the maintenance office, Nader explained that all was okay with the radio problem. We stayed there until Specialist Lane came.

Lane was a team leader with 15th Transportation Corp Battalion (aviation maintenance) and he would get me settled in. Knowing that I was all set, Nader headed for the flight line to catch his flight back to Charlie battery.

Lane helped me with my bags and got me a bunk. Then he let me know that I was to help him. He was on the night crew and would be starting on my aircraft that night.

By 2100 hours (9 p.m.), everything that I needed to help with was finished and I headed for my bunk. I stayed up writing a letter to mom. I was not even sure what time it was when I turned out the light to try to sleep.

Morning came early with John Holland rousting me out of my bunk. "Are you the Crew Chief for 054?"

My reply was one of surprise. "Yes, I am. Why?"

Holland was quick to answer. "I am the team leader for the crew working on your bird today and we need you at the aircraft. Go get some chow and then meet me at your aircraft as soon as you can."

After a breakfast of powdered eggs, I headed for the maintenance area where I found that the night crew had pulled all the rest of the inspection panels. Avionics was working on the FM radio problem and was checking all the wires that had anything to do with the radios. By noon, they had found the problem. There was a wire in an area where they had repaired the airframe before they assigned me as the Crew Chief on the aircraft. The damaged wiring had gone unnoticed and the break had caused the intermittent radio problems.

I spent the next three days waiting for the sheet metal crew to repair the roof of my aircraft and installed the new greenhouse window. Because there was not much I could do, I spent most of my time just hanging around talking with Lane and Holland.

I did not get much time to do any letter writing. However, I heard many stories about things that had happened. They talked about how great they thought it would be as a Crew Chief. They were sick of doing test flights and wanted to know if the ARA needed Crew Chiefs.

I told them that I did not know anyone who was leaving, but I knew a few guys who wanted out of being a Crew Chief. Holland came from a family that owned fix wing aircraft used to spray crops. He already had a pilot's license and loved to fly. If he had a love of flying, then why had he not gone to flight school? That was something I just could not understand.

Lane told me about a Crew Chief that came to 15th Transportation Corp Battalion (aviation maintenance) for an engine change and ended up staying for three engines. Every time they installed a new engine into the aircraft, something was wrong. They finally caught the Crew Chief putting trash in the intake of the engine causing the new engine to blow up. When I asked why he did that, Lane told me that the Crew Chief was afraid of flying and did not want to go back to his unit. The result was a court martial and he received a big fine for what he did. They made the Crew Chief pay the cost of the engine plus other charges.

This is why 15th Transportation Corp Battalion (aviation maintenance) changed their way of doing things and made the Crew Chief fly on the test flight after repairs. They felt that if the Crew Chief knew he had to fly on the test flight that maybe he would not try to destroy anything. After all, who would be crazy enough to scuttle an aircraft in which he was about to fly?

14

MAXWELL SYSTEM

Zero Five Four was an old B Model, but she was ready to return to action and so was I. The repairs were complete. She was sitting on the tarmac and I was waiting with it. I was thinking about the flight down and wondered, "Would the trip back be the same? Would I be in the front seat and maybe get some more stick time?"

This is the roof of 054 and shows, the angle of the damage caused by enemy.

This was a first for me, going off to have work done on my aircraft. I knew that sometimes pilots that were not scheduled to fly to ferry the aircrafts. Would Mr. Nader be coming after my aircraft, or would they send another pilot? I tried to pass the time away by walking along the flight line but stayed close to my aircraft.

I had noticed a Chinook parked within walking distance. For some reason this bird was different from your run-of-the-mill Chinooks. It looked like one of the Guns-A-Go-Go helicopters. They had once landed at the far end of the runway at Tam Ky but I did not get a chance to get a close look at them. Yes, I knew it was one of the Guns-A-Go-Go birds. Here was my chance, so I wandered over to look at it.

Sure enough, this was one of the Guns-a-Go-Go aircraft with Easy Money painted on either side and the tail number was 13149. What an awesome looking aircraft! I could see it used its payload capability to its full advantage. It was not only loaded with heavy weapons, but had armor to protect the crew and vital parts. What a treat! I was looking at the last bird of its type. There were only two Chinooks ever converted to weapons platforms. On February 22, one of these aircraft that had the "nose art" title of Birth Control had been forced down near Hue.

I had been told that our unit controlled the missions that these aircraft were assigned and recalled being on a mission where they were being employed. This aircraft sure could bring heat. I had been awed watching it work out. Now I could see why.

The armament on this bird was just breathtaking. It had a 40mm mounted on the nose, two fixed mount 20mm cannons and two nineteen round 2.75-rocket pods on the stub wing pylons. There were two gunner positions, one on each side of the aircraft, with a .50 caliber machine gun in each position and M-60 machineguns as backup. It had a .50 caliber on the back ramp with another M-60 for backup. There were twin M-60 machine guns rigged through the cargo hatch to help protect the belly as it went over the target.

I was thinking I should have had my camera so that I could take a photo of the aircraft. It was to be an opportunity lost though. I never did get that picture. Before I could finish my walk around, I heard Mr. Nader. "Warriner, you ready to head back to the unit?"

I replied quickly, "Yes, Sir" and headed for my aircraft.

Nader thought he would check the repairs and the books before he did a preflight of the aircraft in case anything was wrong. The first thing he needed to do was check the books.

Suddenly Nader spoke. "It looks like they gave us the log books for another aircraft. It belongs to the 1st Squadron 9th Calvary. They must be on their way to pick it up."

Nader hesitated then added, "Look, it is parked right there. I wonder what they would say if they got our aircraft in place of theirs?"

Before I could comment, Nader added, "It looks like they did a good job on the repairs on your aircraft. We better take our aircraft home and stay out of trouble. Wait here and I will go exchange the books. It should not take me long."

I figured he would be back within a few minutes so I just took a spot inside my bird to wait.

Shortly he was back. We finished our inspection of the aircraft and were ready to pull pitch. I put my flight helmet on and untied the main rotor, "Clear and untied sir."

Nader hit the starter button and called, "Coming through". Soon the turbine engine sprang to life with the usual puff of smoke and pop as the fuel ignited and the blades started to turn. As soon as I was sure all was okay, I went around to right side of the aircraft, slid the armor plate forward and closed the door for Nader.

Going around to the left side, I climbed in the left pilot seat and closed the door, which was not easy from inside, but I managed. Next, I slid the armor plate forward just in case we went over an area where the bad guys wanted to use us for target practice.

Nader was still joking about taking the other aircraft in place of mine. After all, it was a newer aircraft and still looked good on the inside and outside. Because the unit that the aircraft belonged to was tough on their aircraft, Nader thought it could be a bad trade.

Soon, we were on our way back to Camp Evans. Nader gave me the controls again for a little more stick time.

I was at the controls and did not realize how close we were to Evans until I heard, "Evans Tower, Blue Max Zero Five Four southeast of your location for landing at Blue Max pad".

Although the maintenance officers had a radio call sign, it was common for them to use the last three numbers of the aircraft they were flying. This told everyone it was a pilot not on a combat mission.

"Roger, Blue Max aircraft, clear for straight in landing, negative traffic your area, winds are calm at this time".

Nader acknowledged, "Roger, Evans Tower, Blue Max Zero Five Four" and changed to our Battery push, "Blue Max Six Three India, Blue Max Zero Five Four on short final".

As soon as operations acknowledged, "Zero Five Four, Six Three India, understand short final, will notify maintenance." I heard, "I have the aircraft."

We had not even shut down when the armament crew was all over us like worker bees. They used the mule to bring the rocket pods and other equipment to my aircraft. Even my M-60 machine guns were waiting for me. I noticed that there were only three banks of six tubes totaling 36 rocket tubes for each side of the aircraft instead of the normal four banks giving me 48 tubes. I knew that they were planning to install the Maxwell System on my aircraft again.

Specialist Ryan was in charge of armament. He spoke with a chuckle, "Chief, I guess you have the luck of the draw again. I guess you know what you are getting. They must like you or something. That is what you get for having a good pilot that can fire the missile".

I knew it had nothing to do with who my pilots were and that all the sections had pilots who could fire the missile.

The Maxwell System was a hybrid or modification of two armament systems, the XM3 that normally had 48 tubes using 2.75 inch folding fin rockets, with 24 on each side of the aircraft and the M22 or SS-11, which had six wire guided missiles with three per side.

Because the M22 system was not used very often and took 2 ½ to 3 hours to get ready, it was not installed often. It seldom stayed on an aircraft, as this made the aircraft useless for regular missions. Warrant Officer Robert Maxwell studied the two systems and figured out that because the two systems were separate, they could be fired independently. With the use of steel plates, Huey skid tubing (with ground handling loop attached) and one bank from the XM3 (with tubes removed), he designed a mounting system for the SS-11 missile.

For the first test run, he removed two banks of the 2.75 rockets before placing the single SS-11 on each side. By the time I was a Crew Chief, there was only one bank of rockets removed to install the system.

After all the armament was mounted, the Maxwell System installed and aligned, I began loading the 2.75 rockets into the tubes, while the armament team mounted the missiles on their brackets.

Most pilots were not happy flying the aircraft with the Maxwell System because it was harder getting it in and out of the revetments. The aircraft was heavier and did not fly as well. Carrying fewer 2.75 rockets also meant less firepower on a normal mission. Not enjoyable but someone had to do it.

Only a few pilots in the battery were qualified to fire the SS-11 missile, which was a help in knowing who your pilots would be. Mostly they used the missile on bunkers. They installed the Maxwell Systems on my aircraft before but I had never been on a SS-11 mission. I never watched it in action. I often wondered what it be like to be on a mission and watch it launch. Would it take off fast or slow?

Two days later, I got my chance. Just before 10:00 am, I had a change of pilots. My new pilots informed me that a mission was going to be coming up soon. I did not ask about the change; that happened sometimes and sometimes the Crew Chiefs did get advance information on missions.

When the horn went off, I was ready and we lifted off as usual.

Right after liftoff, Captain Adams was on the intercom, "Chief, we expect to be firing the SS-11 on this mission. I do not know if you have ever been on one of these missions. These missions are run differently than any other mission, so listen to what I say."

Now I knew why my pilots had switched places with another crew. I usually clicked my intercom twice to let my pilots know I understood but this time I answered, "Yes, Sir".

I enjoyed flying with Captain Adams. He was the platoon leader of the first platoon with the radio call sign of Blue Max Six Seven. If he was aboard my aircraft, then I knew he was not only in charge of my aircraft, he was also in charge of the mission.

I was listening to Adams talking to his pilot, "When we are on station, I will set up the run. I want you to take over the aircraft and fly straight and level. Pay attention to your flying, not where the missile is going or what I am doing. Do not change direction or anything unless I tell you to do so. Even if we are taking fire, do not do anything unless I tell you to do so. If you don't stay straight and level, I could lose control of the missile."

Switching to the radio, "Quick Silver Seven One, Blue Max Six Seven in route your location, zero five mikes out. Request you pop smoke, over."

The response was quick, "Roger, Blue Max Six Seven. Quick Silver Seven One, I have you in sight. Smoke out".

Seconds later, Adams spotted the smoke. "Quick Silver Seven One. Blue Max Six Seven. We have purple smoke."

I knew it was always important that we identify the smoke. If Charlie was listening and the ground unit told us what color smoke they used, Charlie could pop the same color smoke and try to confuse everyone. That, in fact, had happened before on several missions.

"Roger, Blue Max Six Seven. Purple smoke. From our smoke, northeast across the rice paddy. We are receiving heavy enemy fire from the window in the pagoda. Every time we try to move, they open up."

Adams replied, "Quick Silver Seven One, I have it in sight. I will be firing the missile over your heads. So keep your heads down." The normal azimuth of attack would always avoid firing over or towards friendly forces for obvious reasons, unless engagement circumstances dictated otherwise.

I could tell Adams was concerned as he spoke to his pilot. "We need to keep the good guys on our left, when we fire these missiles. If they mess up, they usually go down and to the right. Oh, and chief, because the good guys are on our left, you will not get a chance to fire your weapon."

I keyed my intercom and answered, "Yes, Sir".

Adams lined up for the run and gave the controls to the pilot. "Quick Silver Seven One, Max Six Seven rolling hot".

There was a roar as the missile left the aircraft. It started out so slow that it looked like you could put a saddle on it and take a ride. I was thinking that if the enemy was in its path, that they had all kinds of time to move away. Then, the missile picked up speed. I could see the wires trailing behind the rocket. Then suddenly, it started to dive to the right.

Captain Adams was on the radio. "Seven One take cover. We have lost control of the missile and we are not sure where it will go."

Captain Adams was trying to regain some control of the missile by pushing on the control stick. I was not sure if he had regained control or maybe it just decided to head off on its own. For whatever the reason, it started to drift off to God knows where. Adams keyed his intercom, "I hope it does not hit any good guys. I think a wire broke on that missile. Let's make a go around and try the second one."

Captain Adams was back on the radio. "Seven One, Blue Max Six Seven. Missile headed away from your location. We are coming around for a second attempt."

SS-11 controls

Missile control stick center bottom of photo

After coming back around, Captain Adams was back on the radio, "Seven One, Blue Max Six Seven. We are rolling hot so keep your heads down."

As the missile left its mount, it started out the same as the first one, dropping and slow but then it picked up speed and leveled off. I was sure that Adams had full control of this missile. I watched it as it headed straight for the target in the window of the pagoda. There was no explosion. My thoughts were that this was another bad round because nothing had happened. Then there was an explosion followed by a secondary explosion.

I could tell Adams was happy. "Quick Silver One Seven, Blue Max Six Seven. Looks like that did it. We will stay on station in the event you still need us."

The troops were now on their feet and I could see them moving towards the pagoda. We were now circling close enough that I could see troops entering the pagoda and checking the area around it for any other sign of enemy activity.

There did not seem to be any trace of the enemy in the area after the secondary explosion. I figured if any of the enemy had survived the explosion, they sure would have been scared off or at least they had dirty shorts. I was sure that the explosion had probably killed or at the least deafened everything in or near the pagoda because I heard it loud and clear from where I was sitting.

We continued to circle the area until they released us from the mission and we headed home. I had not fired my M-60. I felt like I was only along for the ride but knew better.

HOORAH for Cpt. Adams!!!

I had a feeling that we had once again accomplished our mission with honor and pride.

15

UNWELCOME CHANGE

By the end of March, we had a new maintenance warrant officer in Charlie Battery. Mr. Winchester had blond hair and looked very young. However, for the most part, we were all very young.

Specialist Lane and Specialist Holland, who I had met at 15th Transportation Corps Battalion (aviation maintenance) while getting my aircraft repaired, managed to make the move to Charlie Battery. Now both had become Huey Crew Chiefs. Lane took to crewing like a duck to water, enjoying every second of his job. Holland on the other hand was not as happy as he thought he would be. However, he was very good at the job, could not wait for his time to end and go back home. This was because his family owned aircraft and he could fly those aircraft.

Changes were taking place every day. There was a rumor that we were getting Cobras to replace our Huey aircraft. With the arrival of the Cobra, the Huey Crew Chiefs would be out of a flying job. This did not make any of us that liked to fly happy. Exchanging a flying job for one of taking care of an aircraft that we could not fly did not sound exciting. We would get dust blown on us and never get up where the air was cool. In time, everyone would be assigned a Cobra and lose the flying position. I was not looking forward to that at all.

Every Huey Crew Chief talked about moving to maintenance or transferring to another unit. No one wanted to be a Cobra Crew Chief. One question was, who would be stuck with the Cobra first? Secondly, when would the switch take place?

The answers to these questions would depend on how quickly the Cobras arrived and possibly how long each of us could keep our own Huey flyable.

One thing for sure, I did not want to be the Crew Chief of any Cobra helicopter. When the first Cobra would arrive in Charlie Battery, I was sure that I was going to be one of the first to get the shaft and my flying days were definitely numbered.

All the rumors started to become reality in the last week of March. Charlie Battery received the first of the Cobra helicopters that we also called Snakes. It was an impressive looking aircraft. From the front, it was sleek and narrow making it a much harder target to receive hits by the enemy. It carried 76 folding fin rockets, 28 more than the Huey. It also had a mini gun mounted in the front turret that had 4,000 rounds of ammo feeding it.

The main rotor system had blades that looked like the Charlie model Huey but there was no stabilizer bar. Other things I noticed were that it had front seat and back seat flight controls and a very narrow area for the pilots to sit. Rumors started to fly around that maybe the Crew Chief could fly in the front seat but I was sure that would never happen.

Some of us were looking over the aircraft and talking when we noticed Sergeant Cole on the flight line. He overheard us talking. "Yes, the rumors from rumor central are true. This is our first Cobra. We will have all Cobras before long, but I do not know how long it will be before that happens. Boerm, you will be the lucky one to crew this Cobra. Forty-forty is in need of some major repairs. This means, The Old Gray Ghost will be leaving the battery for good.

Jerry did not seem happy at first. Then he thought about things a few seconds and changed his mind. "Sergeant Cole, I don't have the MOS to work on this aircraft."

Sergeant Cole must have figured that was coming. "Most of the systems on the Cobra are the same as the Charlie model Huey. You should not have any problems with it. Besides, I know you do not like flying on missions. There is going to be an in-country school for the aircraft. You will be going to that course and you will not be alone."

He hesitated and smiled. "I think there is only one Cobra qualified enlisted person in Charlie Battery. That enlisted man is in maintenance and he will be staying in maintenance. Get used to the idea! All of you Huey Crew Chiefs will be assigned a Cobra."

Jerry had been a Huey Crew Chief almost as long as I had. 64-14040 was in bad need of repairs. Jerry did not mind flying but never liked flying combat missions. I knew he wanted off and here was his chance.

The next question was who would get the next Cobra that was on its way to Charlie Battery? Only time would answer that question. I prayed it would not be me. Before the sun went down, the second Cobra arrived. Sergeant Cole answered the question by announcing that Specialist Padilla would be leaving the flying status. I was relieved because I lucked out. How long before I lose my job. A job I enjoyed so much!

They seemed to be picking the oldest birds first and that meant my number would be coming up soon. Not right now but in the near future. I hated the thought.

Leaving the flight line, Sergeant Cole turned and added, "Warriner, I know you want to stay flying, but one of the next Cobras will be your aircraft." My heart sank into my shoes. I had a feeling my flying days were over.

I sensed my time had come. Within hours of the first Cobra arriving, they painted the Blue Max logo on the transmission cowling. It was now official. This Cobra was now our bird and 4040 was gone from sight. It was like saying goodbye to an old friend and just knowing you would never see him again. I was thinking, how lucky those Crew Chiefs before me had been. Maybe they were not so lucky, but I felt they were. They were able to complete their tour on flight status. It was nice, collecting the extra fifty dollars a month, but having the wind in your face out-weighed any other reason to fly.

Before the week ended, one of the new Cobras flew wing to my aircraft. I was not sure why the two Cobras were not flying as a team. They were much faster than my old Bravo or Charlie model Huey. It was not for me to ask questions and it would be a chance for me to see the Cobra in action.

The next day started out quiet. Only one mission came down in the morning. With very little happening and on standby, I stayed on the ground. Then, as I was trying to eat my lunch, all hell broke loose. This bounced several sections at once.

They shipped my section in one direction and everyone else headed in another direction.

Arriving on station, the radio conversation told me we had a large number of NVA regulars in the open. With no place close by to hide, they were open targets for us. If we did not run out of ammo or the enemy shot us out of the sky, we had a good chance to end the fight fast.

My pilots made the first run at that target. Coming around for a second run, I was watching the Cobra unleash its massive firepower on the enemy. It was no wonder why they named it the Cobra. It was impressive with its venomous snakebite.

The next couple of weeks turned into a living hell. Someone decided that since the Cobra needed directing in and out of the revetment by the Crew Chiefs that every aircraft needed guidance out of the revetment. Everyone seemed to hate this idea and even the pilots complained.

Getting dust and dirt blown all over your body was not a good feeling. I felt that our take off time was much slower than what it should be. To help with the take off time, some Crew Chiefs that were not flying would put their helmets on to direct the aircraft out of the revetments while omitting the wait for the Crew Chief to climb into the aircraft. Besides, if the aircraft started to go a little sideways, the pilots could correct the problem long before the hand signals registered in their minds. Convincing the pilots to stay at a hover while the Crew Chief climbed in also saved valuable time.

I was not sure who started this maneuver first but it was not long before many of the Huey Crew Chiefs were directing the aircraft out of the revetment and climbing on the skid at a hover. The pilots seemed to like this. Once they felt the Crew Chief's weight shift the aircraft center of gravity, they would nose it over and start to take off.

Some Crew Chiefs even started to ride the skid on landing. I felt that this was not a good move. What if there was a hard landing? The Crew Chief could slip off the skid. No matter how you looked at it, there could be bad repercussions. I only did it as a way of showing we kicked A** on the mission.

Like everything else that made the job of crewing fun, all this ended when some of the higher ups got wind of it. A directive came down from the commanding officer stating that anyone caught riding on the skid would face the consequences.

Then to top it off, the Battalion found out many Crew Chiefs used loose seat belts to hang half way out of the aircraft on missions. Another directive came down channels that unless you were wearing a monkey harness, you would wear your seat belt tight. Who were they trying to kid? With a tight seat belt there was no way I could fire my M-60 in the areas needed to protect my aircraft. I was guilty of flying with a loose seat belt, pushing it to the max and not giving much thought to chances of falling out of the aircraft.

I disobeyed these rules from Battalion. I hated the monkey harness. Besides, I did not know where to get one. If I fell out, I did not want to die from the beating that I would get against the bottom of the aircraft or my pilots setting the aircraft down on top of me when they landed. Therefore, I just continued to do as I had always done. What were they going to do, send me to Vietnam?

Holland seemed to favor switching to a Cobra or going to work in maintenance. Sergeant Cole said he was not going to play musical aircraft. If two Crew Chiefs wanted to switch, he would consider letting that happen. However, only those who had flown as a Huey Crew Chief could switch.

Because we only had a few Cobra qualified pilots, it seemed like the pilots switched around a lot trying to get them qualified. One day you were flying with 1st Platoon pilots and the next you were with 2nd or 3rd Platoon. This was not a good sign. It was a sign my Huey Crew Chief days were numbered.

I was stuck flying with Captain Hardass so many times that it was not funny. He had the radio call sign of Blue Max Six Seven and was the first Platoon Leader. He had taken over the platoon from Captain Adams when he rotated back to the states. He had prior service as a Marine Sergeant before entering the army, going to OCS and flight school. This fact really showed in his actions. Hardass arrived in Charley Battery as a Lieutenant and ready for promotion to Captain. Being a regular officer, they placed him in a command spot and he soon became a section leader.

We nicknamed him Captain Hardass because it was his way or else. You have no idea what it was like flying with this hard ass.

Oh, he knew what was going on and what to do when someone was in trouble. However, flying with him, you felt like your life could end at any second. You said a prayer before going into a rocket run because he would not pull out of the run until the moment in time.

The aircraft would be going so fast that when he would pull out of a rocket run, we always received mast bumping. The main rotor hub would make contact with the mast. In an extreme case, the main rotor could separate from the mast from the constant pounding causing the aircraft to crash. This was something you never wanted to happen to anyone.

No Crew Chief wanted to fly with Captain Hardass.

Even though no Crew Chief wanted to fly with Hardass, it seemed that no one wanted to rock the boat and risk the consequences of going to the Battery Commander. Each time I flew with Hardass, it was the same thing. Pulling out of the run, the aircraft would shake and I was sure it would come apart at any moment.

If the pilot was at the controls and pulled out at a sensible time, Captain Hardass would grab the controls and start yelling at the pilot. I was trying to figure out how to solve the problem. Maybe a few pieces of hot brass spraying from my M-60 down his neck would get his attention. If I was lucky, I could get him to change his ways.

Yes! That will work. I will put my plan into action on the next mission with him. I will have to make sure my rounds will not hit our troops, but it will work.

I did not have to wait long. I had trouble holding in my thoughts as I watched Hardass doing his preflight of my aircraft. I knew there was a chance I could get into trouble but felt it was better than to die with an idiot at the controls of my aircraft. Maybe he would get the message on the first dose of medicine.

Arriving on station, it looked like I was in luck as the enemy was in an area far enough away from our troops. Sometimes getting hot brass to hit a pilot happened by accident but it was not going to be this time.

Pulling out of the dive, I opened up with my M-60 while I looked to make sure my weapon was clear of the aircraft and then rotated the side into position. Take that! Yes, the empty casings were hitting Hardass on the helmet by the dozens. I knew that some of the brass was making their mark.

The pilot was looking back at me. I just knew that he knew what I was up to but I heard nothing from either pilot. I would do it again if I had to. Maybe the hot brass would smarten him up.

Neither pilot said anything about what had happened when we returned from the mission. Did Hardass get the message or not. I did not know. When I told Ben what I had done, I found out most every Crew Chief had tried it. Then Ben told me of how he had once taken his big two-foot long screwdriver and had hit Hardass on his helmet with it.

Why had Hardass kept quiet? Was the message sinking in?

The next day as Hardass was about to climb into his seat, I was right behind him. He turned around to confront me. "You think I don't know what you were up to yesterday! If you do it again, I am going to report you to the CO".

I did not care at this point. My life was on the line as well as everyone else on board. "Sir, no disrespect intended to your rank, but if you report me to the CO, there are several Crew Chiefs ready to tell the CO about how you are flying our aircraft and risking everyone's life."

Hardass got red in the face, did not respond, turned and climbed into his seat.

For some reason, I never heard any more about the issue. Captain Hardass started to pull out of rocket runs a little quicker. The mast bumping stopped and so did some of his crappy attitude towards the pilots that flew with him.

I was not sure when or whose message finally sank in. Did one of the pilots get the point across? Maybe my message was the message that finally hit home. After all, he was always telling other pilots they did not know anything and needed to learn to fly. Whatever it was, I was sure I had a hand in making it happen.

I felt a little safer with Hardass but still preferred to fly with people like Captain Whitling, Captain Barloco or Lieutenant Comer.

I was always amazed at how pilots like Captain Whitling could listen to all the radio chatter without missing anything. Whitling never missed anything. Even if Whitling had a radio switch turned off to one of the radios, he still seemed to know everything that was happening. This baffled my mind.

Now, here I was on another mission with Captain Whitling. There was so much talk on the radios that turning off a couple of switches was the only way to know what was happening. I could hear a little bleed over from those radios that were off, but could not piece anything together.

One radio had chatter from aircraft putting in a lift of troops nearby. Whitling told his pilot to listen to the lift aircraft so we would know where they were. Whitling wanted to stay in contact with the troops on the ground, as we were there for them. Suddenly Whitling let his pilot have it, "I told you to listen to that radio. Did you hear Yellow One calling us?"

I could only guess, but figured that the pilot had been so busy listening to Captain Whitling that he had not heard Yellow One at all.

I got the message loud and clear and I am sure the pilot did too. I had never seen Captain Whitling so upset but he sure had a reason to be upset. We needed to know what was happening around us because we did not need to fly into another aircraft.

Author beside one of the first Cobras in C Battery

16

VALLEY OF THE SHADOW OF DEATH

On the morning of April 19, I was working on my aircraft doing routine maintenance when I heard the sound of a large group of helicopters coming. Looking up, I noticed two flights of lift aircraft each with two ARA escort aircraft. I thought it was strange that Charlie Battery was not in escort of the lift. All our aircraft were on the ground waiting for missions or in maintenance.

Going back to what I was doing, I heard another group coming. It seemed like every group of lift birds had an escort of ARA aircraft protecting them. I knew another battery must be in support of the missions because most of our aircraft were on the ground. I was sure they were ARA aircraft because, as far as I knew, we were the only aircraft set up with the 48 rocket tubes. As I understood it, other units tried to get this setup but could not have them because the ARA was the only unit authorized to have them.

There were so many aircraft in the air transporting troops, equipment and doing air support that it looked like a swarm of bees. When one group would be returning for more troops, another was going out loaded with troops. As I watched the timing of all these groups of aircraft, I figured there had to be at least sixty or more of the UH-1D and H models, which carry 6-8 combat troops. The H being an upgrade of the D with a bigger engine and giving it more power most likely was carrying more troops. I counted eight or more CH-47s. I could not see any sling loads under any of them so I figured they were carrying 30-35 troops.

There was a rumor that there was a BIG PUSH going into the A Shau Valley. This had to be the mission of these aircraft. I was sure the rumors were true because the aircraft were flying in the direction of the valley.

None of our aircraft were involved with this first push, but the next day all H**L broke loose. Every aircraft that could fly was busy. There was no rest for anyone. To make matters harder for the aircraft and their flight crews, fog would close the Valley every day. Timing was of the utmost. If we did not time things right, the fog could cause a possible trap for those in the valley. It was a guessing game! We had to take timing, weather and the mountaintops at the sides of the valley all into consideration.

The many years of erosion caused by Rao Loa River formed the A Shau Valley. The mountains of the Chaine Annamitique (Annamite Chain) rose abruptly to heights of over five thousand feet on both sides of the valley floor and a flat strip of bottomland covered with man-high elephant grass covered the bottom. The mountains covered by triple-canopy rain forest, the usual mist covering and the thick stands of bamboo presented many hiding places for the NVA.

Only highly secretive and equally hostile native Katu tribesmen lived in the valley and they were firmly on the side of the NVA.

The A Shau Valley was a major NVA staging area and infiltration route into Southern I Corps. Highway

548, which started in Laos and ran the length of the valley, was a major branch of the Ho Chi Minh Trail. Corduroy logs as well as steel planking, reinforced sections of the hardened-dirt road. The trees on either side of the road had their tops tied together to form an overhead canopy which concealed truck movement from over-flying aircraft.

As I understood it, the Special Forces had a CIDG (Civilian Irregular Defense Group) camp located in the valley. In the A Shau, there usually were Montagnards, Mao, or Hmong tribesmen. The NVA placed pressure on the camp from the very first day. Overrun and abandoned in 1967 as indefensible because of the especially poor flying caused by almost year-round weather made air support nearly impossible. Now, the 1st Cavalry Division was about to prove that the A Shau Valley could be taken back by the Americans.

As we flew in and out of the valley, we would have to fly over these mountains. Sitting in the door of my aircraft, I found the air very cold. If I was flying with pilots like Hardass, I knew we would fly at an altitude way over the 6,000-foot mark that others flew.

Newly promoted Captain Hardass was one of the only pilots I really hated flying my aircraft. What choice did I have? If my aircraft commander was Hardass, then that was the way it was. Having Hardass meant I usually had Warrant Officer Lackey as my right seat pilot. He was a good pilot and I would have to depend on him to keep us out of trouble.

UH-1C, 65-09436 had the Maxwell system (modification made by our Battalion weapons officer) mounted on it because the Charlie model was faster than the UH-1B models we had at the time. However, the problem with 436 was getting it off the ground. Even with only 600 lbs. of fuel, the aircraft just did not want to fly.

It was an extremely humid day. The aircraft assigned to the stand-by section was 36, under the command of Barloco. The "alarm" went off. Operations relayed the fire mission, "An enemy convoy of 100 trucks in the A Shau Valley."

This was a large number of trucks. They needed the Maxwell system. Operation called Barloco to launch his section.

Because the overcast sky and the valley mountain range were some 6000 feet above sea level, getting into the valley was not easy. The Charlie-Model was having problems getting off the ground. The Crew Chief and door gunner jumped out and actually started to push the aircraft along the runway, while Barloco kept it light on the skids. The tower thought they were insane but cleared traffic as we attempted to get the aircraft pointed into the wind. Here was a helicopter that the crew was pushing down the runway, first slowly, then faster and faster. When the aircraft picked up speed, the chief and door gunner jumped aboard. Finally achieving enough lift for transition for flight, they lifted off.

Meanwhile, the rest of the flight of three waited for them to gain some altitude. Everyone accepted clearance to climb until breaking out on top of the cloud layer. At 9500 feet, they turned to the valley, found a hole in the clouds and let down to engage. However, they simply could not find the enemy convoy despite their repeated contacts with the ground elements in the valley. They searched and searched but to no avail. It just was not to be.

Down to only enough fuel to get us back to our home at Evans, everyone finally departed without firing so much as a single shot. The problem was that 36 did not have as much fuel as the other aircraft. Climbing up to 9500 feet, following our ADF back home and letting down was not an option. Therefore, Barloco climbed to 6500, tipped the nose over and prayed that he and his crew would not run into the side of those mountains. When he was certain that we were clear of the mountains, he lowered the nose and began a rapid descent to get back as soon as possible.

When Barloco broke out of the clouds, he found himself at low level, stopped his descent and opened his side window to get a look outside the aircraft. Much to his dismay, they were actually below the foothills that rolled between the valley and our base camp. The windows had all fogged over from the cool weather and humidity at that altitude. No one was aware that the crew had accidentally descended into a slight depression and was only seconds from colliding into one of the foothills. He jerked up on the collective to gain some altitude and cleared it by only feet.

Following the ADF to base camp, Barloco contacted the tower informing them they needed to go to the refuel point. As Barloco turned into refueling and brought the aircraft to a hover, the engine died from fuel starvation. Barloco performed a hovering autorotation and set the aircraft down. The chief jumped out, opened my door – as was our protocol, and asked why he had shut down the aircraft.

Barloco simply replied, "Just pump some fuel chief".

Amazing, to think how close they came to not making it back was nothing but incredible.

Day after day, we went into the valley and most every time we stayed on the ground between missions. There was a fuel point where they tried to keep a fuel blivet or two for those of us who needed the fuel. Sometimes, we went to the rearming point and other times a crew would bring us what we needed after each mission. Waiting in the valley was an experience that I was sure I would never forget. I just knew the enemy was all around us. We always had two minutes to be in the air if they called us for a fire mission. Being in the valley put us closer to where they needed us in a short time. This saved lives and valuable time.

Every day that I went into the A Shau Valley was a day that I knew the meal would be C Rations. I learned to get to where the food was fast. As soon as they opened the case of C's, I always tried to get a choice meal and not be stuck with Ham & Lima Beans, or something else that was not any good in my book. If they shipped the C Rations to the Valley in my aircraft, you could bet your last buck that I would pull out something I wanted. I also usually carried a few C Rations in case the crew needed them. I learned to switch meals that I did not like for something I liked without anyone even knowing I made the switch.

Staying on the ground in the valley could be tough. You never knew when they would hit us with the rockets or mortars. Trying to get off the ground during incoming, always made me wonder, "Will we make it without getting hit and blown out of the air?"

View from 6000 Feet above part of the A Shau Valley.

As the second week of the A Shau Valley campaign started, I was on a fire mission with Warrant Officer Lackey and Captain Hardass. We were in support of some grunts working the east wall of the valley near the top. I heard a mayday call coming from one of the lift Huey aircraft. Looking down, I could see the aircraft in question. The main rotor blade was turning so slow I could almost count the turns it was making and I could see they were about to crash. Just before they hit the trees, the main rotor stopped turning and the aircraft exploded into flames. My heart went to my throat.

Were there any troops aboard? If so, I was sure no one had made it out alive. I did not want to ask my pilots about the crash. I was sure that I would not like to hear the answer I got so I tried to block it out of my mind. I prayed the crew had not suffered. It was all over quickly for all those involved and maybe no one became a POW.

I tried to push the incident from my mind, but the thoughts of the crew kept intruding into my mind. "If I have to die, please let it be quick." Then my mind kicked into the other mode, telling myself that you are going to make it out of this mess, just stay focused.

I was just getting the Huey crash out of my mind when I was on another mission. There I watched a CH-54 (Flying Crane) fly into the side of the mountain just after a .51 Cal hit the aircraft.

Before the A Shau Valley, I was okay and did not feel threatened. Now I was getting very uneasy. I did not feel safe flying at any altitude.

Flying at any altitude was scary. Seeing antiaircraft flak coming at us and just knowing that at any second I could be shot out of the sky really scared the crap out of me. Knowing this always kept my pucker factor working. Pucker factor was a term I had heard others speak. The explanation I heard was having your butt cheeks seemingly squeeze a piece out of the seat you are sitting on. Yes! That sure sums it up for me. Never had I been this scarred in my life. On most missions, it seemed like the crap was coming from everywhere.

On the day of the shoot down of the Flying Crane, the radio transmission from my wing aircraft was funny but scary, "Our Charlie Echo says they are firing basketballs at us." He was right. It sure did look like basketballs coming at us. No one thought it was very funny while the crap was coming at us. Afterwards, when we had landed, everyone laughed about it.

I was flying with Captain Hardass, Blue Max Six Seven when I heard, Six Eight and Six Eight Papa on the radio. "Six Eight Papa, Six Eight you have something hanging under your aircraft!"

We were not in position to see what was going on. However, I knew that Blue Max Six Eight, Captain Whitling was the platoon leader, aircraft commander and the section leader of the mission. I knew that Six Eight Papa, Captain Thornbird, was the aircraft commander in the wing aircraft. I also knew that his pilot was Warrant Officer Hartley and the Crew Chief was Specialist Stevens. I knew that neither aircraft had a door gunner aboard.

I could not see where they were. I figured they were either landing at the other end of the valley or off somewhere to the right side of my aircraft. If I could not see the other aircraft, then I could not help and even if I could see what it was, I could only let my pilots know. Besides, we were low on fuel and on our way to refuel and rearm.

After landing, refueling, and rearming we shut down to wait for the next mission. I was finally able to piece the story together, when I heard Warrant Officer Hartley telling my pilots what had happened.

Hartley was saying, "We had made a run on an enemy position. The enemy had us in their sites, were firing everything they had at us and I knew they had come close with their rounds."

"When I turned around to check on the Crew Chief, I could not see him anywhere. Maybe he switched sides. I checked the other side. When I did not see him, my thoughts were that he had fallen out of the aircraft. The call from Six Eight was all I needed for me to know. Our Crew Chief was the something that was hanging from our aircraft."

"Checking the instruments, I realized, we had taken a large caliber round in our fuel cell. We were losing fuel at an alarming rate."

"Then right after Six Eight called us on the radio, we heard a wsssssssh that sounded like air rushing over an open microphone coming over our intercom. There was nothing we could do, we were low on fuel and needed to land quickly or run out of fuel and crash."

"We came in fast to land. I was sure that we would kill the Crew Chief on landing. To my surprise when I looked back, the Crew Chief was back in his spot in the doorway. I thought that either I was seeing things or the Crew Chief had just been in a spot where I had not noticed him before. I told Thornbird to set the aircraft down, the Crew Chief is inside."

Then Specialist Stevens started to tell his side of the story. "I am glad I was wearing the monkey harness that I managed to get. I used to sit on my back plate section of the chest protector but after I got my hands on the monkey harness, I put it back. I think I felt safer with my back covered then sitting on the plate. I had climbed out on my skid as I sometimes had done before. At the time of all the crap, I was hanging out of the aircraft firing my machinegun. It was a good thing that I had the back plate in my chest protector because a round hit me in the back, knocking me out of the aircraft."

"I was hanging by the monkey harness but was able to reach my microphone button. The noise you heard over the intercom came when I tried to let you know where I was. Just before we landed, I was able to pull myself back into the aircraft."

Everyone stopped talking about what had happened and the talk switched to a rumor that we would have to spend the night in the A Shau Valley due to the weather closing in the valley. Not having left earlier may have messed up our chances of leaving.

This did not sound very good. There were too many enemy in the area and that thought did not make me happy.

I was not sure if leaving the valley or spending the night was safer but I was opting for the leaving side of the coin. That is, if I had a say in the matter. Leaving could be a disaster waiting to happen. If the weather closed in while we were coming out of the valley, we would find ourselves looking for a hole to get on top of the clouds and then looking for a hole to drop down through afterwards.

Every time we got into the soup as we were leaving the valley, my mind would go into overdrive wondering if we would clear the mountain or crash into it. Would there be another aircraft in our flight path? We were always in a flight of two and the pilots usually had a plan to split our paths and get separation so we would not collide with the other ARA aircraft. However, what about someone else leaving the valley, where would they be?

I already had one flight out of the valley in the thick soup. We lost track of our wing aircraft and was not sure if we had cleared the mountains. No one knew if anyone else was coming in or going out of the valley at that same time. The pucker factor was in full swing. Everyone aboard the aircraft was on their toes watching for anything that may have been in our flight path. We worried if we were clear of the mountains, would another aircraft be above us, or would someone be below us trying to gain altitude to get above the clouds.

I did not relax that day until we were above the clouds. I felt great once we were above the clouds, but then I had realized we had to get back down through the mess to land. There did not seem to be any way down through the thick soup, but then we found a hole and dropped down through it. We did not know where Camp Evans or any other land for that matter was because the soup had completely closed in everything.

Thankfully, Evans had just installed a new electronic way to guide us home called a GCA. No one had had much of any training on the equipment but the tower said someone had some training and soon our feet were back on the ground at Camp Evans.

Many thoughts go through one's mind when something like that happens or is about to happen.

These thoughts are never good ones and my mind was constantly in overdrive. Some aircraft from other units had already been lost due to bad weather. Luckily, none of Charlie Battery aircraft had been lost in this manner. I did not want to be one of the first.

I did not know if they had tested the GCA and or even how much training anyone had in using the equipment. Now the big question remained, would we get back to Evans in one piece without crashing and what if Evans were to be socked in?

It would be good practice for everyone to be involved in a GCA approach to Evans but I was not sure whose pucker factor was working the hardest. I was sure that my pilots were running a close second to myself on pucker factor or maybe they had surpassed me in that area. I was sure the men at the Evans tower were concerned about not having a crash on their watch. One thing for sure, the pucker factor sure would be in full swing for all involved and it would be a big relief to put feet on the ground again.

As we got close to Evans, the runway came into sight. My pilot wanted to see how good these guys were with this system and we continued the approach to the tarmac. Once we were almost to the ground, my pilots contacted the tower, thanked them and we did a go around to land at the Charlie Battery Pad.

On May 7, I was flying with Captain Hardass, when an infantry unit engaged a large enemy force. Crap was coming from everywhere. It was as if the hills of the valley had enemy in every tree line. The crap started just as we pulled out of a rocket run.

I would locate where the enemy rounds seemed to be coming from and as soon as I dumped a few rounds on the location, we would start to get it from another area. I was surprised when Hardass commented that I had done a great job. Was he feeling ill or something? I had never heard him say anything good about anyone.

Three days later on May 10, we were coming out of the Valley again and Captain Hardass as my AC when he said, "Chief, keep your eyes open and keep an eye on us. The oxygen is thin up this high. We don't want to pass out from lack of oxygen."

"Yes, Sir. I will, Sir." I did not want to tell him that I thought he was full of it and that I was more concerned over how he always flew my aircraft. Besides, I always kept an eye on my pilots to make sure they were okay. I had never heard of anyone having problems breathing. I had been at higher altitudes than this without experiencing any trouble and was sure that you had to be flying a lot higher than this if we were to need oxygen. Keeping an eye on my pilots was something I felt was my job. I did not need a pilot crashing my aircraft for any reason. It would not happen on my watch if I could help it.

Then the word came that we were pulling out of the A Shau Valley. I would never forget the many images already etched in my brain. I would never forget the Valley of the Shadow of Death.

I felt very lucky. Many ARA aircraft received so many rounds that they looked like Swiss cheese. Some were able to fly out on their own for repairs. My aircraft only took a few hits and none put me out of commission. For the most part, I was sure the ARA had been very lucky and managed to survive the Valley of the Shadow of Death.

Waiting for a mission in the A Shau Valley

Heating lunch in the A Shau Valley

MY AIRCRAFT UH-1B 64-14054
A SHAU VALLEY 1968

FUEL
BLADDER

WARRANT OFFICER
GARY LACKEY

Crew Chief view of rocket as they hit target

17

BATTLIN' BRAVO

I was at my aircraft early as I had a few things I wanted to do.

When I looked up, I noticed Lieutenant Comer coming towards me. "Chief, are you ready to go fly? I hope so. You need to get whatever gear you want to take with you. We are going to Bravo Battery for a few days with your aircraft. Hawkins and I will be your pilots. Bravo Battery is short on flyable aircraft and Charlie Battery needs to bail them out. I do not know what it is about these other two batteries but they cannot seem to keep their aircraft flyable."

Here was my chance to let Comer know how much I enjoyed flying with him. "Yes, Sir. Maybe being away from here will be a good change. At least, it will be a change of view. I am going with an Aircraft Commander I enjoy flying with."

Recently commissioned, First Lieutenant Comer came to Charlie Battery as a Warrant Officer. I had flown with him several times and felt he was a good pilot. I sure did like to fly with him because he liked to fly down close and personal.

I had heard him make comments about the other flight platoons. He was always giving the other flight platoons crap about their flying nosebleed high. Yes, maybe flying down low was taking a chance, but up there at nosebleed altitude, it was like shooting in the dark. You did not even know if you were even scaring anything in the area. I had heard there were only two places to fly that were remotely safe, down low where the enemy did not have time to draw a bead on you or up high where the rounds ran out of power. Anything in between was what they called a kill zone.

As Comer always was saying, "Flying up nosebleed high is not getting the job done."

This made a lot of sense to me. I could not see the use in flying anywhere else but down close and personal. I guess several of the other Crew Chiefs felt like I did that the M-60 was not effective at these high altitudes. Besides, you could not see what you were shooting at or where your rounds were hitting. I was sure that the rounds that did reach the ground were definitely not effective. Many times, I had been on missions where all I could do was watch my tracers as they burned out long before they hit the ground. Then I drew an imaginary line from there to the target.

Grabbing a few things from my bunk area, I returned to my aircraft, just in time to find Lieutenant Hawkins doing a preflight of my aircraft. "Sir, I hear you are flying up to Bravo Battery with us today?"

Hawkins, who was not very tall in stature compared to most of the pilots in Charlie Battery. He was a good pilot, and sported a mustache, as did many of the ARA pilots. I had taken a photo of him holding a seventeen-pound warhead rocket a few days earlier and the rocket was almost taller than he was.

Hawkins was another one of several pilots that I really enjoyed flying with on missions. His answer told it all, "Yes, I need a rest from all the flying. Maybe I will get some while we are there."

Lieutenant Hawkins

I knew he was kidding. The other battery had been flying just as much as Charlie Battery. There was talk that their maintenance crew was not as good at keeping the aircraft flyable. They would not take a part off another aircraft that was waiting for parts, not even if it meant more aircraft would be flyable. I did not know if this was true, but they needed a replacement aircraft or I would not be going there. Other comments that Charlie Battery had the best record in the Battalion for keeping flyable aircraft spread through the battery. Charlie Battery would not keep an aircraft from flying if they could borrow a part from a downed aircraft. To me, cannibalization made sense in cases where a single part could make more aircraft flyable.

I placed my gear inside my aircraft and was about to ask Hawkins if he needed anything when I heard Lieutenant Comer say, "Hawk, is the pre-flight done?"

The answer Hawkins gave, said all that Comer needed. "I am almost finished. My stuff is all set up. I will finish the preflight. Get your stuff set up."

Hawkins finished the preflight and climbed into his seat, "Okay chief, untie and let's crank."

I untied the main rotor and gave the, "Clear and untied". The familiar sound of the igniters snapping could be heard as the turbine began to spring to life and the rotor started to beat the air into submission.

After I closed both pilot doors, I took up a spot in front of the aircraft and waited for the signal. The wait was short and I almost had not gotten into place when Comer gave me the thumbs up.

I gave them the signal to pick the aircraft up to a hover, guided them out of the revetment and gave my pilots the signal to turn the tail. As soon as my side of the aircraft swung towards me, I climbed onto the skid while the aircraft was still at a hover and climbed aboard taking up my position in left side cargo door.

As I plugged in my helmet, I could hear Evans Tower. "Blue Max Six Eight Golf, winds calm, negative traffic your area, cleared for takeoff at pilots' discretion."

We pulled pitch and headed north away from our Battery area of operations for another fun filled day in the life of the ARA with no indication on when we would return.

As we flew along, I was deep in my thoughts about what the day would be like at Bravo Battery. Would I have a day like the one I had at Alpha Battery? Would it be a laid-back do-nothing-day or would I be busy? Maybe I would be put out of commission by a well-placed bullet by Charlie like had happened at Alpha Battery? I sure had hopes that would not happen.

Comer's voice interrupted my thoughts. "Jane Tower, Blue Max Six Eight Golf inbound from the south for landing at Blue Max pad".

"Roger, Blue Max Six Eight Golf, cleared for straight in approach, winds calm, negative traffic at this time."

Comer changed the radio to the Bravo Battery push (frequency), "Blue Max Four Three India, Blue Max Six Eight Golf, short final your location."

The response came back quickly, "Roger Blue Max Six Eight Golf, Four Three India, when you land Four Three wants to see you in Operations. We are sending one of our Crew Chiefs out to meet your Crew Chief".

Mike Russell

Almost before the main rotor had stopped turning, I noticed someone approaching my aircraft and before the main had stopped, I heard, "I am Mike Russell, Crew Chief of one of the Bravo Models here in Bravo Battery".

Then he said nothing for a moment. I could see a puzzled look on his face as if he was trying to get answers to his own thoughts. "Hey! Don't I know you?"

I knew I had seen him somewhere before. "Mike, I am Specialist Warriner but prefer to be called Russ. Yes, I think I have seen you before but I am not sure where."

Then Mike asked, "Russ, have you eaten yet? Maybe we can figure out where we met before over some of that mud the army calls coffee. After we go to the mess tent, I will take you to the Crew Chief tent. If you are staying overnight, you won't want to sleep in your aircraft."

As we started down the flight line, I thought that if Mike had taken a Huey course somewhere before Vietnam, it must have been Fort Rucker. I decided to ask. "Mike, where did you take the aircraft mechanic courses? You have the Huey 67November MOS, don't you?"

The answer I got gave me a feeling that Mike thought I was onto something. "I took the basic aviation and my Huey course at Rucker. Where did you train?"

I had an idea that we had met at Rucker, "That must be where we met. I also took my basic course at Rucker and then my Huey course right after that. When were you at Rucker?"

His expression changed. "I don't remember the dates but I think I finished my Huey course the end of August or something like that."

Now, I was sure. We had met at Rucker. I needed to feed him some more information. "I finished my Huey course at the end of August, but then became a hold over for a couple weeks. After going home for a leave, I finally got in Country in mid-November. Do you remember who the class leader was for either class?"

"Russ, a SP6 was in charge in the basic class but I can't remember who the class leader was in the Huey course."

Now I was positive that Mike was at Rucker with me. Was he in my class or with Padilla? I just had to know. I decided to test Mike with a few more questions. "Was the basic course class leader a pitted faced SP6 that was headed for the Mohawk course after the basic course?"

Mike interrupted, "Yes, sure was and some of us went to Panama City, FL to the beach. Some of us got sun burned pretty badly. We went down in an old grayish blue Chrysler station wagon that one of the guys had. We were not even sure we would make it in that car."

I interrupted, "Did one of the guys try to prove that farts were a gas?"

Now Mike was laughing. "Sure did. He burned the hairs on his ass. Boy did that stink. We must have been in the same basic course."

Okay, so now I know he was in the same basic class as I was. Now I needed to find out if he was in my Huey class or not. "How about the Huey course, do you remember anything that happened?"

"We lived over on Tank Hill in the old wooden barracks. The class leader marched us to classes every day, with someone calling cadence. I remember we had someone who did not like to take showers but we fixed him. We gave him a blanket party and GI shower with a floor brush and some lye soap. I think the class leader was a PVT but I think he made PFC at the end of the course."

Now, I was sure he was in my class or with Padilla. One thing for sure, he had to have gone through at the same time. "Was the building on Tank Hill right across from a building that housed a Warrant Officer Flight Class and an airfield behind their building with the helicopter used for the training?"

I could hear the excitement in his voice. "Yes, it sure was! The building had two floors. They split our group into two after our basic course and each group had a floor to themselves. I was in the group that had the bottom floor and the class leaders had their own room. As I recall, the class leader upstairs shared his room with another classmate."

"Some of us needed a haircut but money was tight. I knew the class leader who was upstairs cut his own hair, so my brother and I asked him to cut our hair. He would not do it. Then I asked to borrow the clippers to cut hair. I gave my brother and another guy such a bad haircut and I mean bad! When I returned the clippers, I begged him to fix the mess I made of my brother's hair. He did not want to but after some begging, he reluctantly fixed the haircut. I think he cut some of the other guys hair after that."

There was no question now. "I think Padilla was your class leader. I was the class leader who lived upstairs and I shared a room with Kidd. I think he was from Louisiana' but I cannot remember for sure. The guy that would not take a shower was PVT Mellon from my group. I spoke to him about taking a shower and he told me that he always took a shower every day. No one ever saw him take one and I was sure it was not true. A few days later, some of the guys gave him a GI shower. Funny, how he never missed taking a shower again. In fact, he used to make sure someone knew he was heading for the shower every time he took one after that. I was the class leader that you borrowed the clippers from."

As we walked, I spotted a Cobra on the flight line, "Hey, I see you guys got a Snake in the Battery, or does that belong to another unit?"

"That is ours or I think it is anyway. That one came in today and we expect another in tomorrow. I don't know who will get that aircraft but I sure hope it is not me."

"Well, let me tell you Mike, we got a couple Snakes in Charlie Battery. They are taking away the older aircraft first. I lucked out and did not get the first Snake. I am afraid I will be next on the list though. I hope you are ready for the BS that has started. We have to stand in front of our aircraft and guide it out of the revetment. Even the Huey Crew Chiefs get to have dust blown all over us. Any Crew Chief that does not have a helmet or eye protection is in for it. Someone up the line of command liked seeing the Snakes guided out of the revetment. Now the Huey guys got stuck doing it."

Mike looked upset. "That is some BS. I sure hope we are not stuck doing that! What a bunch of BS. By the time the pilot sees the hand signal, he has already hit the revetment. To top it off, they have to slow down to get around us standing there in the middle of where they need to go. Then they have to wait for us to get into the aircraft."

"Well Mike, you better count on it because I think it came from Battalion. I am sure it did not come from the company level."

Mike did not say another word but you could tell he was thinking.

At the end of the flight line and entering the Bravo Battery area, I spotted a sign that got my attention. It read {Welcome to ARA Hill, Home of Battlin' Bravo, THE BEST ARA BATTERY IN THE WORLD}. Now, every battery within ARA battalion wanted to be known as the best. Charlie Battery was the best. If it was not, then why did so many want to transfer to Charlie Battery? I sure thought it was the best.

I decided to yank Mikes' chain a little. "Now there is some crap. Everybody knows that Charlie Battery is the best in the Battalion. It must be the best battery. Otherwise, why do so many guys beg to switch to Charlie Battery?"

Mike laughed and changed the subject. "Hey Russ, do you remember my brother Frank? He was at Rucker with us and was in the same class as I was. He is with the Big Red One down south. I am trying to get him transferred to Bravo Battery."

I did not think the army let two family members serve in combat at the same time and questioned it. "I thought the army would not let family members serve in combat at the same time. How did you both end up in Nam at the same time?"

Mike never answered my question. We were in sight of operation so I added, "I am sure that I would know your brother if I saw him. Look, I knew that I had seen you before but did not know where. I better go to operations and see what is planned for my aircraft."

Just as I was about to go into the bunker, Comer came out of the bunker. "Chief, stay where we can find you. We are on stand-by. We are not going anywhere for a while unless the s**t hits the fan. Go get some coffee or something, but stay where we know we can find you."

I replied, "Okay, Sir. I am headed for the mess tent for a coffee. After that you can find me at the Crew Chiefs tent."

The coffee tasted like it was at least a month old. "That is some bad coffee!"

Mike laughed and suggested, "Let's head over to the Crew Chiefs tent. I need to check to see if anyone is hiding out on me. I am in charge of the Crew Chiefs now."

That was when I noticed his promotion. "How did you pass me in rank?"

"I guess it was luck. Maybe it is from being in the right spot at the right time. You made PFC out of school and I did not. When I joined the Cav, they promoted my ass to PFC and it did not take long to move me up after that. They wanted someone to be in charge of the Crew Chiefs and that is when I got made a sergeant."

Sergeant or not, he had gone through school with me and got lucky. However, was it lucky? Now he had to make sure those under him were doing their job. As we entered the Crew Chiefs tent he said, "What are you guys doing in here? Don't you have something to do?"

One of the men grabbed something off his bunk and ducked out the back of the tent muttering something about needing something. Then, Specialist Smith spoke up, "My aircraft is being sent to the 15th Transportation Corps Battalion (aviation maintenance) for repairs. I was getting a few things to take with me."

Mike already knew this. "I heard you had a problem we could not fix here. How soon are you leaving for the repairs?"

Smith answered, "I guess soon. They told me to get whatever I needed and get to my aircraft. I don't know who is flying my aircraft into Da Nang."

Almost before he had those words out of his mouth, Specialist Hill stuck his head in the doorway and seemed to be in a hurry, "I figured I would find you guys here." Then, he paused to catch his breath and directed his next statement at me. "You must be the

Charlie Battery Crew Chief. I am Phil Hill, the battery RTO. Your pilots are at the aircraft. Operations released the aircraft and you can go back home. I needed to get out of that bunker for a few minutes so I asked if I could get a coffee and come find you. Now I have to get back to Operations."

Phil Hill in Bravo Battery jeep

I thanked Hill for letting me know and headed to my aircraft, with Mike tagging along. Walking at a brisk pace, we continued to talk. It sure was a great to hash over old times that we had only a few months prior, yet it seemed like it had been years.

We said goodbye and made a promise to stay in touch. Yet, I had a feeling that I was sure I would never see him again. My stay with Bravo Battery was over almost before the dust had settled from our landing. Nevertheless, that was how things were in the ARA. You never knew where you would be next.

I untied the main rotor and gave the call, "Clear to crank".

As we flew back to Charlie Battery, I thought about my short time with Bravo Battery. It had been even shorter than my trip to Alpha Battery. This time I had not even gotten off the ground on a mission. Finding Mike was great. Now if we could stay in touch and both make it home, I was sure that we could be friends for a long time.

After all, we had made the usual promise to stay in touch. I was sure Mike had the same thoughts as I was having about never seeing each other again. At least I had his home address and he had mine. Would either of us lose track of the other's address? If not, there was a slight chance that maybe someday we would meet again. Neither one of us was sure about staying in the army. Both of us had talked about getting an early out of the service by staying in Vietnam long enough to make it happen.

My thoughts brought me back to reality, when I heard Comer calling for clearance to land. Soon I would be back to the daily grind.

Huey flying wing coming back from B Battery

Note: As usual, I did not have a door gunner on the right side of my aircraft. You can see the M-60 hanging in the doorway.

18

FLYING DAYS END

The trip to Bravo Battery had been uneventful but I had reconnected with Mike Russell. I now knew where four of my Huey school classmates were located and this gave me a good feeling. However, I was too busy flying missions to dwell on any of the days stationed at Fort Rucker.

Charley Battery had two Cobras. Word around the battery area was that more Cobras were due in any time. I tried to keep busy. I did not want to think about who would be the unlucky Crew Chief assigned the next Cobra that came in. However, I could not help but think about it every time I walked by one on the flight line. Watching it take off on a mission or coming in for a landing was a constant reminder.

There was one thing for sure; I did not want to give up my Huey ride for the daily dust bath. Nevertheless, I was sure it was coming and faster than I wanted it to. After all, Sergeant Cole had informed me that my turn to give up my Huey was going to happen. That thought did not make me a very happy camper.

Every time a Cobra came in to land, I prayed that it was not a new one. I looked for our unit markings. If it had our markings, then I was still in the clear.

Returning from the fire mission, my mind was on my aircraft. It was due for a regular scheduled 100-hour inspection. I wanted to get the inspection panels off and get this inspection over quickly. Maybe if I got the inspection over with quickly, I could get back to flying. By doing this, maybe someone else would get the next Cobra.

As we came in for the landing, I noticed two new Cobra helicopters. The number of Cobra helicopters on the flight line had increased. My mind was racing. I hurried to remove the first of the inspection panels. When I looked up, I noticed Sergeant Cole coming towards my aircraft. My heart was in my throat to the point that I was having a hard time functioning. "S**T, one of those Cobras is going to be mine."

What I feared the most had happened. I was now hearing those dreadful words, "Remove your gear from your Huey and put your personal things in your bunk area. The battery is turning your Huey in. That Cobra on short final is your new aircraft."

"Okay Sergeant Cole, but I sure would like to get back to flying, if a Huey opens up for a Crew Chief."

I would rather go to maintenance than crew that Cobra. However, I knew that if I went to maintenance, my chances were little to none that I would get a chance at any Huey that opened up. Oh, if asked, I was willing to go into maintenance. However, I was sure that it would blow my chances of a Huey ride again. Being a Crew Chief on a Cobra could possibly give me a chance to crew a Huey for a day when the Crew Chief was away. At least there was a possibility.

Sergeant Cole informed me, "Warriner, you will be heading to Vung Tau to attend the Cobra maintenance training school along with Boerm. You will be leaving tomorrow morning. Make sure you are ready to go. Now, you need to pull your gear, put it in your area and go look at your Cobra. The maintenance crew will take care of what needs to be done on this aircraft."

Walking past 520 to put my gear in the Crew Chief tent did not make me feel too good and I had a knot in the pit of my stomach. I wondered how old the aircraft was and where it had been before arriving in Vietnam.

My gear put away, it was time to go check out the Cobra I was to crew. I pulled out the logbooks and I noticed the full aircraft number was 67-15520 and it only had 149 hours on it. At least there were low flight hours on it. Maybe it would not need a lot of TLC right away.

The first time the aircraft lifted off on a mission, it gave me a sick feeling that my flying days were gone forever. Maybe when I went off to Vung Tau, I would feel better about things.

Sure enough, two days later with bags in tow, I was off to Vung Tau. This ended up being a fun time away from Charlie Battery. I thought it was a waste of time for the Army because Huey training was almost the same thing. Anyone could pick up what information they needed for the Cobra and many of the systems were the same. In fact, the Charlie Model Huey had almost the same rotor head and hydraulic systems. Anyone who could read could get what was needed out of the manuals and a little common sense sure helped.

Listening to the instructor going over things that I already knew and that anyone with any common sense could figure out by just reading the manual made no sense to me. However, that was the army and not for me to question. There were the usual manuals that came with every model of aircraft the army had and besides a little common sense goes a long way.

Each day, as I sat in a classroom, I had all I could do to keep my mind on the work at hand. My mind would wander off. Why worry about this, when there were the manuals to fall back on to answer any questions? No, I had better pay attention. There could be something to learn here. I knew there were always changes that came down to the units. These changes usually came about because they found out that something would work better another way or the environment we were working in created a reason for an adjustment. Sometimes, parts needed inspection due to the extra stress put on that part caused by combat conditions. This usually happened because some aircraft had the parts fail quicker than they thought it would or should.

The C Model had one major change. They found out the tail rotor worked better on the other side of the aircraft. This change required a new tail boom.

The two weeks of school seemed way to short. Every night, I sat back and enjoyed the area. I sure was enjoying the nearby ocean that was just outside the classroom. Our classroom was hot. This made me glad that the instructor let us out every hour for a few minutes. We were having a break from class, sitting, looking out over the ocean, when "The dock of the bay" started playing. Funny, I heard this song just as I happened to be sitting on the dock having a cold drink. It was just perfect for that moment in time.

When the two weeks were over, it was back to our unit and back to daily fire missions. Nothing had changed except that I now had to watch my aircraft leave on missions, wait for it to return, refuel it and rearm it without a chance of having cool air blowing in my face. I sure did miss flying with the wind in my face and the excitement of the hunt for Charlie.

I tried to get used to it but just could not seem to enjoy any of what I was doing. What was I going to do? I had already put in for an extension to stay in the unit because I liked flying and thought it would be better than going back to the states and put up with all the stateside inspections. Polishing shoes and having my uniforms all lined up, just the way the army wanted them to be, did not appeal to me. Now, here I was stuck getting dirt blown all over my sweat-covered body with no way to cool off. Things were not going to be easy until my time was up in this country unless something changed.

I thought I was going to hate the rest of my time in Vietnam, but then my luck changed when Sergeant Nader walked onto the flight line. "Warriner, do you still want to go back flying? Specialist Ayers is leaving and that leaves 436 without a Crew Chief. We want someone who already knows what to do. Do you want it?"

I had been watching 36 as it landed and took off and knew it had some kind of problem with losing power. "Doesn't it have a weak engine? I think it is about to have an engine failure."

Sergeant Cole had a response I thought made sense, "I adjusted the bleed band control and it is fine now."

Maybe he was right and all is okay. "Yes, I will take it." At least I would be back flying. Chances are, if the engine was bad, I could figure it out before it went south completely. Now I was the Crew Chief of a Charlie "C" model Huey. I would have preferred being a Crew Chief on a Bravo "B" model, but I was back flying in the left door of a Huey and enjoying the wind in my face.

In some ways, I liked the Charlie Model better than the Bravo "B" model that I had been the Crew Chief on before. The B model that I crewed had leaky blade grips, causing an oily mess. Dust and dirt stuck to the oil that was slug all over the aircraft. If the leak was bad and they had not scheduled the aircraft to fly, some Crew Chiefs would put a Kotex around the blade grip to keep it from dripping. When I found out the Kotex came from the PX, I thought this was strange. We seldom ever saw any women other than the Vietnamese and they could not buy anything from the PX.

The Charlie model did not have oil in the main rotor blade grips, had larger main rotor blades and a slightly larger engine. They both had a Lycoming power plant but the Bravo Model had a 960 Shaft Horse Power T-53-L-5 and the Charlie Model had a T-53-L-11with 1,100 Shaft Horse Power.

I had to learn the ways of new pilots because changing aircraft meant an assignment change into a different primary flight Platoon. I found this came easy. I had already flown a few missions with some of these pilots and had gotten to know most every pilot in Charlie Battery.

It felt good to run to my aircraft when the horn went off. I knew I would be getting off the ground, protecting my aircraft as it pulled out of a rocket run and cooling off from the breeze that came from the cargo doors.

Yes, life was okay again. Time seemed to pass faster when I was flying and I had high hopes that I would stay on the Huey until the end of my tour.

I think most every Crew Chief got some kind of goodies from home from time to time. I would get packages from my mom as well as friends. I never knew what I would get in them. Usually there was some newspaper packing around a coffee can full of cookies or whatever else was in the package to keep them from breaking.

My family baked me great cookies called Congo Squares. Each time a package arrived, I looked for the coffee can that the family packed. Each coffee can had pieces of bread mixed in with the cookies. This would help keep the cookies from drying out because the bread would dry out first.

I had just come back from my aircraft after a mission when I spotted a package on my bunk. I was eager to see what I got from home. Opening the package, I found the usual newspaper packing. I was ready to throw the newspaper away when a thought went through my mind that I could get a chance to see what had happened back in the world (states). Everyone commonly call the states, the world.

Nothing looked like it was worth reading. Then, I spotted an ad from a Ford dealership that was near my hometown. It seemed funny that some of us had been talking about buying a car when we got to the world (states). I guess you could say I was a Ford man because that is what I liked the best. I thought I could at least check it out.

I decided to write to the dealer and asked for some information. Some of the Crew Chiefs thought I was crazy. Most of them figured I would never even hear back from anyone at the dealership. Maybe they were right. What did I have to lose except a few minutes of my time? Jerry Boerm thought it was a great idea and thought he would write home and ask about the new Fords. Jerry was a Ford man also and wanted a new full size Ford.

I started my letter by telling them who I was and where my family lived. I also informed them that I was an enlisted man serving my country in Vietnam as a door gunner and Crew Chief on a Huey gunship. Then I went on to inform them that I was not sure just what I wanted for a car. However, I thought I wanted something sporty, plenty of power, four-speed standard transmission and maybe a convertible. The color had to be something that stood out in a crowd and was sharp looking.

As I dropped the letter into the outgoing mail, I had a feeling that I would never hear back from anyone much less find what I wanted. I figured it was best not to tell anyone back home and sure did not want to tell my mom and dad about the letter. If I never heard from the dealer then my parents would not know anything about it. If I did hear from the dealer, maybe I could line up a new car and buy one when I came back home. That is, if I made it home.

To my surprise two weeks later, a letter caught me off guard. It came with a return address of Sweeney Ford in Lopez, MA and above the return address, I found the words, Warren Thomas, new car sales.

I opened the letter and read. "Dear Specialist Warriner. My name is Warren Thomas. I am in new car sales at Sweeney Ford. My boss gave me your letter to answer. The enclosed envelope contains some information about some of the new automobiles. I know you asked about something with a BIG ENGINE. We can get one for you but I think you will be happier with a car like the one in the enclosed photo. Your insurance will be very high for a car like you are interested in."

As I opened the envelope that was enclosed, there was a gold 1968 Ford Torino GT photo with my mom and dad standing next to it. The photo was at my parents' home, which was a good twenty plus miles from the dealership. In the background was the garden that I had spent many hours helping to take care of. I was trying to figure out how Warren had located my parents. Then I remembered that I had told the dealership that I was from Williamsburg.

To my surprise, there was a note attached that read:

Son, Your Dad and I hope that you like this car because we are going to purchase it. When you come home, all you will have to do is take over the payments. If this is not what you want for a car then we will keep it ourselves. I like driving it and will use it for work until you get home. Love, Mom.

After showing the information to Jerry Boerm, he decided he would write a letter home and try to line up a car for himself.

I was surprised how that coffee can full of cookies wrapped with newspaper and shipped to Vietnam could have had such an impact on so many people.

Author by Torino after Vietnam

19

MAYDAY-MAYDAY-MAYDAY

I had been crewing 436 for only two weeks. The missions were scattered, which kept me from getting off the ground very much. The switch from being a Crew Chief on a Cobra to a Charlie model Huey had caused another switch. I would be in the third platoon, but that was okay with me because I knew many of the pilots in the Battery already. Even though I had not flown with them all, I had flown with many of them at one time or another.

Every morning, each aircraft had a new set of pilots assigned to fly it. Every morning, I watched to see who my pilots would be for the day. Every aircraft that was flyable had flight gear in it, and I enjoyed watching the pilots switching their gear to another aircraft or getting their gear out and taking it back to their tent. Every flyable aircraft was ready to go at all times.

As usual, I was on the flight line early checking my aircraft over and noticed that my right seat pilot was Warrant Officer Littlefield. I was glad to see this because I was sure my aircraft commander would be Warrant Officer Bill Summerfield. Summerfield used the radio call sign of Blue Max Six Nine Romeo One.

I enjoyed flying with Summerfield. I felt that he was an excellent pilot because I had flown with him several times before. Usually his co-pilot was Warrant Officer Littlefield. Summerfield sported a mustache like many of our pilots. Summerfield never seemed to be afraid of anything. I felt he knew the limits of every aircraft he flew and was able to push these limits if need be.

Mr. Littlefield and I were doing the preflight of the aircraft together. We had just finished the preflight when Summerfield showed up with his gear. "Chief, we are in the Hot Section right now because the hot section is on a mission. I hope you are ready to take off. Is the preflight finished?"

"Yes, Sir. We are just finishing up."

I had climbed down and Littlefield was just starting to climb down. Almost before I had the words out of my mouth, the horn went off. As I ran to untie the main rotor, I could see my wing aircraft crew coming on the run. I wanted to let my pilots know I had untied the main rotor and we were all set. "Clear and untied!"

Usually whoever was the first pilot to the aircraft would start to crank the bird. If the aircraft commander had started to crank, then the pilot would take over and finish cranking. This gave the aircraft commander a chance to get on the radio and get the mission. Summerfield was already in his seat and ready, "Coming through" as he hit the starter button.

As the turbine began to whine, I could hear the distinctive sound of the igniters snapping and the main rotor began to turn ever so slowly. Then, with a puff of smoke, the turbine sprang to life.

When Summerfield gave me the signal that they were ready, I directed the aircraft out of the revetment and gave the pilots the signal to turn the tail. I could see that Summerfield was at the controls, so I knew that after turning the tail he would hold the aircraft at a hover while I climbed aboard. As soon as

Summerfield knew I was aboard, he nosed the aircraft over and headed southwest towards some low mountainous terrain. I took up my spot in the left cargo door, buckled my seat belt loosely, grabbed the M-60 and loaded it with a 200 round belt of ammo.

As we slowly climbed up to an altitude high enough so we could get over the mountaintop, Summerfield spoke over the intercom, "Chief, we will be shooting for troops on the other side of this mountain. They are somewhere in the valley just beyond this mountain. Keep an eye out for the smoke. With that, he radioed the troops and asked for them to pop smoke."

Summerfield spotted the smoke just as I was about to key my intercom, so I just waited for his instructions. The foliage was so heavy that it was hard to figure out the exact location of the troops and completely impossible to even see the troops.

Warrant Officer Summerfield was a good AC and always seemed to find a reference point to help guide him. I was sure he had already marked a spot in his mind but was not surprised when Summerfield requested them to pop a second smoke.

Summerfield marked a spot in his mind and we rolled in with a marking pair of rockets. Swoosh! Boom! Then I heard the call on the radio, "Cease fire!"

Many times my pilots had fired only a pair of rockets on the first run and waited for confirmation that we were on target. However, this was the first time I had heard anyone call cease-fire as we rolled in. As we went into an orbit around the area, I was thinking about what had just happened. Must be the smoke was spread out so much from the heavy foliage that we were firing too close to the troops.

Moments later, the radio broke silence again. "Blue Max Six Niner Romeo, this is Delta Four Three. We have wounded from your rockets. I have the enemy position spotted and will direct your fire."

"Roger Delta Four Three, Blue Max Six Niner Romeo, pop smoke over."

"Blue Max Six Niner Romeo, Delta Four Three, roger smoke out."

"Delta Four Three, we have yellow smoke."

"Roger, from our smoke the target is 20 meters due north."

Summerfield set up to make his run. We rolled in with a marking pair of rockets. Swoosh! Boom! Again, the radio silence was broken. "Cease fire!"

I thought to myself, this was not a good sign. We must have wounded more troops. For a few moments, which seemed like minutes, the radio was silent. As we circled above the troops, my mind raced with thoughts of whether we had killed the radio operator and wondered how they were going to get the wounded troops out through the trees.

After what seemed to be forever in my mind, I heard, "Blue Max Six Niner Romeo, this is Delta Four Three. Can you stay on station and act as MEDEVAC for our wounded? The MEDEVAC aircraft is busy and cannot come for the wounded for some time. We need to get the wounded out of here as soon as we can."

Now we knew the truth of what had happened. We had two friendly units working an area and they were fighting each other. The heavy foliage in the area caused two elements to lose track of each other and each thought the other was the enemy.

We were in an orbit above the area and I was thinking about what had just happened. We needed to stay on station until MEDEVAC could get on station. If the MEDEVAC did not arrive to pick up the wounded, then we had to act as the MEDEVAC aircraft. We did not have any equipment to pull the wounded out and there was no place to land anywhere near the wounded.

Word from the troops interrupted my thoughts. We were staying on station while they cleared an area so we could pick up the wounded. Summerfield was on the radio with the troops.

As we continued to circle above the area, I could see the grunts working to clear an LZ large enough to get a helicopter in close enough to pick up the wounded. The trees fell as the troops used explosives to clear a landing zone. I could see the area starting to open up. After several minutes, which seemed hours, I could to see the grunts continuing to clear the area.

Now my mind was into overdrive because I knew there would be stumps to contend with when we came in to pick up the wounded. This was going to be a tough spot to land. Maybe we would have to hover to pick up the wounded. All this made me nervous. The idea of how we could get these guys aboard weighed heavy on my mind.

My mind was racing with all these thoughts and a good 45 minutes to an hour had passed. I knew we would be cutting it close on fuel and the longer we stayed on station the tighter things would get.

I kept telling myself, "When the time comes, I will deal with it somehow. We may have to hover as low as possible while the wounded are loaded."

The radio interrupted my thoughts. "Blue Max Six Niner Romeo, this is Delta Four Three. Dust Off One Seven is in bound. You are free to go get fuel and rearm. Thanks for sticking around to help."

I never had pulled wounded out of an area before and I was glad that I was not a MEDEVAC Crew Chief. The only time I had been on one of their birds was when I returned to Tam Ky after the flare incident. They had landed to pick up wounded and it had not given me a good feeling, even though the wounded they picked up that day were not badly hurt. I did not even want to think about how badly these guys were injured from our rounds and tried to stop thinking about it.

Leaving station and getting out of the valley was a good feeling, until we were about to clear the mountaintop. That is when I heard that dreadful sound no Crew Chief wants to hear. This time it was coming from inside my aircraft, "Mayday-Mayday-Mayday, Blue Max Six Nine Romeo One, engine failure".

Summerfield was on the radio and both of my pilots were working hard to keep control of the aircraft. They were trying to maintain an altitude that would put us over the top of the mountain and trying to keep the main rotor speed up enough with the engine out. The pilot was watching the gauges and talking to my AC while both were trying to find a spot to land. We were too close to the mountain to change direction and all there was on this side of the mountain was trees. We needed to make it over the top and into the flat area on the other side or we might not survive.

Just as we were about to cross the top of mountain, I looked down to see the skids clearing the rocky ledge of the mountain. That was close. I was positive that I could not have even placed a small box between the skid and the ledge. Then I felt the aircraft drop as Summerfield bottomed pitch and went into full auto-rotation. He was trying to speed up the main rotor that was starting to slow down causing the low RPM warning to scream through the head set. We needed to build the rotor speed up again or crash. Summerfield picked a spot and headed for it. Trying to land without hitting the trees was not easy. There were no rice paddies or open areas to land. The best we could hope for was to walk away.

As we touched down, the main rotor wash cut a path through the trees and bushes, brushing them as we landed. When we finally stopped, the main rotor blades were still touching the bushes, but there was no major damage and no one was hurt.

That was some good flying by Summerfield. There was no time to say anything because I had no idea where the enemy was.

I grabbed one M-60 and as much ammo as I could carry. Littlefield grabbed the other M-60 and more ammo. We took up a spot on top of our aircraft, where I thought I could have a good view of the area. After sitting there a few moments, a thought went through my mind that we were sitting ducks. If the enemy was in the area, we had better find a safer spot.

Our wing aircraft was flying overhead, but I knew they were low on fuel. Within moments of landing, a Cav Hunter-Killer team, working in the area, was on site. This made me feel much better but still not fully at ease.

I was very pleased to see two more of our aircraft circling overhead within moments of our aircraft touching down. I knew the recovery team was on their way to retrieve my aircraft along with the crew.

When the recovery team arrived, I climbed aboard the aircraft and soon was back in the Charlie Battery area.

They told me that they would sling load my aircraft to 15th Transportation Corps Battalion (aviation maintenance) for repairs. This maintenance unit had just moved to Evans and we could see their area from ours.

When the inspection of the turbine engine was finished, they discovered the engine had let go internally. No adjustment would have prevented the engine failure. The inside damage was not evident until the engine was pulled apart. Therefore, no one was to blame for not finding it before.

Because they thought there were more repairs to my aircraft then 15th Transportation Corps Bn (aviation maintenance) could fix, it was going to get shipped somewhere else for major repair work.

I removed all my gear from the aircraft. I loaded my equipment in a jeep and moved it back to the Charlie Battery. Then, I returned to work on the aircraft until they shipped it out for the other repairs.

Once my aircraft was ready for shipment, I watched as the crew slung it out over our battery area. Then I headed for Charlie battery area. Much to my surprise, they gave me a Bravo model that had come in to replace the Charlie model. I did not get a Cobra. Yea!

My new Bravo model Huey was not new. It was older than the one I had crewed before. It had come from Fort Belvoir in the states. The aircraft seemed to be in good shape but had an HF radio and an antenna that was mounted on the outside of the tail boom.

Now I was on an aircraft that had something that no other aircraft had. However, I was not sure what good this extra antenna would be in Vietnam. I had never seen one of these antennas before. I was not even sure what it was until I flew mortar patrol that first night after starting to crew the aircraft.

They warned me not to let the pilots use the radio while on the ground because of the high output of the radio. Everyone had to be careful walking close to the tail boom because there were brackets for the wire to be mounted. There were four brackets on each side of the tail boom and they stuck out like little arms.

UH-1 62-02048 with HF antenna on tail boom

The first night on mortar patrol was very interesting to say the least as my pilots would call the states and other places with the HF Radio.

20

R & R TO MANILA

Just after moving north, I put in for an R&R. I wanted to go to Hawaii, but only married GIs received these R&Rs. None of the other places sounded enjoyable. The best choice for me was to go to the Philippines. I knew that April was not going to work because I would not have enough time in country until maybe early May.

I wanted and needed to get away as soon as possible. Maybe I'll have a chance to go in May. Yes, it should work. I will be just over the six-month mark in country. Yet, they still could turn me down.

As May arrived, so did word of my R&R approval. I still did not know just when I would be leaving for my much needed rest and relaxation. I started packing my bags almost before the words had finished coming out of the platoon sergeant's mouth. Who cared? I was going on R&R soon.

I felt like a kid in a penny candy store trying to figure out which candy was the best to buy for the five cents that was burning a hole in my pocket.

On the fifth of May, just after returning from a fire mission, I refueled and was busy rearming my aircraft when I heard, "Warriner, go get what you want for your R&R, and catch a ride with the mail truck that is leaving in a half hour." Sergeant Cole paused then added, "Don't worry about finishing your rearming. I will finish and get someone to cover your aircraft."

They did not have to tell me twice. I was on cloud 9 and almost at the Evans Airstrip before Sergeant Cole had finished.

Waiting for my flight out of Evans, I watched with anticipation and wondered whether it would be a C-130, C-123 or ride a Chinook. Man, I did not care. Whatever! Just get me out before the sun goes down. Watching several aircraft come in, land, and take off again, my eagerness to get out of Dodge was eating at me. The wait was taking forever in my mind.

As I stood on the runway awaiting my flight, I noticed I was standing next to body bags. An uneasy feeling came over me. My mind went into overdrive. I do not want to go home that way. What a terrible feeling for their families. I hope my flight is soon.

I could not imagine my parents hearing, "I am sorry to inform you that your son was killed in action while serving in Vietnam."

Even though I was leaving this war torn land for R&R, I would be back and could leave that way the next time. Yes, it sure was going to be nice just getting away from the rat race of combat for a day or so.

A mongoose that a soldier had as a pet interrupted my thoughts as I focused on the animal. It was the first mongoose I had ever seen. What a strange animal.

The GI noticed I was watching the mongoose. "He is my pet and having him gives me something to think about besides combat. He helps the time go by a little faster and before long, I will be back in Maine."

I was shocked! I had found someone from New England. "Maine, I am from Massachusetts!"

Talking about how we missed seeing snow and the changes in the seasons in New England had taken my mind away from the body bags, for at least the moment anyway.

The conversation abruptly ended. "Some of you who are headed south to An Khe will be boarding the C-130 on short final. Wait for us to unload and the load master to tell you to board."

With anticipation, I said goodbye to my new friend, grabbed my bags and was ready to head for the ramp.

Yes, I am aboard! Now find a seat. Right side has seats. Better grab one quickly or I may end up off the aircraft. Do not want to wait again. Then I relaxed when I realized the loadmaster had been counting people and he already knew how many he could get on the aircraft.

What is the hold up? Everyone is aboard and in a seat. The body bags; they are loading the body bags! A strange feeling went over me as I realized the body bags were going south with me. I tried hard to think about my R&R and tried to take my mind the bags that were now only a few feet away from my feet.

Before I entered the service, I had never left New England. I had never thought of being anywhere else. My travel after entering army life was limited at best. Thinking I need to get my mind off that cargo, I talked to my inner self. What is the name of my new friend? Man, I cannot remember his name. I must be losing it.

Try to think of something else. Then it will come back to me.

The flight to An Khe was uneventful other then the noise the aircraft was making. An Khe had not changed much from when I had last been there. Now my mind had new thoughts. What do I do now? Where do I go from here? Boy this sure is not Cav Country anymore. Where will I have to stay tonight?

Suddenly a voice interrupted my thoughts. "I am Specialist Scott. You look lost. Can I help point you in the right direction? I am from the 173rd Airborne Brigade and you will need a place to sleep tonight because there are no more flights out today. Come on back to our area. We will find you a place to lay your head for the night and someone will bring you back to the airfield in the morning."

I cannot believe my eyes. Am I still in Vietnam? Here is a man standing there with spit shined boots and clean, starched, and pressed jungle fatigues. I took a quick look around. Yes, I am still in Vietnam. I know that this is the An Khe Mountain. Where is the 1st Cavalry patch?

Being back at An Khe, our old 1st Cavalry Divisions area, now belonging to the 173rd Airborne Brigade gave me an uncomfortable feeling. I had a feeling deep down inside I could not put my finger on. Was it that these guys did not like those of us in the 1st Cavalry Division? If that was the reason then why should they? From what I could see, they were like a state side unit with clean pressed uniforms and spit shined boots. What was the matter with these people? Did they not know they were in Vietnam? Boy, this sure is not Cav country any more.

Back in their unit area, I was getting out of the jeep. Their commanding officer met me and my feet had no more then hit the ground when he spoke, "Welcome to the 173rd Airborne Division. This is Sergeant Jones, one of our platoon sergeants."

"Sergeant Jones, will you see to it that this 1st Cavalry troop has a place to sleep tonight? In the morning, he will need a ride to the airfield."

Almost before he had finished, he was gone. It all happened so fast that I did not even catch the commander's name.

Sergeant Jones seemed more receptive to me. "Warriner, let's see if I can find you a bunk for the night."

Entering a tent used as enlisted men's quarters, Jones spotted Specialist Smith. "Warriner, this is Specialist Smith." He paused then said, "Smith, show this 1st Cavalry soldier where Johnson's area is. Show him where the mess tent is and see if you can find him some chow."

The 173rd Airborne Brigade chow sure was not the same as what my unit chow but at least it was filling.

After chow, I sat in the bunk and tried to write a letter home but just could not seem to keep my mind on what I was writing. I put my writing tablet away and lay my head down.

I was very uneasy sleeping in another man's bunk. Where was this man? Guard duty, patrol, wounded, or on his way home in an OD bag like those I came south with? I did not want to know. Restless, awake more than I was asleep and glad when morning came. I had missed chow, which was okay, as I wanted out of the area as soon as I could.

Back at the airfield, I awaited a flight out. Soon I was on another C-130 and listening to the rumble of the engines with thoughts of Cam Ranh Bay. Had it changed any?

When we touched down at Cam Ranh Bay, my thoughts were on what it was going to like being back in the area. How long will I be here, a few hours, a day or several days? It was not long before I heard part of the answer to my question. "You need to get bedding and find a bed. You are staying overnight."

Sleeping here reminded me of when I first arrived in this war-ravished land called Vietnam. It was easy to tell the new guys from the old guys. The new guys had a scared look and the old guys heading home had a hardened look anyone could spot a mile away.

Two days went by. Then, I finally was able to board the plane for the Philippines. Finding a seat and knowing it would take a while to get there, I introduced myself to the guy sitting next to me. "I am Specialist Russ Warriner from the 1st Cav. What is your name?"

Holding his hand out, "Sergeant Smith, 1st Infantry Division but please call me John. Where are you from back in the world? I am from Nebraska."

Sergeant E-5 Stripe

"I am from Williamsburg, a small town in Western Massachusetts. I cannot wait to get back there for good."

Freedom Bird

John noticed I had crew wings. "Do you fly? I have been on many helicopters but only as a ground pounder and often thought I would like to be a door gunner."

"Yes, I am a Crew Chief and door gunner in the Aerial Rocket Artillery."

John was not in aviation but wanted to know more about what it was like flying. Then we switched the topic away from Vietnam. This made me feel better as I did not want to think about Vietnam for a few days.

As soon as the wheels of the plane touched down, an announcement came over the intercom, "Remain seated until someone comes aboard to talk to you. You will be briefed on what you can do and what not to do on your R&R. Listen to the representative as this is for your safety."

When the cargo door opened, an Air Force guy with two stripes on his arm entered the plane. Again, we heard what and what not to do while in the Philippines, but he kept stressing on what not to do.

One suggestion was to pick a buddy, stay at the same hotel and travel around the city of Manila with him.

John and I looked at each other. Sure, why not stay at the same hotel and check things out together? After all, we did not know anyone else on the plane.

Mister Air Force continued, "After you enter the terminal, you will be briefed again. I suggest you listen to the words and let them sink in. Maybe you will stay out of trouble by following the instructions."

Getting off the plane, I asked John, "Why are we being told all this over and over again? Let us just get on with our R&R and stop burning it up."

With the talks finally over, they released us.

Exiting the terminal, we found several cars lined up near the building. They were like vultures waiting to strike their prey. "John, which one do we grab? It doesn't matter to me."

John pointed to a 62 Chevy. "Let's take that 62 Chevy. It looks like a good one."

All the other cab drivers were trying to get us to use them. As we walked by, John and I told them "No" even though the one we picked was in the middle of the pack.

Entering the cab, I said, "Boy, John, it sure is strange to see an American automobile in the Philippines. This driver sure must be proud of his car to keep it this clean and shiny. Look at those chrome hubcaps. Just look at these seat covers."

The driver took our bags and placed them in the trunk. "Get in. We go."

Our driver spoke broken English. As he got in the car, he spoke, "I Mr. Samuel. You call me Sam. We need go. You no take front car. Make them mad."

Sam was still talking as we had pulled away from the terminal. "I take you to hotel now. What hotel name? You need time clean up? You want food or something? You want girl? Sam find you good girl."

John answered before I could speak, "I want to get cleaned up, go get some good food and then find a bar for some drinks."

Sam agreed, "You smart GI. GI drink, no eat. They sick."

John laughed. "Okay Sam. You are a good guy and I like you. We will clean up and then you can find us some good food. Then find a bar."

A relaxed feeling went over me about our choice of cabs. Sam seemed to be well educated about the area and polite. His English was a little rough but he still seemed like an okay guy.

Sam knew the hotel and told us it was a good choice. Some of the other hotels were not as good.

We were at the hotel almost before we knew it.

"This your hotel. I get your bags out car. I no come hotel. They take good care you. I be back two hours or you want sooner?"

John and I agreed that that was fine. Sam said something to the attendant, got in his car and was gone.

My room was 419. I needed to take the elevator to the fourth floor. As I exited the elevator, I needed to take the left hallway to the end, turn right and my room would be the second door on the left.

John was already waiting by the elevator. "Russ, I am in room is 415. What is your room number?"

"That's good. I have room 419. At least we are both on the same floor."

Exiting the elevator, I noticed our rooms were in opposite directions and commented, "It looks like your room is down the hallway in that direction and my room is just around the corner someplace. It looks like we have time to take a nice hot shower and rest a few moments. I will see you in a while."

I headed for the shower almost as soon as I entered the room. The nice hot water of the shower felt so good I did not want to get out. Reluctantly, I finally stepped out and dried off.

I was sure I had been in the shower a long time. Then looking at the time, I realized it had only been a few minutes. Was I that used to taking a fast shower?

After getting dressed, I told myself that I had plenty of time to rest.

Laying there with my eyes shut, I found myself in a restless mode, checking the clock next to the bed repeatedly.

Unable to sleep, I got up and went down stairs to wait for John. To my surprise, John was already in the lobby. "I see you couldn't rest either."

"No. Still in combat mode, I guess. I am going to the barbershop and see if I have time to get a cut."

John agreed, "Good idea. We never get much time to get a haircut in Vietnam. Besides I don't trust the Vietnamese barbers."

I laughed, "I know what you mean."

We were getting our hair cut at the same time. I was telling John about my first day getting an Army haircut. Just as I got to the part about Mr. I-don't-want-my-hair-cut, I heard, "You want shave?"

Thinking for a few moments, I finally answered, "Sure. Why not."

I was nervous. I never had a shave by anyone and here I was letting someone who did not speak much English give me a shave. Things were going smooth. I began to relax, and then I felt the razor on my left ear. "What the H*** do you think you're doing?"

"You hair ears. I shave."

Reluctantly, I told him to finish but let him know I wasn't a happy GI.

I could not wait to get out of the barbershop. I paid without leaving a tip.

Outside, John finally spoke," Man you were pissed and I would have been too. You need a drink and I sure could use one. Let's see if Sam is here yet."

Sam spotted us just as we exited the hotel.

"Where you want go?"

John answered before I had a chance to say a word, "Find us some good American food. I want a good American Steak. Then, find us a good bar. I want a drink."

Sam knew the area well, "I take you where get American steak. Then go club. You no same other GI. They drink, they eat. They sick."

John agreed, "Okay, take us to where we can get some American steak. I haven't had one of those in months."

I was not about to tell John that our unit had a cook who seemed to know how to get steaks. Nor would I tell him that I had a steak just before I left the unit.

After Sam spoke to the waitress at the first place where we stopped, he remarked, "You no eat here. Sam find better place."

I asked, "Sam, why did you tell us not to eat at that place?"

Sam did not hesitate, "No like American GI. Give bad food. You be sick. Trust Sam, I take care you. You pay Sam. I stay with you."

After finding another place to eat and having a great meal, we were off to a local club. Sam came into the club and joined us, to my surprise. "Sam stay. Keep you out trouble."

Because I had turned 21 in Vietnam, I had never been in a place like this. I noticed several girls lined up at one side of the room. Sam noticed that we both looked at the girls. "Nice girl. You want girl?" Sam waited a moment, "Which you like?" and motioned to the girls.

John picked out a girl to sit with us, but I did not feel right with Gloria waiting at home for me. My mind was in a spin. Gloria will never know. She has a new boyfriend anyway. Is she waiting for me? I am only going to sit with a girl, not sleep with her. These are not round eyes. I am sitting alone while John has company. Pick one out stupid! It will be okay.

Something was not right back home. The letters from Gloria were few and far between, coming in groups and were not the same as her first letters. Yes, something was wrong. After a few drinks, the idea of having a girl sitting with me began to look better and better.

Finally, reluctantly, I gave in and picked out a girl to sit with me. I tried to justify what I was doing. She is only sitting with me. This is not so bad. She is a nice girl. I am only talking with her. I had no idea this meant I had committed to having her back to my room for the night.

Sam convinced me that picking a girl was a smart move. She would stay with me as long as I was in Manila and keep me out of trouble. She would act as guide and would be good company.

When we returned to the hotel with the girls in tow, I was a little under the weather. My mind was cloudy with thoughts of being faithful, combat, and wishing I was home with family.

The next morning, the girls went back to their homes. When Sam came back, the girls were with him. John and I wanted to see the American Cemetery and Memorial in Manila. It was a spectacular sight and I had never been to a place like it in my life. Looking at all the grave markers lined up in a row and seeing the hemicycle at Fort William McKinley was just breath taking.

American Cemetery and Memorial in Manila

Walking around the hemicycle area, I read the names inscribed of all those laid to rest. It was hard to believe so many Americans had lost their lives and laid to rest in this sacred place that was so far from home. Outside there were rows and rows of crosses, all in perfect alignment. They were so straight, that it was truly amazing.

Sam asked where we wanted to go to next and John responded, "Can we go to the Base exchange? They must have a place to get some booze."

I was not sure what to get. Turning twenty-one after arriving in Vietnam, I had partaken of only a few drinks with friends and that was only to prove I could get away with it before I was twenty-one. Sam asked us to pick him up a small bottle of Beefeater Gin. Because I was not sure what to get, I picked up the small bottle of Beefeater Gin for Sam and I settled on a BIG bottle of Beefeater Gin for myself.

Sam said that the local pub liked it when you brought your own bottle in as long as you bought the mix from them and left whatever was left of your bottle with them. This sounded okay to me. What had happened the night before was really eating at me. Why had I taken a girl back to my room? I just wanted to wash away all the guilt of the night before.

Just before arriving at the pub that night, I told Sam, "No girl for me tonight."

No matter what Sam or anyone else said, I was going back to the hotel alone. Almost as soon as we arrived, I commenced drinking the bottle of Beefeater Gin. My conscience was weighing heavy on my mind. I still was not sure what was going on with Gloria, but I felt so wrong about what I had done last night.

I am not sure how long we were at the pub. ALL the girls were mad at me. They asked if I wanted a different girl. Wanted to know what was wrong with the girl I had picked out before.

All these questions and hounding just made me drink more in an attempt to drown my guilty feelings. Before the night had ended, I had polished off my large bottle of Beefeater Gin, was drinking some of what John had bought and was working on Sam's pint.

By the time Sam drove us back to the hotel that night, I was totally hammered and did not know what time it was; where we were and I did not care. I was telling everyone I was fine. Right! I was seeing double, triple, stumbling over my own words and who knows what else I was doing.

My head out the window as we arrived at the hotel, I said, "This is our hotel right there. See, I am not too drunk." I took a deep breath and headed for the elevator, trying to hide how drunk I was but knowing everyone had his or her eyes on me.

As the elevator headed for our floor, John asked, "Are you okay?"

I replied, "Sure, I am fine." Who was I kidding? I was plastered.

John tried to help me to my room but I would not hear of it. "I am okay. I will make it okay on my own."

Taking a deep breath, I headed down the hall towards my room stopping every few feet to take another deep breath.

I looked back just before I turned the corner. There was John, who looked like two of him, still watching. "Are you okay?"

Turning the corner, I found my room. I told myself. You're okay. Only a few steps to go. Just get the door open.

I tried to open my door but was unable. My mind started to race. Maybe I have the wrong room. No, this is it. You are drunk, stupid. I hope there isn't anyone watching me. Then I heard the voice of the chambermaid who was working late. "Here, let me open it for you."

As soon as she opened the door, I entered, sat down on the bed and thought I would feel better if I lay down. That is when it happened. The room started to spin. Okay, putting my foot on the floor will help to stop the spinning. When that did not work, I put both feet on the floor.

The chambermaid knew what was coming and grabbed the trash can. "Here, in case you sick." However, before the trashcan was near me, up it came.

It was bad enough that I felt like I wanted to die but now I had made such a fool of myself.

I guess the chambermaid had been through this before. "You shower. You feel better. I clean up."

To my surprise, the chambermaid helped me into the bathroom, undress and helped me into the shower.

As she picked up my soiled things, she said, "I fix bed now. I wash these. I bring back. I check you."

When I did get out of the shower, the chambermaid had changed the bedding. My things were all laid out for me and she was gone.

John met me in the lobby the next morning. "Do you want me to go get some more Beefeater? Man, you were plastered."

Just the thought of booze made my stomach churn. "I think this will be a no booze night for me. In fact, I think I will spend the morning trying to recuperate from the ordeal. I don't think anything will stay down right now."

John agreed. "Okay, go lay down and I will check on you later. Maybe you will be ready to attempt to eat by then."

Heading back to my room was an effort. I felt so bad I just wanted to die and get it over. To my surprise there were all my clothes from the night before, cleaned and pressed, lying on my bed. Without even moving them, I crashed on the bed and awoke at 14:00 hours (2 p.m.) to a knock at the door.

It was John. "Are you ready to eat yet? Come on. Some food will help you feel better. I am buying. Sam is picking us up shortly."

Reluctantly, I said okay and we headed out.

When Sam arrived, I was surprised to see both the girls from the first night already in the cab. John and Sam had set it up while I was resting.

We went out to eat. John thought it was better than getting drunk again or sitting there doing nothing. He wanted me to enjoy my last night in Manila.

After the meal that I was not sure was going to stay down, we headed to the pub. Drinking only coke and returning to the hotel alone was my plan, but the girl I was with insisted, "You no pay. I want take care you."

I told myself, she feels so bad about things. I already was with her. She thinks it is her fault. She feels guilty that I got so drunk. So, what is the harm?

So when the night ended, she returned to my room.

When morning came, we all went for breakfast and said goodbye to the girls. Then it was back to the room to get our stuff and check out. I left the chambermaid a BIG tip. After all, I did not think it was her job to do much of what she had done for me.

Boarding the plane, I knew we would soon be back in Vietnam.

Landing at Cam Ranh Bay, we spent the night and left the next morning for our units. John and I made promises to stay in touch but knowing deep inside this would never happen. Somehow, I lost his name and address even before I got back to Charlie Battery.

21

ATTACK ON CAMP EVANS

I felt my R&R had been far too short. Canceling thoughts of Vietnam had been impossible. The flight back to South Vietnam brought all the thoughts flooding back into my brain. Images I had tried to wipe from my brain were so vivid that it was as if I had just witnessed them.

Getting off the aircraft after landing at Camp Evans, I gasped for air. There were many unforgettable smells in the war torn countryside. However, being downwind of shit burning containers was the most horrific of all odors. I had no idea who came up with mixing diesel fuel with shit and burning it. Yet, every outhouse in Vietnam had at least one of these cut in half 55-gallon drums under it. Mixing this smell with the sulfur smell from weapons of war should have made everyone within smelling distance sick with a headache.

Several troops in combat gear were waiting on the runway for transportation out to God knows where for another combat operation. A flight of six Huey lift birds was waiting for word to head out. Perhaps they were going to take the waiting troops.

I had been praying not to see body bags again. Yet, there they were. There were also pallets of supplies awaiting transportation to where needed.

I told myself, "It is okay Russ. Your tour is half over. Now, find a ride back to Charlie Battery and stop thinking about it. Maybe a crew will be returning from a mission, and I can catch a ride. Maybe I should ask the tower to contact the unit. Yes, that will be the best thing to do."

An air force sergeant near the tower seemed to be controlling things arriving and leaving the runway. Approaching him, I asked, "Can you contact the ARA for me? I need a ride back."

To my surprise, he said, "Yes. A flight of two just radioed in that they are inbound. I will see if one of them can swing by and pick you up."

God, it felt good to be in an aviation unit at times like this.

Moments later I heard, "There you are. That's your ride landing now."

When I looked, I noticed a Huey was on short final. It looked like one of our birds. It had the pod with 48 rocket tubes. I wondered which aircraft it was.

I was feeling a sense of pride. The markings on the aircraft were of Charlie Battery. Not only was I riding back to the battery area in an ARA aircraft, I was riding in a Charlie Battery aircraft. When I noticed the tail number 048, I felt even more pride. I would ride in the Huey I had been crewing.

I looked around as I climbed aboard. She sure looked okay to me. No major battle damage was visible. At least the enemy had not put her out of commission while I was on R&R. My only question was how quickly I would be back in the saddle again. If I were a betting man, I would bet it would not be very long.

Camp Evans was located on our maps at YD 541-318, along Route 601, in Thua Thien Province. It seemed to be a very busy place. Was it always that way? Maybe it was since the 1st Cavalry Division had taken over the area.

On Ho Chi Minh's birthday, May 19 of 1968, just after I had returned from my R&R, the enemy hit the area with a mortar and rocket attack. The attack came from the direction of the A Shau Valley where I had gone on several missions. The enemy seemed to find many hiding spots making it very hard to find him.

I was sitting on my bunk when the attack started. Following my first thoughts, I bailed off my bunk, hitting my head on a case of soda that would not fit under my bunk.

When the lull in the incoming came, I jumped to my feet and made my way towards the bunker. In the mass confusion, I ran into several others trying to get there.

Even though none of the rounds had landed near Charlie Battery, everyone tried to get into a bunker.

The first rounds hit in a scattered pattern on the LZ. The second batch seemed to be concentrated on the far side of the LZ. This was in the area near the main ammo dump that was about a mile away. This action caused many of the officers and enlisted men to move to a spot where they could get a better view of the fireworks. Several officers brought out lawn chairs that they had picked up at the PX.

Many set up a seat near a bunker in case things changed and the rounds started to land near us.

Several officers seemed to be joking about how Charlie was such a bad shot. Charlie was over shooting the area, and not even coming close to important things.

From my vantage point, I could see the area to the north side of the LZ was taking a pounding. Charlie was getting closer to the ammo dump. I expected the fire mission horn to go off any second but there was no horn. No one ran for the flight line.

When the first rounds hit, one lone aircraft had cranked and lifted off. Could it have been two? Maybe it was the first of the mortar patrol aircraft. Now, I was not sure. After all, we usually had at least one section airborne within moments after receiving incoming.

Our tube artillery started firing rounds only moments after Charlie's first rounds hit the ground. Our artillery rounds were landing in the area that I thought the mortars were coming from. Would they hit the enemy? The outgoing and the incoming rounds seemed to be crossing right over our heads. Where was our fire mission horn sound? No one seemed to be alarmed. Those coming from the direction of the valley had to be the enemy. Was Charlie still out there firing at us?

Some of the Crew Chiefs stayed in the bunker, others stayed near the bunker and some did not seem to care about staying near their bunker. Maybe the danger was over and maybe it was not. One thing for sure, Charlie did not seem to be hitting our side of the LZ.

I decided that staying in our bunker was a good idea even though it had never been finished. At least it gave some protection. The Crew Chiefs used the outside wall of the second flight platoon's bunker. I picked a spot next to the window that connected the two bunkers and settled in.

Because the roof was not finished, I could see large explosions on the far side of Evans. This was an area where most of the ammo was stored and we commonly called the ammo dump. From what I could see, the target Charlie was after was the main ammo dump. For this reason, no one seemed worried, as the ammo dump was about a mile away. What were the chances that anything that far away could bother us?

I could not see any aircraft circling around above us but every once in a while I could hear one. I figured it had to be our aircraft. I listened to hear the second mortar patrol aircraft cranking. Why has the first aircraft not come in for fuel? Where were they? They must be getting low on fuel! My aircraft was down for repairs and this meant I would not be going out. Yet, I was worrying about it like a fool. Hearing an aircraft coming in and landing, I finally relaxed.

I could hear the pilots as they passed our tent as they headed for their bunker.

Was it all over? I was not sure. I was questioning my own thoughts. Should I stay in the bunker? Maybe just being close to the bunker would be the best. Relax stupid, your aircraft is in maintenance and you do not need to go anywhere. Okay, I will stay put and everything will turn out okay.

The ammo dump continued to have explosion after explosion as the rounds continued to cook off throughout the night.

All of a sudden, there were several secondary explosions and the sky lit up. The incoming rounds stopped and everyone thought it was over.

Then there was a gigantic explosion. The concussion felt like mega sticks of dynamite had gone off. Seconds later, dust emerged from the window leading to the officer's bunker along with lots of commotion.

Man, what was that?

After the dust settled, everyone started to check to see who was there and who was not. A Warrant Officer asked, "Has anyone seen Tommie?" Nobody had. They ran to the bunker where Tommie was just before the big explosion and found him under all the dirt and debris.

They also found Warrant Officer James Krull lying under some of the debris.

The explosion had sent flying pieces of metal all over the LZ and destroyed some two hundred helicopters.

Rumors were that only one Charlie Battery aircraft got off the ground and that was the crew getting ready to fly mortar patrol. That aircraft did not have a wing aircraft and could not get permission to fire rounds into the area. Therefore, they were just flying around burning up fuel. Warrant Officer James Krull was the aircraft commander. He had grabbed a Crew Chief that just happened to be on the flight line at the time. He also grabbed Warrant Officer Tommie Allen Rolf who was doing a pre-flight on another aircraft that was to fly mortar patrol later in the evening. Warrant Officer Rolf was new in country. He had arrived in Charlie Battery only four days earlier and this was going to be his first night flight.

In the late hours of May 19, Warrant Officer Bob Hartley was talking with Warrant Officer Tommie Rolf along with other pilots when there was an explosion that shook the area. Rolf started for the refrigerator saying, "Bob, that calls for a coke. Do you want anything?" All of a sudden, the roof caved in. Dust and dirt was flying all over the place. This sent the pilots scattering in all directions.

The large explosion had caused a 155mm round to become a projectile. The round became a missile and tossing all the way across the base camp and a mile from the ammo dump. The round came down in our Battery area, punched a large hole through the roof of the officers' bunker, hit Tommie Allan Rolf and killed him instantly. This round did not have a fuse on it so there was no explosion. The round fell to the floor. As the round entered through the roof, it had broken a support beam. That beam hit Warrant Officer James Krull in the leg as it hit the floor.

They placed Mr. Krull on a MEDEVAC helicopter and I never heard from him again. This left Charlie Battery with two less pilots.

After the dust settled, we had some aircraft that needed repairs. Some of the aircraft had major damage and others had no damage at all. Within a few days, we were back in full swing again.

The round and support beam on bunker floor of the officers' bunker

Two days later, Warrant Officer N. G. Brown came into Charlie Battery from Bravo Battery as a replacement pilot. Mr. Brown was not only Huey qualified but also had Cobra training in the states before coming to Vietnam.

22

MOVING SOUTH

By 26 October 1968, the "First Team" received word that we were to move again. We proved again that the 1st Cavalry Division could do a great job of beating "Charlie". I am sure only a select few knew where we were heading. It was always on a need to know basis and most did not need to know. The rumors were that we were moving south where the NVA were crossing the border into South Vietnam and we needed to stop him.

Wherever the 1st Cavalry was moving, it was to prove once again that we were the best unit in the US Army. There sure was no question that the move was taking place. We packed up everything except for what we needed to do our missions. We were still doing all the regular missions in support of the troops and yet a lot of the equipment was packed or being packed. The ARA had already proved that we could move to a new location and do our job in a short time frame.

We now had eight Cobra and four Huey helicopters in Charlie Battery. We were due to be an all Cobra Battery soon. I was crewing one of the last Hueys, a Bravo model with the tail number of 62-02048. Just like the move north, I was to be one of the advance party aircraft on the move south.

I had no idea where our final destination would be, but figured I would enjoy the long flight to where ever it was we were going.

As we lifted off from Camp Evans and started the flight south, I was enjoying the sights of the country. Vietnam was a beautiful country when you could see the area that the war had not destroyed. We were flying high enough that I could see a long distance when the weather was right. There was a covering of lush trees and rice paddies everywhere, except where Agent Orange or the rockets and mortars had destroyed the area. My pilots wanted to fly near Tam Ky where Charlie Battery had been located before we moved north but could not because we did not have any extra time. One of my pilots said he had flown near there less than a week after we moved north and everything was gone including the hanger that we worked so hard to build. There was not even one stick of wood left.

Although all the ARA Batteries supported anyone who needed us, Alpha Battery was considered part of 1st Brigade. Bravo Battery was part of 2nd Brigade and Charlie Battery was considered part of the 3rd Brigade. When the ARA first landed in Vietnam, it was set up this way and it would remain that way until the 1st Cavalry left Vietnam.

Landing at Quan Loi was a day that I am sure will be engraved in my brain forever. I was not ready for what was about to take place and neither were any of the pilots.

We were on final approach for the north end of the runway. I was watching the area around the aircraft to make sure no other aircraft was in our approach path.

Just at the bottom of our approach, suddenly a huge dust cloud that our rotor wash had created consumed my aircraft. I attempted to close my cargo door, but the cloud had already enveloped us. Even though I held my breath when I saw the dust coming into the aircraft, my lungs filled with the dust. I could not see anything because there was so much red dust caused by the rotor wash. The red dust came into the aircraft and covered everything in the aircraft. It got in our eyes, lungs and stuck like glue to our sweat covered clothing.

This was my first encounter with the red dust which was about to become present in every day of our lives in the south.

Was this going to be our new home? How will I keep this dust out of my aircraft?

Within an hour of landing, it was official. This was the new home of Charlie Battery.

I needed to find a way to keep this red dust out of my aircraft. I decided to try leaving my aircraft doors shut when it was not going to fly. However, the dust raised by the passing aircraft would seep into the aircraft and settle on everything anyway. In addition to the problem, with the doors shut, the inside of the aircraft was like an oven. It was so hot, I was sure you could fry an egg on the floor.

Within a few days, they sprayed the area with a mixture of JP-4 (aviation jet fuel) and tar that they called pentaprime. This held the dust down some but caused another problem. It got all over your boots when you walked. This made your boots feel like someone had tied lead weights to them. Our aircraft had this black pitch all over it from the black-pitch-covered-feet. If you dropped anything, you could bet the black pitch would be on it. The only way to get it off was to wash with something like JP-4 or gasoline.

The Big Red One (1st Infantry Division) occupied this same area before us and stayed on until we were settled in. We were now in the III Corps area. Within a short time, 1st and 2nd Brigade moved south. Bravo Battery moved into Phuoc Vinh and Alpha Battery moved to Tay Ninh, which was the most western part of our new area of operations. They based Headquarters Battery out of Phuoc Vinh for this phase of operation. It was Bravo Battery's turn at the same base as Headquarters Battery. Alpha Battery had their turn when the ARA had landed in 1965. Those of us who were in Charlie Battery had our turn while in the Camp Evans area of I Corps.

We had not been at Quan Loi Airstrip long before we were going on fire missions. I went on several missions before either of the other ARA Batteries arrived in the area. In fact, several of our aircraft had not arrived in the south when I started going on missions. The troops in the area learned fast that the ARA was the best air support they could get. They were surprised how quickly we could and would respond when called on for support.

Charlie Battery had moved about 570 miles from Evans before arriving at the Quan Loi Airstrip. Once again proving the 1st Cavalry could make a move and remain operational. At first, we had to scrounge to get ammo. Everyone who was not doing something else of importance was putting together rockets. A torque wrench was required to tighten the warheads, but no one ever used one. Instead, we just twisted them quickly in a snapping action when the warhead was almost together. When snapped correctly, this snapping action made a popping noise. This we called "popping rockets".

Back at Camp Evans, some officer found out we were not using a torque wrench to put the rockets together and the Ammo Sergeant and Ammo Officer were called on the carpet about it. They proved that popping the rockets made the warheads tight enough. There was no way that we had time to use a torque wrench on every rocket. Taking time to torque each rocket would cause problems by making the aircraft wait for ammo.

Taking a shower was a joke. I would take a shower but before I got back to my tent, I felt like I had never taken a shower. The red dust would cover my body before I could get back to my tent and dry off. When it was dry, the red clay, turned hard with a fluff of dust on top and would make little dust clouds when you walked. Having any dampness made the dust stick to your body like glue. It was a no-win situation. I had to find the best way to live with it.

Showers were a premium and the timing had to be just right. More than one time when I went to take a shower, I found there was no water. If you managed to get there when there was water, it could be cold because the heaters had not been on at all or not long enough. If the water truck had just dumped a load of water into the tanks, the dirt inside the tanks stirred and you could bet you would get dirty water coming out of the showerhead.

Moving into III Corps was just like when we moved north into the I Corps area. We were under attack by the enemy almost as soon as we got there. I had the feeling that the 1st Cavalry Division had an image that followed it everywhere as the meanest mothers in Vietnam. The First Cavalry would not let the enemy get away with anything and the enemy knew it.

We had only been at Quan Loi a short time, when Division Headquarters decided that an area where there was a lot of enemy contact needed Agent Orange. They needed an aircraft and they chose my aircraft for the job.

Before I knew it, they were setting up my aircraft with spray equipment and the liquid was loaded aboard. I was going on a mission to spray this toxic liquid. However, to my surprise they asked me to give up my spot aboard the aircraft because a special crew would take over my aircraft for the mission.

Now I felt like a Cobra Crew Chief watching my aircraft as it left on a mission and not getting the joy of the cool air. I was devastated. I had extended to crew a Huey and not spend my days on the ground.

When my aircraft returned from the Agent Orange mission, I was ready to pull the PE (100 flight hour inspection) and get back to flying in the left door.

After the crew returned from the mission, I removed my gear and helped move it into the maintenance area. We had just started on the inspection when our Battery Maintenance Officer approached me. "Warriner, I have some bad news for you. This aircraft is going to Headquarters Battery and a Cobra will replace it. You have a choice of continuing as a Crew Chief and take over a Cobra or moving to the maintenance team."

This cutback on our Huey helicopters meant the end was near for all the Huey Crew Chiefs. We were down to three Huey helicopters. I knew other Cobras were not far away from arriving.

I did not want to crew a Cobra so my response was, "Okay, then I prefer to go into maintenance."

Although my Bravo model Huey was due to leave the Battery, our Battery Maintenance Officer was fighting to keep it. He wanted to keep my aircraft for the aircraft parts runs because it was hard carrying parts in a Cobra.

This was a hard sell because each line battery had their TOE (Table of Organization and Equipment) changed from 12 Huey aircraft to 12 Cobras and there was no slot for a Huey. Headquarters Battery was still using the Huey and had three of them.

The argument about the line batteries having a Huey worked. Although they assigned my Bravo model to Headquarters Battery, Charlie Battery was able to keep it. Unfortunately, this lasted only about two weeks.

I had asked for a transfer to maintenance. However, I was not a happy camper. I wanted away from the flight line and maybe some of the dust. Now, I was turning wrenches and working with a group of mechanics, half of them fresh out of aircraft maintenance school. I would finish the rest of my tour in Vietnam and maybe things would get better.

Troop insertion

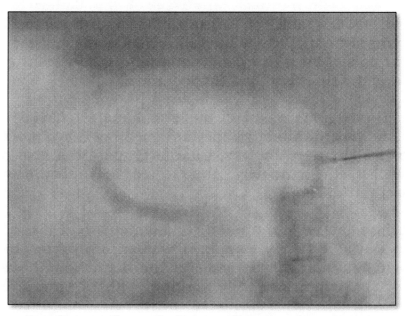
Landing at Quan Loi caused major dust storms

23

MEMORIES FROM THE NORTH

Now that I was no longer a Crew Chief, memories from the north came back and filled my brain.

Being in Vietnam was a different experience for everyone. You never knew what you would see or what would happen. Seeing water buffalo working the fields or the enemy using them to carry supplies was very common.

In the north, Charlie Battery's living area was located at the end of a runway that Alpha Troop 1st Squadron 9th Cavalry used. They had a gun platoon that used UH-1 Bravo and Charlie model Huey helicopters as well as two Cobra helicopters. Their lift platoon carried the troops to and from the field with Delta and Hotel model Huey aircraft.

The unit also had grunts (Infantry) and a platoon of Blues. The Blues were always a small group of men that seemed to try to sneak into the area that they were working. They would seek out, find the enemy and collect information about how many enemy troops there were and the types of weapons they had. All the time they were doing this, they tried to stay out of contact with the enemy and report what they found to Division Headquarters.

Depending on what they found, they sent in Grunts (Infantry) to fight the enemy or artillery would be called in to destroy the enemy and their supplies. As Aerial Rocket Artillery, the Blues only called us in when they needed support fast. Sometimes they made contact with the enemy and the situation became one where they needed to get out of the area quickly.

If there was no field or open area where a helicopter could land, the Blues used ropes to repel into the area. Usually these areas were thick with trees and foliage. If the team did not have time to get to an open area or there was no field or open area close by, the teams used these same ropes. The troops used a harness to assist them that they called a McGuire Rig. Sometimes, these ropes were up to 200 feet long. This would allow them to get into an area where the helicopters could not land. As the helicopter would hover above the treetops, the Blues would descend into the jungle below.

If the enemy was not waiting for them as they slid down the ropes, they would slip off into the area and seek out the enemy. I am sure they never wanted to find the enemy waiting for them as they reached the jungle floor, but there was always a chance of it happening. I think the scariest part of being in a Blues Platoon was not knowing where the enemy would be and if they could be waiting for them as they slid down the rope like sitting, or should I say, hanging ducks.

Sometimes at night when I would be on mortar patrol, I could hear these patrols on the radio. They would speak almost in a whisper, letting Division know they were about to be found and needed help to get out of the area as quick as possible. Sometimes, they would call in artillery that was near them in the hopes they would wound or kill the enemy and not the patrol.

If they used the ropes to extract the teams through the jungle canopy, they would be hanging on to the ropes for the flight back to base camp. I could not imagine being 150 or 200 feet below a helicopter with all my gear on and flying along at 80 knots for 10 minutes, much less for 30 minutes. I had been at Evans a few times when they came in and it never seemed to bother them.

I was sitting in my area writing a letter home one evening when I heard a helicopter coming in for a landing. Because it was close, I knew it was from the unit next door. I also knew there would be some dust kicked up because of the closeness of the helicopter to our tent. I grabbed my papers to keep them from blowing around. Suddenly, I heard a bunch of yelling and screaming as the helicopter passed my tent.

I put my papers away and I ran outside to see what was going on. I was just in time to see our volleyball net take a direct hit by a Blues member. Then I watched in horror as the helicopter dragged two of the Blues down the flight line along with our volleyball net.

I was sure that the pilots knew how long the ropes were on any insertion or extraction. I could not imagine what had happened. Had the pilot forgot he had these troops hanging under him? Did he think the ropes were shorter? I just could not imagine hanging from a rope, finding that the pilot was fifteen or twenty feet off the ground and expecting me to drop the rest of the way.

Sometimes these troops had bruises caused by the trees they hit on an extraction. However, this time these troops had made contact with the volleyball net and the hard dirt of the runway.

These Blues had bruises but they managed to get up and walk away. I never did hear how things had turned out from this but I am sure somebody got their tail chewed out for that little deal.

These men did things most of us would not have even thought of doing. They were always a small team of three or four men and spent time in the jungle at night hiding from the enemy and seeking him out. They would then call in the troops to take care of the problem.

You would always know when they were leaving because they had on their camouflage war paint and camouflage fatigues.

It was nothing for them to bring back the enemy for interrogation. I heard stories of how they would catch more than one enemy and how only one would make it back for interrogation. Somewhere along the way, the other would fall out of the helicopter with the help of a South Vietnamese soldier that was part of the team. Was this true or not? I did not know but it sure made me glad that I was in the Aerial Rocket Artillery and not in the Infantry. I was also extremely glad that I backed out of going to Ranger School. Yes, I was glad that I picked aviation as my MOS with the help of the recruiter.

On a normal troop insertion, the Artillery would fire into the area where the troops were going to land. Just before the aircraft landed, the Artillery stopped and the ARA would roll in with a final volley and then the gun ships would escort the lift birds into the area. We would also be part of the escort and save part of our rockets in case the enemy was in the area.

If the troops made contact with the enemy, we would fire our rockets and were ready to call in another section if needed. The lift aircraft Crew Chiefs had their hands full on all missions. However, if trees or stumps were in the LZ, things could get downright scary because the aircraft had to hover over some stumps while dropping off troops.

I do not think I will ever forget the day that I noticed a tiger that was lying across the sandbags near our end of the runway. I had just returned from a mission and was walking back to my bunk area. A group of troops had gathered around an area not far from my tent. When I was close enough, I could see a big tiger. The tiger looked to be full-grown. Someone had killed him and now it was lying across the sandbags. I was very surprised because I did not think I would see a tiger in Vietnam. The sight of the dead animal made me sad to know that someone had killed such a beautiful animal. I did not even like killing animals for food.

When I asked where it came from, the story was that one of the troops from the 1st Squadron 9th Cavalry Blues had killed the tiger. The ground pounders heard a noises coming from behind them. Not knowing if it was the enemy or not, he had waited in ambush. Moments later the tiger came into sight and met with gunfire. This caused everyone to panic in the small group of troops. When the panic was over and the shooting stopped, the tiger lay dead so the team decided to have one of the lift aircraft bring the trophy back to Evans.

The tiger lay across the sandbags for a few days for everyone to see. It probably stayed there until the CO got wind of the display and gave the word to dispose of the body. This was a good thing because there was an odor that was starting to be very hard to deal with.

Tiger on display for all to see

They placed another display at the end of the runway on another occasion. This time it was an enemy. As luck would have it, this display was gone within hours of it being placed there. This was a sad reminder of the fact that we were in a war and a sad reminder that it was kill or be killed. This image made me churn inside and made me sick. I was sure that I was going to lose my lunch so I hurried off to find something, anything to wipe the image from my mind.

One of my good memories from the north happened in July. I had to stand formation with several others who were getting medals. I had no idea why I was getting a medal. What had I done? No one had told me I was getting a medal.

Everyone and anyone who was receiving a medal of any kind were in formation. Those receiving the highest medal stood in the front row. I was in the third row and did not expect much of a medal. Besides, there was an underwritten battalion policy that the regular officers always got the highest medals and that warrant officers and enlisted personnel did not get anything because they were only doing their job.

As I stood in the formation with my steel pot on my head, I could not wait for it to be over. Why were we waiting? I was not sure. Suddenly, they called us to attention. I watched out the corner of my eye. I could see the Battalion Commander as he moved down the line of troops. He stopped at each one and gave them a medal.

When it was my turn, I was very surprised as Captain Miller read the orders and they pinned the Army Commendation medal with "V" Device on me.

"Attention to orders Department of the Army, Headquarters 1st Cavalry Division (Airmobile) APO San Francisco 96490. General Orders Number 8139 dated 13 July 1968, Award of Army Commendation Medal for Heroism. The following award is announced, WARRINER, RUSSELL L. RA11960898 (SSAN: ***-**-****) SPECIALIST FOUR E-4 United States Army Battery C, 2nd Battalion, 20th Artillery is awarded:

Army Commendation Medal with "V" Device. Date of action: 7 May 1968, Theater: Republic of Vietnam.

Reason: For heroism in connection with military operations against a hostile force in the republic of Vietnam. Specialist Four Warriner distinguished himself by heroism in action on 7 May 1968 while serving as a Crew Chief of a UH-1B helicopter during a fire mission in the A Shau Valley, Republic of Vietnam. When an Infantry unit became engaged with a large enemy force, Specialist Warriner provided accurate suppressive fire on the enemy positions. He repeatedly located and engaged many enemy locations, contributing immeasurably to the success of the operation. His display of personal bravery and devotion to duty is in keeping with the highest traditions of the military service and reflects great credit upon himself, his unit and the United States Army.

Authority: By direction of the Secretary of the Army under the provisions of Army Regulation 672-5-1.

I had no idea who put me in for this medal, nor could I remember who the pilots were on that mission. I tried to think back to the A Shau Valley, but I flew with so many different pilots that I just could not figure out which one I could have been with on that day.

Funny, but not so funny, was the fact that many us that went into combat in Vietnam, seemed to get a rush out of taking chances. Some of those in Charley Battery were no exception to the rule.

It did not matter where you were from or what rank you held, you could receive a tag name like wild or crazy.

Maybe I was not that crazy or maybe I just never heard anyone say I was. I was not sure why some people received a tag of crazy or wild. However, I was sure this would remain a mystery. I did some of the same things that the others did like standing on my aircraft skid or leaning over the rocket pods while firing the M-60. It must have been something else that they did to get the nametag.

We all did things that we would never even think of doing before going into Vietnam.

I think the LOH pilots made it to the top of the crazy list. They would use the skid of their aircraft to lift the roof off grass huts and just beg Charlie to stick his head out so they could shoot him. Then, if he comes out, the gun ship would roll in on Charlie.

Flying nosebleed high or right down on the deck was the safest place to be. I figured that on the deck meant at tree top level, but had no idea what the term nosebleed high meant. When I asked, they told me that was anywhere about 2000 feet above the trees. The area between these two, we called the Dead Man Zone and this was where Charlie had the best chance to shoot you out of the sky.

Two of our pilots decided to land their aircraft in the middle of the enemy position and collect weapons. When they landed, one pilot and the Crew Chief got out of the aircraft. The remaining pilot took off with the door gunner, while the other two ran around picking up enemy weapons.

All the time this was happening, the enemy was shooting at them and the aircraft and the wing aircraft circled above the two. When it was over, the aircraft looked like Swiss cheese. Regardless, they did collect several enemy weapons as war trophies.

Before they landed back in the Battery area, almost everyone knew what had taken place. Of course, the higher ups found out about what had happened and the stuff hit the fan.

Crew Chief Group after receiving medals at Evans
Author center front

24

STATESIDE LEAVE

After a few days without an aircraft to fly in and working in maintenance, I began to think about my options. I had been in Vietnam almost one full year and was going to be here for another half year. I was not sure that I could get a stateside leave. However, it was worth the effort of putting in for one and let the chips fall where they may. The most that could happen was they would tell me no.

I would need to ask the Maintenance Officer because I was now under his leadership.

Early in the morning, I headed out to find our maintenance officer. I found Captain Hanscum in his office.

Captain Hanscum had come to the unit with no Cobra training but had received On the Job Training. At least, that was the story that I had heard.

I was not sure how Captain Hanscum was going to take me asking for a stateside leave. "Sir, is there any chance I can get a stateside leave?"

Hanscum smiled. "What makes you think you deserve an R&R?"

I did not expect the reply that I received. I fired the answer back at him that I thought was the best response. "Because I have been here in Vietnam for almost a year and have only been on one R&R."

I must have had a strange look on my face because Hanscum laughed. "I can't let you go anywhere. I need you here to help keep the aircraft flying."

Figuring he just wanted to yank my chain, I protested, "But sir, I just need to get away from here for a while."

Hanscum figured that I had had enough and said, "I will go talk to the CO and see if I can get you a leave. Until your leave is approved, I want you guiding these new recruits with proper maintenance procedures."

I rendered a snappy salute. "Yes, Sir, I will do my best." I exited his office before he could change his mind. I had a good feeling that maybe I would be out of the area for a few days soon.

I had no idea how long I would have to wait to get an answer, nor how long a leave I would get. I was not sure my Commanding Officer would let me go to the states on leave. However, I had high hopes that it would happen. The fact that others had gotten a stateside leave by extending was on my side.

The next day, Captain Hanscum was waiting for me by his office. "Specialist Warriner, come in my office."

I was not sure why Captain Hanscum wanted me in his office but I had my fingers crossed. Had my leave had been approved?

Captain Hanscum spoke almost before I was inside. "Specialist Warriner, I just came from the Commander's office. He is not sure about letting you go home on leave. He is going to think about it and let us know later. However, he did not seem to favor letting you go home on leave and seemed to think an in-country R&R should be good enough."

I was not happy. "Sir, can you put a good word in for me and try again?"

As I left the office, I had bad vibes that I was not going on a leave any time soon.

Then, less than a week later, I found out my stateside leave had been approved. I would leave for the states in mid-December. I felt good that I would be home before Christmas and that I was getting 45-days away from this place that had turned into a living hell.

When I put in for my extension to stay in Vietnam, I had been flying all the time and enjoying my job. Therefore, I figured it was where I wanted to be. In addition, I thought that if I tried to stay longer, that I could get out of the service before my time was up with what they called an early out. I would have to extend again to make this happen. After all, they gave others an early out if they had only a short time left in the service after leaving Vietnam.

I packed what I wanted to take home with me on the trip and was ready.

I would be leaving right after my second birthday in Vietnam. I wanted to be home for that day but I could not make it happen.

I tried to stay busy. As long as my mind was busy, the time would seem to pass faster. All I could think about was that soon I would be on a plane headed back to the states.

On the day that my stateside leave arrived, I was ready. I would be on a plane that would make a stop or two along the way and soon would be back in New England. I was ready to see the New England weather. Maybe it would snow before I got home!

My trip was long. They stopped in Japan for fuel, again in Alaska and finally I was at Fort Lewis. After checking in at Fort Lewis, I was on another plane making the final leg of the trip that took me through Chicago.

All the way home, my mind was running wild. When I arrived home, what would I find? Would Gloria meet me at the airport or would I see only my parents when I got off the plane? Why were the letters from Gloria coming in so sporadically? I was sure that I already knew the answer but in my mind, I did not want to accept it.

These thoughts continued until I exited the plane at Bradley International airport in Connecticut. Just as I suspected, mom and dad were waiting but not Gloria.

"Where is Gloria? Did she give you a reason for not coming?'

Mom wanted to defuse things. "Leave it alone son. It will be better to forget it."

However, I had made up my mind already. "When we get home, can I take the car and go see Gloria? I want to talk to her."

In the parking lot, there was the car that mom and dad bought. To my surprise, mom handed me the keys. Then she told me it was mine as long as I took over making all the payments after I returned to the states for good.

On the way home, mom filled me in on what had happened while I was away. She also tried to get me to talk about Vietnam, but I just changed the subject and tried to evade the issue.

When we arrived home, I grabbed a bite to eat and headed out the door.

Since it had snowed and the roads were still a mess, the neighbor told me to take one of his 4-wheel drive pickups because it would be safer. He would remove the plow from the newest truck and I was free to take it.

As I traveled the road that took me into the hills where Gloria lived, my mind was still running full throttle. I just knew she would not be there or something would be wrong.

As I drove in the yard, Brenda met me. "We are eating supper. Why don't you wait here and I will tell Gloria you are here."

Why did Brenda come out to tell me this information? Where was Gloria?

I thought it was strange that they did not invite me in. Usually I was more than welcomed into their house. Moreover, if Gloria really loved me, she would have come out right away. "Okay, I will go for a short ride and then come back."

I decided to go over to the farm next door. I met the family after I started seeing Gloria and we had become good friends. I wanted to let them know that I was home on leave. Besides, I thought that maybe I could find out what was happening with Gloria.

The neighbor was happy to see me. However, I was not able to gain any information about Gloria.

When I arrived at the farm, the father had started the milking and one of his sons was feeding hay and grain. Although they both were glad to see me, I could tell I was not about to get any answers to my questions.

Returning to Gloria's home, I honked the horn to let them know I had returned. As I sat there, a strange feeling went over me, a feeling that Gloria was not even home. I did not want to intrude so I continued to wait.

My thoughts and emotions were churning inside. This made me unaware of the time. Then the door opened and Brenda came out of the house. "Russ, Gloria is not here. I thought that I could get her to come home but she does not want to. I think we need to talk. Can we go for a ride and talk?"

I did not think it was right to take Brenda in my car because I was still officially dating Gloria, "Why don't you get in and we will talk right here where your family can see us?" I paused, "If I am engaged to Gloria, I do not think it is right to drive off anywhere with you."

Brenda reluctantly went around the truck and got in.

Brenda sat there a few moments and said nothing. Then she reached into her pocket to pull out several of my letters. She spoke with caution, "Russ, you should know and maybe you already do but I will tell you anyway." She paused then continued, "There are about four letters here that are still unopened."

I tried to cover my true feelings. "The mail must be slow, if Gloria has not opened those yet!"

Now Brenda was almost pleading, "Russ, please let's go for a ride and talk! I have a lot to tell you. It would be better to get away from here and talk. I am sure our talk will clear things up."

I started the truck and as I was pulling out of the yard, Brenda started to talk. I knew that Gloria did not like war but I did not know all that Brenda was about to tell me.

Brenda explained, "Your letters were sitting on Gloria's dresser unopened for weeks at a time. The fact that you joined the service bothered Gloria so much that she did not want to go out with you anymore. She does not want to marry you. She started seeing someone else as soon as you left for basic training. I could not stand the fact that you were in the war and have her lying to you. I know some guys do crazy things when they are in a war after they hear their girl has left them for someone else."

She paused then added, "Russ, you are a great guy and I am proud of you for serving our country. I was sick of seeing your letters unopened and not answered. Gloria said that she did not care how you felt and I could open the letters and read them if I wanted to."

I was not sure what to say because now she knew everything I had written to Gloria. I was lost for words. "So you wrote to me!"

Brenda smiled as she responded, "Yes, I started writing to you pretending I was Gloria. Gloria started seeing Greg the day after you left for the Army. I think it is wrong that she did not tell you. I would like to date you and see how it works out."

Brenda and I went out a couple of times after that but we did not strike a connection. I just could not get a good feeling about dating Gloria's sister.

A few days later, Dan Black introduced me to Yvette. I seemed to hit it off with Yvette and felt closer to her then I ever had to Gloria. Was this an omen? I wanted to stay beyond my 45-day leave.

However, I was afraid that I would be in trouble by staying too long and not going back to Vietnam. Now I was sorry I had extended my stay in Vietnam. The paperwork was complete and I could not change that. I needed to move on and try to forget the mistake.

I was young and must have not been thinking straight because Yvette and I made plans to marry before I was due to return to Vietnam. Maybe subconsciously I thought that if I married her, it would keep her from running off with someone else. She sure did seem to love me.

I guess being young makes you do some crazy things and makes you think you can stop things from happening.

Two days before I headed back to Vietnam, Yvette and I were married. She seemed so pleased. I was floating on air. I was sure I had met the girl of my dreams. I was sure she would be waiting for me when and if I returned from Vietnam. She did not seem to care how long I would be gone. She would be ready and waiting for my return.

On February 5, I was on my way back to Quan Loi and landed at Tay Ninh. I had to wait for a flight to Quan Loi. I was sitting next to my duffle bag waiting for the flight when I heard a voice. "Russ, is that you?"

This caught me off guard and I thought it was one of the men from my unit. However, when I looked up, I was very surprised.

When I turned to see who had said my name, I was surprised to see Jon Kmit. Jon was from my hometown. His real name was Chester Jon Kmit but everyone call him Jon. We had gone to the same school. He had also been the assistant athletic instructor for my class. Now Jon was standing in front of me in the same airport as I was and we were on the other side of the world.

As we spoke, I found out he had just come back from R&R in Hawaii. He was on his way back to the front lines. He was a Specialist Fourth Class, an 11C20 and was in full gear. He had only a few months left to go in Vietnam.

After arriving back at Quan Loi, I received a letter from my mother. She wrote that Jon had lost his life near Tay Ninh a few days earlier. I was sure that this had happened the same day I saw him. This hit me hard.

Chester J. Kmit

FEB. 10, 1969

Williamsburg GI Killed In Action

Spec. 4 Chester Jon Kmit, 23, husband of the former Mary E. Link, of 21 Berkeley St., Easthampton and son of Mr. and Mrs. Chester Kmit of Petticoat Hill Rd., Williamsburg, was killed in action in Vietnam.

Mrs. Kmit received word Saturday morning that her husband was missing in action, and Sunday she learned that he had died of wounds received in enemy combat.

Kmit was born in Williamsburg April 11, 1945, where he resided all his life. He attended the Anne T. Dunphy Elementary School and graduated from Williamsburg High School in 1963.

Kmit received an associate degree in physical education from Dean Junior College, Franklin, in 1966. He also attended the University of Bridgeport.

After entering the U.S. Army in November 1967, Kmit was given his basic training at Fort Dix, N.J., and advanced infantry training at Fort McClellan, Ala.

Kmit and Miss Link were married Dec. 23, 1967 in Notre Dame Church, Easthampton.

On May 13, 1968 Kmit left for Vietnam. He was killed while serving with the 1st Air Calvary Division there.

Kmit was a member of the Hatfield Junior Drum Corps, and the Commander Drum Corps of Haydenville.

Surviving besides his wife and parents are one sister, Mrs. Richard Bernier of Higganum, Conn., and several nieces and nephews.

Funeral arrangements are being made by John F. O'Connell Funeral Home, but are incomplete pending arrival of the body.

Daily Hampshire Gazette Northampton MA.

25

SHAKE-N-BAKE

When I returned from my stateside leave, I noticed that Specialist Lane had received a promotion to Specialist Fifth Class. This was okay because he came to the unit as a Specialist Fourth Class and I had no idea how long he had held the rank. Then, I noticed others had received a promotion. I thought that I had received a promotion and they just had not told me yet. Had they caught on to the fact that I had overstayed my allotted leave time? I was late in returning to Vietnam. I had a problem getting a flight back to Quan Loi. Maybe they knew this information and pulled my promotion.

Photo taken in front of Maintenance Office

A week went by and then another passed. No one said a word about a promotion. I figured I had missed the boat. Maybe I will receive a promotion when the next list comes out.

I was sitting on my bunk reading a letter from my mom when Lane entered the tent.

Lane smiled as he continued to joke around. However, this was not anything new for Lane. He was always joking around and pulling little pranks.

"Did you notice that I was promoted while you were gone?"

I answered as if it had not bothered me at all. "Yes, but now you have more to worry about. I am still a lower ranking peon. Now, when you pull guard duty, you will be in charge."

Lane was still smiling. "Maybe so, but I will not be pulling KP duty anymore."

I was trying hard to hide how bad not receiving a promotion was bothering me. I had worked hard trying to make it up the ladder in rank.

I could not help but think about how some enlisted men received a promotion and they passed others over.

If I had not taken a stateside leave, maybe I would have received a promotion. Maybe they would have pinned Sergeant Stripes on me instead of Specialist Fifth Class Lane.

If I were a hard-stripe (Sergeant), it would give me more say in things, even though Specialist Fifth Class held the same pay grade. Some had gotten even higher up in rank in the same time that it took me to get this far. Mike Russell made Staff Sergeant. He had even skipped a grade along the way.

The Army was funny. If you were in the right spot, at the right time and the right people were in charge, you could make rank fast. If you were not, then you could stay a lowly peon forever.

I was working for a couple of Specialist Fifth Class troops. However, I thought they had just spent time in the states before they came to Vietnam. I was sure that they made rank by having time in grade and promoted the normal way.

I had never heard of a "Shake-N-Bake". I figured they had worked hard to get their promotions, so that was okay. Instead, it all boiled down to chance.

It seemed strange that the people who were in charge were still wet behind the ears. They did not act as if they were knowledgeable about their jobs or the aircraft. Why were they asking so many questions of people like me?

When I found out that I was working for a Shake-N-Bake, I was a little putout about it. I had been the class leader, had been one of the top ones in class and I had not moved up the ladder like that. What kind of crap was this anyway? I was lucky because I was working with Specialist Don Stein who I liked. He came to me with questions and I was willing to work with him. Some of the others I did not like because they threw their weight around.

Shortly after I returned from the states, I received my promotion orders to Specialist Fifth Class. I would stay working in maintenance under these two men because they had time in grade over me. What kind of crap was this anyway? They were still wet behind the ears and had no clue as to what was what. These enlisted troops had made Specialist Fifth Class out of school, skipping Specialist Fourth Class and who-knows-what other rank they never held. I had worked hard to get to where I was at and did not get the Shake-N-Bake treatment. I just could not believe that they had jumped over ranks and received a promotion to Specialist Fifth Class right out of school just because they had finished the classes.

Specialist Don Stein

Don was different. Even though we both held the same rank, he out-ranked me by having more time in grade. He respected me because I had more hands on training. They put me working with him because they knew I would get along with him. Don worked with me without a hitch until some of the other Shake-N-Bakes found out they had time in grade over me.

Then, one day Specialist Lane asked me what the date was on my Specialist Fifth Class orders. When he found out the date, he told me that the date was wrong. They had promoted me at the same time that he received his promotion. Since I had gone on leave, they changed the date and gave the promotion to another enlisted man. Now, why did I not see that coming? I would have had my promotion in my hands before if I had not left for the states. They did not know that I would find out that my personnel 201 file had the original orders. I would not know that until after I left Vietnam and I looked at my file.

After some complaining to the sergeant above me, they gave me hard stripes. That made me an acting Sergeant E-5 and was the same pay grade, but gave me a little more power.

I figured this would work for me but some of the troops still did not like it. Charlie Battery was short a few TI (Technical Inspectors), which was a slot for an E-6. They gave me orders making me a TI for the battery.

We had a night maintenance crew. We worked in the hanger or on the flight line under the lights. However, sometimes we worked with only flashlights.

At one point, the crew changed a main rotor blade assembly in the early evening.

Working with flashlights was hard. It was easy to miss something that you never would have missed in daylight hours. Safety wire twisted the wrong way, too tight, too loose or broken could go unnoticed. This made my work as a TI a little harder, but I felt it sure was better than having some Shake-N-Bake telling me to do something that he could not or would not do himself.

Changing main rotor assembly in the early evening

I would check out the completed job and signed-off maintenance work saying that it was completed and all work was proper. This made me nervous. I was unsure of the items that I had not worked on myself. These enlisted people did not have to fly in the aircraft.

Therefore, why should they care if they fixed it properly or not?

Not long after becoming a TI, Charlie Battery got a Staff Sergeant TI and he worked with me. Staff Sergeant Alfredo had a couple fingers missing on one hand. Sometimes an item would get a Red X, meaning the aircraft could not fly until fixed or someone signed saying it was okay to fly. Many times these items were not a safety issue. However, if a pilot had placed a Red X on the aircraft, it was one of my jobs to check to see if it truly was a good reason for the aircraft not to fly. I did not want to sign off these issues as I felt they were too much of a safety factor. Nevertheless, this Staff Sergeant would sign them off as okay to fly.

A few more weeks went by and then the Battery got another Staff Sergeant who had been a TI before. He took the other slot. They pulled my Tech Inspector orders because there were no more TI slots. It was a Staff Sergeant slot and I thought that maybe if it had remained empty, I would have received a promotion. Now, my chances were gone.

I knew I did not want to go back to maintenance unless it was the last spot to go. However, I knew that that was where I was going.

On January 30, there was a promotion for some. Warrant Officers Brown, Hartley, and Bottomlift received a promotion to Chief Warrant Officer 2. It is funny that I had not even noticed that they were only Warrant Officer 1, or as we called them, "Wobbly Ones", before this took place. We always called them Mister Brown, Hartley, Bottomlift or whatever their name was. Others received promotions before this, but

I had never noticed. Now, I began to notice what the rank of each those officers I knew had.

I was only nervous flying with new pilots. They were the ones that did not know the area, and for the most part, were fresh out of flight school. I could see why the WO1 was nicknamed "Wobbly One". I thought that some should remain a Wobbly One because they sure could not fly very well. Oh, they could get the aircraft off the ground and back again, but they were all over the place doing it. Then there were those that flying just came natural to them.

I also found out that some regular officers had gone through some kind of quick course or cross training. Although they did not receive what I called a normal promotion in rank, in a manner of speaking, this was but a Shake-N-Bake program. For the most part, most every pilot that I had flown with was entitled to a lot of respect. When one of these pilots did receive a promotion, he deserved it.

People like Captain Hardass and others like him, no matter if they were officer or enlisted, were the ones that bothered me. Hardass always seemed to get a fixation on the target while not paying attention to airspeed and other things. Pulling out of a rocket run when it was almost too late in the game would make the aircraft almost shake itself apart.

26

R&R to HAWAII

I had only just returned to Quan Loi, and I wanted to spend as little time there as possible. Quan Loi was receiving incoming enemy rounds almost every day. It was not a good spot to be located. It seemed like our enemy was not happy with the punishment the 1st Cavalry Division was inflicting on them. It was also as if they knew that the ARA was the one causing much of this damage. Why else would the enemy attack the three ARA line batteries so often? Now was a good time to ask for an R&R. At least, I could get away from the madness for a few days of quiet time.

Revetment after rocket attack

Tree that took a direct hit from the enemy

Medal fragments after enemy attack on Quan Loi

Many troops did not care where they went for an R&R. Therefore, since I had recently married, maybe I could get an R&R to Hawaii. I thought that it was important to see my wife if I could and not just run off and have a good time without her.

I put in for the R&R to Hawaii. Within a few days, I received word of my R&R approval. I could not wait to see my wife. The change of scenery would be a good, and maybe, the only chance I would ever get to see Hawaii in my lifetime.

I immediately wrote a letter to my wife to let her know that I had an R&R to Hawaii and the date I should be there. She needed to make arrangements so she could meet me there. I had not even thought about what it would cost her to get there from New England, nor did I figure in any other expenses. I knew my wife wanted to go to Hawaii some day, and here was the chance for both of us. Now the big question, can she get everything lined up in time. Seeing the islands of Hawaii should be a wonderful experience. I landed there en route to Vietnam, but I was not able to get off the aircraft.

The date was set and when it arrived, I needed to make my own arrangements to get to Cam Ranh Bay. I always thought it was strange that we were responsible to get from point A to point B on our own. I managed to catch a flight out of Quan Loi on the ash and trash run to Tay Ninh. Then, I caught another flight to Cam Ranh Bay. Heading away from the rockets and mortars sure was a good feeling.

When I reached Cam Ranh Bay, I had to wait two days for my R&R flight out to Hawaii. Hurry up and wait. That was always the way it seemed to be in the Army. No matter how many times I had been through this hurry up and wait routine, it never made sense to me and I had a hard time getting used to it.

By the time my scheduled flight left, I was a bundle of nerves. As we lifted off from Cam Ranh Bay, I thought that it sure would be nice to not see or hear helicopter blades beating the air into submission, hearing the fire mission horn, or dodging incoming while running to the bunker, for a few days.

My mind was full of thoughts of war, how Gloria had not been at the airport waiting for me when I had gone home on leave and wondering if my wife would be there waiting. As my plane landed in Hawaii, I was trying to focus on my R&R and seeing the island.

Had my wife made it to Hawaii on time? Was she waiting for me? At first, I did not see Yvette waiting as we got off the plane. In fact, no wife was waiting. I soon found out that we had to board a bus that would take us to where family members would be waiting. We had to check in and go through a checkpoint to make sure we had not brought any firearms with us from Vietnam.

As I boarded the bus, I felt better, but still did not know if Yvette would be waiting for me as I got off the bus. Just before the bus stopped, they informed us that we had to enter a building and check in. Our family would greet us as we got off the bus. However, family members could not be with us until we checked in and they briefed us. Therefore, we needed to make our encounter brief and save what we wanted to say to them after we had checked in. As I got off the bus, I did not spot Yvette and my heart sank. Then, I spotted her and a sigh of relief went over me. I gave her a hug and a kiss and told her I had to check in before we could leave the area to go to the hotel.

As soon as they released me, my wife and I headed for the hotel. I told Yvette, I wanted to shower and change into something that was not military. I wanted to relax. When I came out of the shower, I found my wife had laid out some civilian clothes for me to put on.

As I got dressed, Yvette started to tell me how she had planned for us to go here and there to see the island.

I was not sure how I was going to have time to do all that she had planned and still get any of my much-needed rest. I decided that we needed to sit down and make a plan of attack. We did not have a lot of time and we needed to make the best of it.

Because Yvette had already been in Hawaii a few days before I had arrived, she had done some exploring. It was already getting late in the day so we decided to go out to eat rather than try to see very much the first night.

That night, a feeling that the marriage had been a big mistake came over me. I did not know if it was just a feeling that I had or if she felt it too. Did Yvette have the same feeling? Had her feelings changed? Was everything the same as it was when we first got married? Maybe it was just a feeling I had. Maybe I was the one that had changed. Whatever it was, I was getting a feeling that something was wrong. Was I the only one with these thoughts? Was she having the same thoughts? Now my mind was racing. Did she find herself another man while I was gone? Did I do or say something wrong? I was not sure what was wrong. However, I was positive that something was wrong.

When evening came, we stepped out onto the balcony. However, Yvette was very nervous about being out on the narrow balcony. She finally moved just inside the doorway. Yvette pointed out a tall building with a top that looked like a flying saucer. Yvette said it was a restaurant at the top. Eating there and sitting next to the windows, you could see in all directions from one spot. The top made one full rotation every hour. I was tempted to go eat there but she told me the prices were out of our league.

The next morning, things seemed better. After breakfast, we headed out to see the island. Yvette wanted to see the aquarium. She thought the aquarium was very interesting but it was not really my cup of tea. I figured that maybe it was because her zodiac sign was Pisces. After all, this was a water sign and maybe the reason why she enjoyed it so much.

When we left the aquarium, we drove around to the other side of the island. We passed some sugarcane fields that looked like they were ready to cut. I did not really know much about sugarcane, so that was only a guess.

In the distance, I could see an island with smoke coming from a volcano and another island in the distance. I wanted to go see one of the small islands. I understood that there were native people that still dressed in nothing but grass skirts and lei. She did not want me to see any women that did not wear a top in public. Therefore, she made up the excuse that we just did not have enough time. A fact that was most likely true.

The following day, Yvette wanted to go to the mall on the island. She had already been there once, or maybe more knowing her. She told me that I just would not believe how big it was or how many shops were in the mall. Reluctantly, I agreed and off we went to window shop. She was correct. It was the largest mall I had ever been in or seen. I was even more surprised when we parked above the stores instead of next to them. My wife wanted to get a muumuu, which I thought was throwing money away. To me it looked like a piece of cloth sewed up the sides with a place for your arms to stick out.

However, no matter what I said, Yvette wanted to get a muumuu. From the way she was talking, I figured that she planned to get one before she left the island of Hawaii.

Once we were back to the hotel, we unloaded all the goodies my wife found for herself. Then, we headed for the gift shop in the hotel. She wanted to pick up a few items to take back home for family and friends. I had not found anything to buy. I felt my R&R was more of way to get away from the war for a few days.

It would be nice to find something for my mom and dad, but I knew they would be happy with a postcard.

I found postcards for all my family and friends back home. Then I thought I would take a couple back to the unit. However, my wife went ballistic when I found a postcard of a Hawaiian girl that was wearing nothing but her hula skirt and Hawaiian lei around her neck.

"I see what you are looking at. You are not getting any of those cards for anyone. Not even your buddies back in Vietnam." She paused and added, "Oh and by the way, don't think you are going to get any of those for yourself either. Cause it is not going to happen!"

I sure did not want to cause any problems. My marriage did not seem to be off to a good start.

The last day of my R&R, we made a trip to see the USS Arizona Memorial. When we arrived, high tide had closed the Memorial.

It was too late to plan anything else. That afternoon, I packed my bags and got ready to leave. I felt the R&R ended excessively fast, but that was how it was, a few moments in time. Soon, I would have no choice but to say goodbye to my wife. I knew I would have to go through a shakedown inspection. God forgive us if we had picked up a personal weapon or something else they did not want us to have.

Before I knew it, I was aboard my flight and headed back to Vietnam.

When I got back to the unit I found out all H*** had broken out. The enemy was hitting us with incoming almost every day; much more than they had before I left.

27

INCOMING

Now that my R& R was over, and I was back at Quan Loi, I realized that what we had been getting before I left for R&R was nothing when compared to the way it was when I returned.

The enemy stepped up their offensive while I was away. They were hitting us with incoming every day. You could almost set a clock to what time the attack would happen. Every day at 1400 hours, everyone needed to be ready to hit the bunkers or at least stay close to one. This was not the only time that the enemy hit us with incoming rounds, but it seemed to be their favorite time to do so. The enemy sure was mad at us.

On March 9, just before daybreak, I was still in my bunk. I was awake, but it was still early and I did not see any reason to get up yet. Suddenly, I heard the distinct sound of a rocket leaving the tube. Seconds later, I heard the unmistakable sound of the rocket as it came in and heard the impact. Crap that was close! That must have hit the motor pool. Almost instantly, there was the sound of another rocket leaving the tube. Then before that one hit us, another one left the tube.

Before I had time to think, I started rolling out of my bunk and onto the floor.

Was the enemy getting smarter? This time, he hit us in the early morning hours when many of us were still in our bunks.

The first round hit near the motor pool. Then the thought hit me, they are trying to hit our ammo dump. Yes, that had to be what they were trying to hit. Our ammo dump is in that direction.

When the second round hit, it was so close to the tent that the concussion had blown me out of my bunk. The concussion was so great that I thought I was a goner.

All the lights were out. It took me a couple of seconds to get my bearings. In the confusion, I could not find my steel pot, flashlight or anything else, and being in total darkness was no help.

I felt to make sure that I had not lost any body parts. Was I hit? No, only my arm bruised. Now that sure was close. I am not going to move until they stop and then I am getting my ass into the bunker.

Then, I heard screaming coming from someone that was hit. The sounds were coming from the direction of the outhouse that was just across the roadway that ran between my tent and the outhouse.

I needed to find my steel pot, M-16, and my flashlight. I wanted to wait for the delay in the incoming rounds, but I also wanted to be ready to head for the bunker as soon I had a chance. Maybe I could help the injured person to the bunker. I was feeling around for what I needed. Crap, there is the sound of more rounds leaving their tubes. They are walking them down the runway! Okay. Stay put. If you can hear them, then they missed you.

Suddenly, there were several secondary explosions followed by a massive explosion. All these explosions came from the area near our aircraft. They must have hit a revetment! Only the rockets that are stored near each aircraft could have caused an explosion like that.

When a lull in the incoming came, I made my way toward the bunker. The screaming had stopped. Maybe whoever it was already made it to the bunker. I did not stop to check the outhouse because I heard the sound of more rounds leaving their tubes.

When I reached the bunker, there was no room at the inn. Our Battery Medic was in the entrance trying to administer first aid to someone. I could not see who it was in the dim lighting. The medic was asking if someone could hold the flashlight, as he needed to have two free hands to work with.

I moved closer and held the flashlight. Then, it hit me. The wounded person was a pilot. Not only was it a pilot, but one whom I had flown with many times. It was Warrant Officer Littlefield. I felt like someone had just hit me with a brick. When my aircraft lost the engine, Littlefield was one of the pilots. He was what we all called a real short short-timer and was leaving for home in a few days. Jokingly, we would say that anyone who was that short had to look up to tie his shoelaces.

Mr. Littlefield had been flying a mortar patrol flight. This flight was his last combat flight and was the last mission of the night for his crew. He had just returned and had gone to the outhouse. The round hit between my tent and the outhouse just after he entered.

Shrapnel had hit Mr. Littlefield in the left knee and left hand. He did not want his wedding ring removed. Therefore, the medic decided to concentrate on stopping the bleeding and not worry about it.

Littlefield kept making comments that he would never play the piano again. He left on a MEDEVAC aircraft and I thought I would never see or hear about him ever again. This bothered me a lot. I knew he played piano before he entered the service. He had plans to go back and play professionally after Vietnam. The army drafted Mr. Littlefield and he volunteered for flight school while he was in Basic.

The first round hit our motor pool. We were lucky that they hit the motor pool and not the ammo dump because it was nearby.

Obviously, Charlie knew exactly where the ARA lived and that we were some of the ones that were messing up his plans. On March 28, I had guard duty and was assigned bunker duty at the south end of the flight line. Most of our aircraft had left for Tay Ninh to work with Alpha Battery for a few days. I could not understand why they did not keep more of our aircraft at Quan Loi to protect us. Nevertheless, that was the way it was.

We were not completely helpless. We had an 8-inch 175 mm Artillery Battery to our west side of the LZ, a 155 mm Battery to our north end and a 105 mm Battery to our south end. We also had infantry on the LZ and they had 81 mm as well as 60 mm mortars. Even with this support, I felt better with some of our aircraft nearby.

Don Stein was not one of the Shake and Bake guys. However, he had come to Charlie Battery at just the right time. On the other hand, maybe should I say the wrong time? The Shake and Bake program, for lack of a better term, started after Don graduated from the school. I had gotten to know him very well.

Now we were on bunker duty again. We were the only two on the bunker at the south end of the active runway. Mr. Brown was the OD (officer on duty) for the night because he was a short-timer with only 5 days left in country. He had requested a non-flying status because of being short. If he was not so close to going home, I am sure that he would have been at Tay Ninh with the others.

As Don and I settled in our bunker, we made plans to take shifts so that he and I could get a little rest. When midnight came, Don and I received word to keep our eyes open as the VC was in the area. They had tried to get inside the wire in a couple of places.

Thirty minutes later, we heard the M-60 from the bunker to our right open up and then an AK coming from the area outside the wire on that same side. We could not see anything moving. However, some rounds went over our heads. The enemy sure was in the area. I alerted the OD and commented to Don about how close some of the rounds sounded to me. Then added, they missed me and asked him if he was okay.

He was okay also. However, neither of us wanted to let our guard down. Even though all the shooting seemed to be over, we were not about to close our eyes for even one second of shuteye.

Then, the OD notified us to watch for Snoopy because the aircraft would be overhead soon. He would be flying without his lights on so the enemy would have a harder time shooting him down.

I had heard about Snoopy, but had never seen it before. I knew it was a fixed wing aircraft with mini guns and other weapons aboard.

Moments later, I could hear the fixed wing as it entered our area. I could just make out the aircraft in the darkness as it flew over my head. The aircraft could not have been more than one hundred feet above the treetops. Suddenly, they began to spray the area with their massive firepower, just to the right of where Don and I were. Maybe it was the fact that it was happening in the hours of darkness, but I felt that I had never witnessed anything with so much firepower. I had witnessed Guns-A-Go-Go in action during TET of 68. This was a lot more intense.

By 0200 hours (2 am), things settled down. Don and I decided that it was okay for one of us to keep watch so that one of us could catch some shut-eye. I would hold the first two-hour shift.

At 0400 hours, I woke Don and asked him to take over as I was having a tough time keeping awake sitting there by myself. Don agreed and I closed my eyes.

Things were quiet for the rest of the night until 0600 hours when I heard Don. "Russ, look at this. The SOB killed my razor!"

Sure enough, his battery-powered electric razor did not work. When Don showed it to me, a round fell out of it landing in front of me on the ground. "Don, now that was too close for comfort. It was even closer than the shot that just missed me when I was crewing."

Don was not smiling. "You are correct, that was to close for comfort. Now I will have to rough it with my old razor until I can get another electric one."

"Not to worry Don. You can have my electric razor. I do not like using it. I would rather shave the old-fashioned way. It is a Norelco triple-header and not a Remington like yours, but it works okay."

Don chuckled, "No thanks, I will rough it until I can get a new Remington. I had one of those Norelco triple-headers before and I did not like it. Let's close up shop. The truck should be by to pick us up soon."

I placed the starlight scope back in the container. We had taken out the fish-pole antenna for the PRC25 radio, as the reception with the short antenna was not good and we thought it would improve our Commo. Folding the seven-section antenna was quick and easy. We finished packing in less than five minutes.

With everything packed and put away, we sat and waited for our ride.

However, Don and I elected to walk back to our Battery area rather than wait for a ride. The radio and the M-60 seemed heavy and I made a comment to Don, "I do not know about you, but I am glad that I am not in the Infantry. I would not like to haul all this stuff everywhere day in and day out?"

Once we were back in the Battery area I said, "Don, you turn in the radio and Starlight scope and I will go clean the M-60. I used to have two of these to take care of when I was the Crew Chief on the Huey. Cleaning one will not take me long."

Two days later, we were under attack again. As I ran to the bunker, I passed Mr. Brown heading for the bunker. As he went by me he said, "I am too short for this crap."

That afternoon, the enemy got through our perimeter and overran our area killing several Americans. However, we survived the attack. When things calmed down, I went looking for Mr. Brown to say good-bye to him because I knew he was leaving soon. However, I found out he had left on the Ash and Trash bird earlier that day. It seems that the Battalion Commander had let him leave a few days early.

Now, I was sorry that I had no address so I could not contact him after I left Vietnam. He was the one pilot who had let me fly front seat many times, even though he should not have. I really enjoyed those times that I was able to fly in the front seat.

Charlie hit us hard many times. He had managed to hit our ammo dump as well as our motor pool. Charlie Battery seemed to be one of his prime targets. Charlie was showing us he knew where we were located and that he did not like the ARA. The fact, that Charlie had hit Quan Loi and our area so many times proved that, or at least in my mind, that he had it in for us.

There were holes in everything. There were trees blown in half and pieces of wood lying everywhere.

Wood above the tent I lived in.

When a round hit a stack of our rockets that was next to where one of our aircrafts normally parked, the rounds started to cook off. Then, there was a BIG explosion. Luckily, our aircraft near there were out looking for the bad guys at the time.

The explosion blew a huge hole in the ground and destroyed many aircraft.

Charlie Battery maintenance hangar was now in little pieces and was hanging from the trees.

The roof of our mess hall had so many holes in it that it looked like Swiss cheese. The metal roof had lifted and then settled back down. The nails that had been holding the metal in place were sticking up and now the mess hall looked like a porcupine.

Battery mess hall

Hole in the runway at Quan Loi

We noticed that the laundry woman would not come in for the laundry pickup on days that the enemy hit us. Then, I found out that they found her lying dead in the wire that surrounded our perimeter on one of the nights that the enemy hit us with incoming. It seems she was a Vietcong. When they found her, she was wearing black pajamas, carrying an AK, and an explosive device that she must have been planning to place in our area.

A few days before Mr. Brown left the unit, an H Model Huey was backing out of the revetment and the tail rotor hit the revetment. That aircraft was loaded with flares for a flare mission in the night skies but luckily, none of them exploded into flames.

Oddly enough, if the attack had happened on that night, there could have been a different ending to the night.

Quan Loi Tower

Tube Artillery @ North End of Quan Loi

Who broke my weapon?

.28.

END OF TOUR DUTY

My year and a half tour with the ARA was winding down.

I had just received word that there was a formation near operations. The maintenance officer told me that I had to be in that formation. I needed to be in clean jungle fatigues, steel pot and shined boots. What was that all about? I had no idea.

When they called formation, I still had no idea why I was there. When Major James Tindall arrived, they called us to attention, and I soon found out that all of us in formation were receiving an award.

Major Tindall presenting Army Commendation Medal

I had no idea what mine was all about, until Major Tindall stepped in front of me and pinned on another Army Commendation Medal.

After everyone had received medals and were released form formation, I returned to the maintenance office. To my surprise, I received orders to take the rest of the afternoon off.

Then, it was back to the daily grind - checking up on those I was in charge of and ordering parts for the aircraft in maintenance.

As the month of June 1969 approached, my tour in Vietnam was about to end. Soon, I would be getting on the freedom bird and heading for the states. I had mixed feelings about everything by this point. I wanted and was ready to go home. Yet at the same time, wishing I were staying longer. I had many friends in the Battery. However, many of those friends had already gone home or were about to go home.

Staying longer had its good points. I did not have to stand inspections. It also had some bad points, I could be going home missing an arm, leg or worse. I could be going home in a body bag.

I had figured out how much more time I needed in Vietnam to get an early out of the service upon leaving Vietnam. I tried to get another extension but they turned me down. Maybe that was a good thing. I was angry inside. I lost friends in this crazy war. They shipped my wounded friends out of country never to be seen again.

The idea of standing stateside inspections with spit-shined shoes and the other garbage that I felt I was going to face in a state side tour did not give me a good feeling.

Now, it was going to happen and nothing I did could change it. I needed to suck it up and go with the flow. Furthermore, I had no idea where my next duty station would be after I arrived in the states.

I was optimistic that it would be a good assignment. Now that I held a Cobra MOS, I did not think that it would be Fort Rucker. I knew that Hunter Army Airfield was the Cobra training school for the pilots. Maybe that is where I will serve next. What would it be like at Hunter?

I tried to figure out what I wanted to do if I got out of the service. Maybe I was better off staying in the Army. Could I handle a state side tour?

I was still only a Specialist Fifth Class. Others had received a promotion by reenlisting and extending. Maybe I still had a chance to do that. No, a promotion comes with added responsibility. I wondered if these guys who got promoted this way would stay in the service and go for 20 years or more.

My mind raced trying to figure out what I wanted to do with the rest of my life. Why had I not figured this out before? Why had I waited so long?

On June 14, I received my orders. I was leaving in ten days. I needed to make sure my bags were packed and be ready in case they let me go sooner.

On June 24, with my orders in my hands and bags in tow, I left Quan Loi on an ash and trash run with the Headquarter Battery Huey. Their destination was Tay Ninh on a parts run and then back to Headquarters Battery at Phuoc Vinh. I needed to process out of there and then catch a flight from there to Cam Ranh Bay.

Within an hour of arriving at Phuoc Vinh, I was able to board a C-7 (Caribou) heading south to Cam Ranh Bay.

I felt good knowing that I was getting closer to getting on the freedom bird. As I exited the aircraft, I realized I was almost there. Yes! I am finally at Cam Ranh Bay.

Now, I had time to reflect back on my time in the Aerial Rocket Artillery. I had been in one of the best units in the US Army. The ARA was a unit that was there when others were in trouble and needed help. I had served in the Aerial Rocket Artillery of the 1st Cavalry Division in Vietnam. This made me very proud.

I was not sure how many combat flying hours I had logged, but I was positive that I had over 1000. I knew that some flying hours did not reach my records. I was sure that the Cobra hours in the front seat never made the records in my name. I was sure all those hours had the name of whoever needed a few hours to collect flight pay.

My first few days in Charlie Battery, I had been assigned to the maintenance section. However, they quickly assigned me to an aircraft as the Crew Chief.

Almost all of the first year I had been a Crew Chief and most of that had been on a Huey aircraft. I knew my flight hours never reached my records on those first months because I was not officially on flight status.

Those months in Vietnam were some of the best of times, but they were the worst of times. Some were times I wanted to remember and others were times that I would rather forget. Nevertheless, I was sure most memories would stay with me for a long time.

The move north in early 1968 and the move south in late 1968 were enjoyable. These Huey rides were on the list of good memories.

As I sat on my bunk the first night at the Cam Ranh Bay personnel center, I was talking to some of those soldiers that were also going home. To my surprise, the conversation turned to air support. When these soldiers found out that I was a member of the ARA, several of them thanked me. What did I do? I was on the ground for the past several months. Nevertheless, some of the soldiers wanted to thank me.

One of the soldiers asked, "Have you ever flown in a helicopter?"

I answered, "Yes, I was a Huey Crew Chief for almost a year. I also have flown in the front seat of the Cobra."

However, the comments and questions ended because we had formation. They told us that there would be no more formations until the following morning. Now that was a stupid formation. Why call a formation to tell us there would be no more formations until the following day?

After chow, I sat on my bunk. My mind started running wild. I thought about flying in the Cobra at night. How could I forget flying nights in the front seat of a Cobra?

I was one of the first night Crew Chiefs. The fact that the pilots were flying many hours prompted an idea for the Crew Chief to fly in the front seat on mortar patrol. Suddenly, I began to log many flying hours in the front seat of the Cobras. Of course, none of these hours made it to my flight log because I was no longer on flying status.

During those days, I was trying to rest because I was up all night. This did not work out very well. Some of the enlisted would slip in the tent during the daytime to smoke some of their left-handed cigarettes. They usually closed the tent flaps to smoke this happy tobacco. Did they think that no one would notice the closed flaps? My God, it was hot with the flaps closed. Did they think this would trap the odor inside the tent and no one would know? I would wake up with a big head and smell this unforgettable odor.

Flying on mortar patrol in the night skies was scary yet fun. Some of the pilots, like Mr. Brown, gave me some stick time. At least these pilots were thinking about the possibility that I could be forced to try to land the aircraft. Right! As if I could do that! I could not tell where we were. How would I find a place to land much less land the aircraft? Some nights it was almost impossible to see anything. The pilot would use the instruments. This was a scary thought because I knew nothing about flying with the instruments. I had been in the back seat of a Huey on instrument check rides, but had not paid attention. My pucker factor was always in full swing. It was close to 99.9% on the scale of 100.

What would I have done if I had a wounded pilot? That could be bad news for both the pilot and me. Could I have gotten the aircraft down safely? Maybe I could do it. Then again, maybe I could not. I was sure glad that I never got a chance to find out.

There is no question that I sure would have done some praying. The pucker factor would have been in full swing at 110% or higher.

My mind shifted gears and I began to think about when the troops found a very large underground enemy complex. Charlie Battery pilots had been on a mission where there had been some major secondary explosions.

When the dust settled and the ground troops were able to get into the area, they found a very large enemy supply area. They sent tunnel rats into the holes to find the enemy. These troops were men who were small enough to fit in the holes. They were usually volunteers and had more guts than brains.

In a matter of a few hours, there was a stockpile of enemy weapons piled near our Cobras on the flight line. It was no wonder that Charlie was trying so hard to defend this area.

The enemy even had an underground hospital in this area, with a very complex set of tunnels going in all directions. These tunnels made it nearly impossible to find these VC and NVA.

Some enemy weapons, some have never been fired

More enemy weapons

Enemy rifles

Enemy tubes

Before I left Cam Ranh Bay and Vietnam for the last time, I picked up a couple of paintings that I thought mom would like, had them packaged and shipped home.

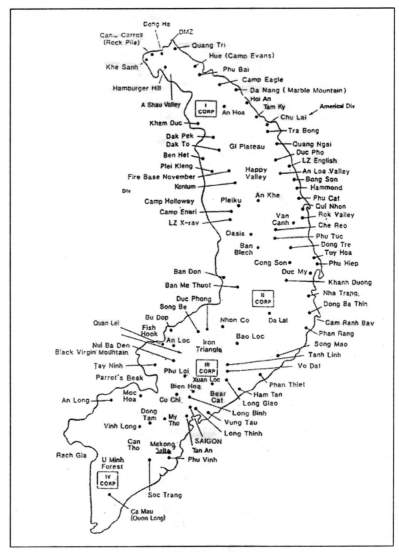

South Vietnam

I had traveled all over Vietnam. I had been as far north as the DMZ and east to the Ocean. I had almost entered Laos and Cambodia, or maybe even crossed the line without knowing it. Then before I left Vietnam, I had served in the south. What a story I could tell about my travels in Vietnam!

I already had a little something of a reminder or keepsake of my time in Vietnam in my duffle bag. One of our aircraft had taken a round in the cyclic stick and that item I had tucked deep in my duffle bag. It would be a great conversation piece.

Somebody was always telling war stories. I was sure that having this item would be icing on the cake for a story.

At every formation, they constantly told us, that we could not leave Vietnam with certain items. Weapons and military property were on the top of the list. They were going to check our baggage to make sure we followed the rules and that we left all these items in Vietnam. If they caught us with any items, we could go to the military jail in country and spend several more months in Vietnam and would count as bad time. There was a bin for these items. By dropping these items in this bin, there would be no questions asked. In my mind however, I had problems believing this to be true.

These comments ate at me. The thought weighed heavily on my mind that they could find my war trophy deep in my duffle bag. It was more trouble than it was worth. The thought that I could be staying in Vietnam finally got to me and I dug it out of the bag. I was sweating profusely not only from the heat but the thought that someone would say something. Was this true? Maybe it was a way to catch offenders and this thought scared the hell out of me. I kept telling myself, I have to get rid of it. At least if I put it where they told me, they said there would be no questions asked and I would leave Vietnam on time.

As I placed it in the bin, I looked to see who was watching. I was shaking like a leaf. No one seemed to be watching. However, I was sure someone was.

After dropping the cyclic stick in the bin and I had gotten on the plane, I realized that they never did check ANY of my bags. I figured it must have been a way for these people who had not seen any action to acquire their war trophies.

Within minutes, we were miles away from Vietnam. However, the sights and smell still lingered in my mind. I tried to shift my thoughts away from the war torn country.

As I kicked back, shut my eyes and tried to rest, my mind went to thoughts of home. What would I face when I arrived there? Eventually, I fell asleep to the hum of the engines. I woke up when the pilot announced, "In a few moments, we will be landing in Japan for fuel."

After taking on some fuel, we lifted off and headed for the states. Where would we land next? Would it be Alaska? Our final destination could be California or Washington. Which would it be? I had been through both places in my travels to and from Vietnam. It did not matter to me just as long as I was heading home.

Hours later, the pilot announced that we were in the jet stream and we would be landing in the Fort Lewis area. We would deplane and get on a bus that would take us to the Fort Lewis processing center.

I was ready for the steak that I knew was waiting for me. I did not care if it was tough or not. I was so hungry that it did not matter as long as it was food. I knew that it surely would not match the steaks that Slingshot cooked back at the ARA.

At out-processing, I heard the same story I had heard so many times before. Do not wear your army uniform while traveling. The civilians do not like anyone who has been to Vietnam. As if not wearing the uniform would hide the face. It was easy to tell we had been to Vietnam. That was a dumb statement.

As soon as I finished processing and had my steak, I headed for the airport.

By the time I got to the airport, the only flight I was able to get out was on American Airlines. My first stop would be the Windy City of Chicago, with a layover before the next leg.

As I got off the plane, I found a phone to make a call to my wife to let her know that I was on my way home. There was no answer. Someone needed to know my flight number, when and where I would land or I would end up stranded at the airport. My only other choice was to call my mom and dad. I would give them the information. That way someone would be waiting for me when I landed.

Mom said she would call my wife and inform her that I was on my way home, and someone would be there when I landed. This was good because I did not have any extra money for a cab and did not think I had any other option.

As I got off the plane at Bradley International Airport, I spotted my wife and parents, all there waiting for me. A feeling that my wife did not like the idea that she was not there alone to meet me hit me like a brick. However, if my wife had been home when I called, I am sure my mom and dad would not have known that I was home until later.

I spent the next few days trying to unwind and visiting with friends and family.

After a week at home, I spent the next few days building a utility trailer to carry my belongings to my next duty station. When I was home on leave, I took my mom's car, gave the Torino to my parents and traded mom's car for a new Ford Ranchero.

My leave ended far too soon. I spent two days packing everything. Then my wife and I were off to my next duty station at Hunter Army Airfield in Savannah, Georgia.

On August 11 of 1969, I signed into the Attack Helicopter Maintenance Company at Hunter Army Air Field, Savannah, Georgia. I had plans to finish my time in the Army and get out. I had no idea what I wanted to do with the rest of my life.

Much to my surprise, there was no pressure to attend formation, no inspection or any other crap that

I thought I would encounter. I reported straight to the airfield every day for work, had no guard duty and everything seemed okay.

I did not know what I was thinking because by November the reenlistment talks sounded better and better. The reenlistment bonus sure sounded good. Things did not seem right with how my marriage was going. Therefore, without discussing it with my wife, by November 27, I had reenlisted for another six years. I must have lost my mind! Only a short time before, I wanted out of the Army.

As soon as I finished being sworn in for another six years, I was off to the Triumph Motorcycle dealer to buy a new 650cc Bonneville.

I made friends with another enlisted soldier on base that had a new Harley. We began to ride our motorcycles to and from work together.

Time seemed to fly by and by May of 1970, I had orders in my hands and I was on my way to Korea.

When I signed out of Hunter, I had a chance to look at my DA form 20.

The form stated that I had served in the Vietnam Counteroffensive Phase III, TET Counteroffensive, Counteroffensive Phase IV, Counteroffensive Phase V, Counteroffensive Phase VI, TET 69 Counteroffensive, and Vietnam Summer-Fall 1969.

The list of medals showed a Purple Heart, sixteen Air Medals (one had a V for Valor) and three Army Commendation Medals (one had a V for Valor). I was surprised at the number of Air Medals. I was sure that I should have had more like at least thirty-five by my count.

Even though I knew the records were wrong, I could not do anything about it. The past would not change. I signed out and soon was on the road to Connecticut to see my wife who had already gone back home. My marriage was rocky at best and I hoped that I could repair some of the damage I felt I had already caused. Now I was on my own to get my vehicle and personal belongings back up north before leaving for Korea.

I would extend my tour in Korea. Extending my tour in Korea only added more fuel to the fire of my already failing marriage. My life continued to spiral downward and I ended my army career after almost nine years because I did not think it was going to work out for me. However, my life after Hunter Army Air Field is another story for another day.

EPILOGUE

After several years, more than one marriage and having problems with jobs, I was diagnosed with having Post Traumatic Stress Disorder. This sent me down a path where I learned to deal with PTSD.

Finding those I served with helped me deal with my PTSD, as did helping others find their service friends. Another outlet that helped me was writing about my memories of Vietnam.

Eventually, I began writing about my unit in the 1st Cavalry Division Association bi-monthly newspaper (Saber) in 1993 and I continue to do so today. This, in turn, guided me to start the Blue Max Aerial Rocket Artillery Association veterans group, which was renamed the Aerial Rocket Artillery Association. I am proud to say that it is still going strong today.

My writings, starting the veterans association, helping organize reunions for the ARA and helping others has helped me deal with my PTSD in way that some may never understand. Sharing experiences helps those experiences to heal. Seeing other veterans you served with also helps to heal the pain for those who could not be there.

In my humble opinion, Vietnam had different effects on everyone who served there. I do not believe that anyone who served in Vietnam completely escaped the effects of Vietnam. It did not matter who you were or what rank you held. I believe that, no two people came away affected in exactly the same way. Although in many ways, they are all similar. In any war, the effects can last forever.

Many of us had more than one marriage or got a divorce and never remarried. I believe that everyone who served in combat has had PTSD to some degree, even if some people do not realize it. Many of us have had flashbacks and nightmares that made us wake up in cold sweats and other symptoms of PTSD.

I hope that reading my story will give the reader a better understanding of PTSD, and in addition, how it affects everyone differently. I hope the reader can understand how each of us handled our experiences differently.

In conclusion, I hope that everyone who reads this book enjoys it. When I started to write, my intention was just to put something down on paper for my family to see and have some understanding of my past. I had no plans to make it a book. However, now I am glad I did. It helped me to heal. Maybe in some small way, it will help others.

May God Bless, Russ

Note: I extracted ALL the KIA data in this book from the 2002 "Coffelt and Argabright Vietnam KIA Database".

GLOSSARY

AC: aircraft commander; usually flew the left seat on Huey, back seat on Cobra

A/C: aircraft

ADF: Automatic Direction Finder

A.I.T: Advanced Individual Training: specialized training taken after Basic Training

AHB: assault helicopter battalion

Air Cav: air cavalry; helicopter-borne infantry; supported by helicopter gunships.

AK-47: Soviet-manufactured Kalashnikov semi-automatic and fully automatic combat assault rifle, fires 7.62-mm at 600 rounds per minute; the basic weapon of the NVA, it has a distinctive popping sound.

AO: area of operations

Assault-can: M-60 ammo box with cover removed and a homemade plate made to clip on the M-60, which holds 200 rounds of ammo.

Base Camp: a re-supply base for field units and a location for headquarters of brigade or division size units, artillery batteries and airfields

Battery: an artillery unit equivalent to a company. Six 105mm or 155mm howitzers, four 8-inch or 175mm self-propelled howitzers, or 12 Aerial Rocket Artillery Helicopters

Beehive round: an explosive artillery shell which delivered thousands of flechettes, small projectiles, "like nails with fins," instead of shrapnel

Bird: helicopters or any aircraft

Blivet: a rubberized bladder used for holding fuel at temporary locations.

Blues: a Aero Rifle Platoon of approximately 24 infantry.

Body bag: plastic bag used to transport dead bodies from the field

Body count: the number of enemy killed, wounded, or captured during an operation

Boo-coo: from the French word "beaucoup" used as Vietnamese slang for many or much

Boom-boom: Vietnamese slang for sex

Bronze Star: U.S. military decoration awarded for valor or meritorious service

C-4: plastic, putty textured explosive carried by infantry soldiers. It burns when lit and would boil water in seconds instead of minutes, used to heat C-rations in the field and to blow up bunkers

C-7: two-engine cargo airplane; the Caribou

C-123: cargo airplane; larger than the Caribou

C-130: large propeller-driven Air Force planes that carry people and cargo; the Hercules

CA: combat assault. The term used to describe dropping troopers into an LZ

CH-54: largest of the American helicopters and strictly for cargo. Also called Flying Crane or Skycrane

Caribou: transport plane for moving men and material

Cav: Cavalry; the 1st Cavalry Division (Airmobile)

Charlie: Viet Cong or NVA

Cherry: slang for a soldier who has never been under fire.

Chinook: CH-47 cargo helicopter

Chopper: helicopter

Chuck: the Viet Cong or NVA

Cobra: an AH-1G attack helicopter, armed with rockets, automatic grenade launchers and machine guns.

Commo bunker: bunker containing vital communications equipment.

Concertina wire: coiled barbed wire with razor type ends

Connex container: corrugated metal packing crate, approximately six feet in length

Contact: firing on or being fired upon by the enemy

CONUS: continental United States

CP pills: anti-malarial pills

C-rations: packaged food intended for use in combat. Each usually consisted of a can of some basic course, a can of fruit, a packet of some type of dessert, a packet of powdered cocoa, sugar, powdered cream, coffee, a small pack of cigarettes, two pieces of chewing gum, and toilet paper.

CS: riot-control gas, which burns the eyes and mucous membrane.

DEROS: date of expected return from overseas. The day all soldiers in Vietnam waited for.

Di di: slang from the Vietnamese word di, meaning "to leave" or "to go"

Di di mau: slang Vietnamese for "go quickly"

Dinky dau: Vietnamese meaning to be crazy

DMZ: demilitarized zone. The dividing line between North and South Vietnam established 21 July 1954 at the Geneva Convention.

Dust-off: medical evacuation by helicopter.

Early-Outs: a drop or reduction in time in service. A soldier with 150 days or less remaining on his active duty commitment when he left Vietnam.

EM: enlisted man

E-tool: entrenching tool. Folding shovel carried by infantrymen

ETS: date of departure from military service

Fatigues: standard combat uniform, green in color

Flak jacket: heavy fiberglass-filled vest worn for protection from shrapnel

Flare: illumination projectile

Flechette: a small metal dart, similar to a nail with fins

FNG: F--king New Guy

Freedom Bird: the plane that took soldiers from Vietnam back to the World

Free fire zone: free to fire upon any forces you may come upon...Do not have to identify.

GCA: Ground Controlled Approach (GCA) is an all-weather landing system in which a ground controller, watching the landing airplane on a radarscope, transmits maneuver orders to produce a proper approach path.

Grids: map broken into numbered thousand-meter squares.

Grunt: infantryman

Hard-stripe: nickname for a Sergeant

H&I: harassment and interdiction. Artillery bombardments used to deny the enemy terrain which they might find beneficial to their campaign; general rather than specific, confirmed military targets; random artillery fire.

HHC: Headquarters and Headquarters Company; higher-higher: the honchos; the command.

Hootch: a hut or simple dwelling, either military or civilian.

Hot: area under fire.

Hot LZ: a landing zone under enemy fire.

Huey: nickname for the UH-1 series helicopters

I Corps: the northernmost military region in South Vietnam

II Corps: the Central Highlands military region in South Vietnam

III Corps: the densely populated, fertile military region between Saigon and the Highlands

IV Corps: the marshy Mekong Delta southernmost military region

IFR: Instrument Flight Rules: a set of regulation and procedures for flying aircraft whereby separation to other aircraft and terrain is maintained

In-country: Vietnam

Intervalometer: control box, which provided electronically sequenced rocket launching of 2.75 inch rockets. The intervalometer could arm, sequence, space firing intervals, and safe rockets electronically. It kept track of which rockets fired and initiated a new firing sequence starting with the next unfired rocket.

KIA: killed in action

KP: kitchen police; mess hall duty

Klick: kilometer

Laager: [**lah**-ger] camp or encampment

LBJ: Long Binh Jail, a military stockade in Long Binh

Left-handed cigarettes: Marijuana cigarettes

Lima-Charles orLima-Charlie: Loud & Clear

Lima-Lima: land line. Refers to telephone communications between two points on the ground

Lima-Lima: low level flight

LT: lieutenant

LZ: landing zone. Usually a small clearing secured temporarily for the landing of re-supply helicopters. Some become more permanent and eventually become base camps

M-16: 5.56mm the standard U.S. military rifle used in Vietnam from 1966 on.

M-60: the standard 7.62mm lightweight machine gun used by U.S. forces in Vietnam

M-79: a U.S. military hand-held grenade launcher

MACV: Military Assistance Command Vietnam

MARS: Military Affiliate Radio Station. Used by soldiers to call home via Signal Corps and ham radio equipment.

Mark 24 flare: true nomenclature MK-24. Canister flares approximately 3ft long and 4.874 inches diameter weighing between 24lb and 27lb depending on model. Burning time was between 150-180 seconds, with an average of 2,000,000-candle power of light. The ejection of the parachute could be set between 5-30 seconds and then the ignition delay was set to go off between 5-30 seconds after the parachute would deploy.

Marker round: the first round fired by mortars or artillery used to adjust the following rounds onto the target.

MEDEVAC: medical evacuation from the field by helicopter

MIKE: Minutes

Minigun: Rapid-fire machine gun with multi-barrels that is electronically controlled, capable of firing up to 6,000 rounds a minute primarily used on choppers and other aircraft.

Mortar: consisting of 3 parts a steel tube, base plate, and tri-pod. By dropping a round in the tube, it strikes a firing pin and causes the projectile to leave the tube at a high angle

MOS: military occupational specialty

Mule: a small, motorized platform often used for transporting supplies and personnel

Nam: Vietnam

Napalm: a jellied petroleum substance, which burns fiercely as is used against enemy personnel

NCO: non-commissioned officer

Number one: the best

Number ten: the worst

NVA: North Vietnamese Army

OD: olive drab

P-38: a tiny collapsible can opener

PE: 100-hour inspection

Perimeter: outer limits of a military position.

Peter-Pilot: right seat pilot; usually with not a lot of experience yet; new copilot.

PFC: Army rank of Private First Class that is immediately above E-2

Poncho liner: nylon insert to the military rain poncho, used as a blanket

Pop smoke: to ignite a smoke grenade to signal an aircraft

POW: prisoner of war

PSP: perforated steel planking

Pucker factor: As explained to me, this expression was used to measure how scarred a person was and expressed in a percentage. At 100%, your butt cheeks would pinch a plug out of your seat cushion.

PVT: An Army rank Private E-1 or E-2

PX: Post Exchange

RA: Regular Army, prefix to serial number for enlisted men

R&R: rest and recreation. Two types: A three-day in country and a seven-day out of country vacation.

Rock'n'Roll: firing a weapon on full automatic

Sergeant: Equivalent to a SP5

Slick: a UH-1 helicopter used for transporting troops in tactical air assault operations. This helicopter did not have armament other then the M-60's, thus it was called a "slick"

Smoke Grenade: a grenade that released brightly colored smoke. Used for signaling choppers. Yellow was a safe LZ and Red was a hot LZ.

SFC: Sergeant First Class

SOP: standard operating procedure

SP4: Specialist 4th Class. Equivalent to a Corporal

SP5: Specialist 5th Class. Equivalent to a Sergeant

SP6: Specialist 6th Class. Equivalent to a Staff Sergeant

Staff Sergeant: E-6

Steel Pot: the standard U.S. Army steel helmet

Rotate: returning to the U.S. after serving your tour in Vietnam

RTO: radio telephone operator

S-1: Personnel

S-2: Intelligence

S-3: Operations

S-4: Supply

Saddle up: put one's pack on and get ready to move out

Salvo: For the ARA, this meant firing all the remaining rockets in pods

Sapper: a Viet Cong or NVA solder who gets inside the perimeter, armed with explosives

Seabees: Navy construction engineers

Search and Destroy: an operation in which Americans searched an area and destroyed anything, which the enemy might find useful

Shake'n'Bake: Officers and enlisted who earned rank after a few months in service, many skipped rank Example: E-5 that never held E-3 or E-4 rank

Short: tour of duty being close to completion

Short-timer: soldier nearing the end of his tour in Vietnam

Shrapnel: pieces of metal sent flying by an explosion

Six: any Unit Commander, from the Company Commander on up; this is how the ARA came up with Six for the Battalion commander; Two-Six Alpha Battery Commander; Four-Six Bravo battery Commander; and Six-Six for Charlie Battery commander

Sky Crane: CH-54, large double-engine helicopter used for lifting and transporting heavy equipment

Strobe: hand held strobe light for marking landing zones at night

TET: Vietnamese New Year

TOE: Table of Organization and Equipment

Top: a First Sergeant (E-8) or Sergeant Major (E-9)

Tracer: a round of ammunition chemically treated to glow so that its flight can be followed

US: prefix to serial number of Army draftees

USO: United Service Organization. Provided entertainment to the troops

VC: Viet Cong

VFR: Visual flight rules: a set of aviation regulations, which a pilot may fly an aircraft in weather conditions sufficient to allow the pilot visual reference to environment outside the cockpit, to control the aircraft's attitude, navigate, and maintain safe separation from obstacles such as terrain, buildings, and other aircraft.

Victor Charlie: the Viet Cong; the enemy

Viet Cong: South Vietnamese Communist

Wake-up: the last day of a soldier's Vietnam tour. Example for 6 days: 5 days and a wake-up

White Phosphorus: incendiary explosive used in artillery round, mortars, rockets, and grenades. When White Phosphorus hit the skin, it would continue to burn as long as it could receive oxygen, even in water.

Mud was a way to seal off the wound and smother the flame.

Willy Peter: Slang for White Phosphorus

WOC: Warrant Officer Candidate

Wood line: a row of trees at the edge of a field

The World: the United States

WP: White Phosphorus

Xin Loi: a Vietnamese meaning "sorry about that"

XO: executive officer; the second in command of a military unit

100 mile an hour tape: duck tape, always silver colored

.50: .50 caliber machine gun

.51: 12.75mm heavy machine gun used by the enemy

60: M-60 machine gun used by US Troops

67A10: Basic aircraft maintenance MOS course

67N20: UH-1, (HUEY) aircraft maintenance MOS course

67Y20: AH-1, (COBRA) aircraft maintenance MOS course

PHONETIC ALPHABET

A   Alfa
B   Bravo
C   Charlie
D   Delta
E   Echo
F   Foxtrot
G   Golf
H   Hotel
I   India
J   Juliet
K   Kilo
L   Lima
M   Mike
N   November
O   Oscar
P   Papa
Q   Quebec
R   Romeo
S   Sierra
T   Tango
U   Uniform
V   Victor
W   Whiskey
X   X-ray
Y   Yankee
Z   Zulu

CPSIA information can be obtained at www.ICGtesting.com
Printed in the USA
LVOW120902140413

328879LV00002B/469/P